# Student Mobilities, Migration and the Internationalization of Higher Education

*Also by Rachel Brooks*

CHANGING SPACES OF EDUCATION: New Perspectives on the Nature of Learning (*with Alison Fuller and Johanna Waters*) (*editor*)

CONTEMPORARY DEBATES IN THE SOCIOLOGY OF EDUCATION (*with Mark McCormack and Kalwant Bhopal*) (*editor*)

FRIENDSHIP AND EDUCATIONAL CHOICE: Peer Influence and Planning for the Future

NEGOTIATING ETHICAL CHALLENEGES IN YOUTH RESEARCH (*with Kitty te Riele*) (*editor*)

RESEARCHING YOUNG PEOPLE'S LIVES (*with Sue Heath, Elizabeth Cleaver and Eleanor Ireland*)

TRANSITIONS FROM EDUCATION TO WORK: New Perspectives from Europe and Beyond (*editor*)

*Also by Johanna Waters*

CHANGING SPACES OF EDUCATION: New Perspectives on the Nature of Learning (*with Rachel Brooks and Alison Fuller*) (*editor*)

EDUCATION, MIGRATION AND CULTURAL CAPITAL IN THE CHINESE DIASPORA: Transnational Students Between Hong Kong and Canada

# Student Mobilities, Migration and the Internationalization of Higher Education

Rachel Brooks
*University of Surrey, UK*

Johanna Waters
*University of Oxford, UK*

palgrave
macmillan

First published 2011 by
First published in paperback 2013 by
PALGRAVE MACMILLAN

Palgrave Macmillan in the UK is an imprint of Macmillan Publishers Limited, registered in England, company number 785998, of Houndmills, Basingstoke, Hampshire RG21 6XS.

Palgrave Macmillan in the US is a division of St Martin's Press LLC, 175 Fifth Avenue, New York, NY 10010.

Palgrave Macmillan is the global academic imprint of the above companies and has companies and representatives throughout the world.

Palgrave® and Macmillan® are registered trademarks in the United States, the United Kingdom, Europe and other countries

ISBN 978-0-230-57844-9    hardback
ISBN 978-1-137-34599-8    paperback

This book is printed on paper suitable for recycling and made from fully managed and sustained forest sources. Logging, pulping and manufacturing processes are expected to conform to the environmental regulations of the country of origin.

A catalogue record for this book is available from the British Library.

A catalogue record for this book is available from the Library of Congress.

*For Betsan, Hannah, Martha and Daniel*

# Contents

# List of Tables and Figures

## Tables

## Figures

# Acknowledgements

We would like to thank Debbie Epstein, Rebecca Boden, Phil Brown and Susan Wright for organizing the seminar in Wales at which we met and first started to discuss possible research collaborations. This book draws partially on an empirical research project we co-directed and we are grateful to the British Academy for its funding, and to Helena Pimlott-Wilson for being such a first-rate research fellow. We would also like to thank other researchers, working in the area of student migration, who have shown interest in our work and helped to develop our thinking.

In addition, Rachel would like to thank her colleagues at the University of Surrey who provided a very supportive environment in which to write this book – especially Roberta Guerrina, Simon Usherwood, Maxine David, Paul Hodkinson, Chris Flood and Peter Jarvis. Thanks are also due to other colleagues, friends and family who have provided various forms of help and encouragement over the past few years: Jebbie Williams, Anne Skeldon, Alison Cook, Wendy and Barry Brooks, Mairi-Ann Cullen, Sue Heath, Diane Reay, Alison Fuller, Kalwant Bhopal and, particularly, Jude Hussain. Finally, Rachel would like to thank Hannah, Martha and Daniel for all their nearly-always-enjoyable distractions from book-writing and, most of all, Jon Coles, for his support, friendship and love.

Jo would like to say a big thank you to her colleagues and friends at the University of Liverpool, especially Richard Phillips, Clare Holdsworth, Jenny Johns, Pete North, Fabienne Marret, Louise Ackers, Andreas Lang, Tinho Da Cruz, Claire Rimmer, Andrea Wall and Jayne Avies, for making her work life such a pleasure. She would also like to acknowledge the fantastic support of Barbara (Grandma), Gary (Dad), Craig, Gavin, Emma and Claire Waters, Kathleen O'Malley, and Chris, Amanda and Sarah Powell. During the writing of this book, two of her beloved grandparents passed away – Joan and Archie Gabe (I miss you both). Finally, thank you to Betsan Cheryl and Richard Powell for their love and kindness.

# Preface

Two years have passed since the first version of *Student Mobilities, Migration and the Internationalization of Higher Education* was published. Over this period, the importance of international student mobility – to individuals, families, nation-states and higher education institutions – has continued to grow. Universities have maintained their route down the path of neo-liberal globalization, state funding is increasingly withdrawn from higher education, and more students are internationally mobile than ever before (Lewis, 2011; Waters and Brooks, 2011). Indeed, over the past decade almost all countries for which data are available have reported an increase in the number of incoming international students (King and Raghuram, 2013). One driver of this mobility has been the continued growth of the middle-class and the 'super-rich' within East and South East Asia (fuelled especially by China) – social groups that have been keen to use their new wealth to gain access to global circuits of higher education and what are perceived to be 'world class' universities. In contrast, other student mobility has been motivated by a desire to *save* money. Indeed, in England, there is now evidence to suggest that the substantial increase in tuition fees from September 2012 onwards has encouraged some young people to move overseas to universities that provide tuition in English, but have considerably lower fees or no fees at all (Brooks, 2012). The landscape is, however, diverse. Despite these overall trends, which point to an increase in mobility worldwide, international initiatives are not uniformly successful: offshore branch campuses in Singapore have been threatened with closure due to lack of funds (Sharma, 2012), while the European 'Erasmus' scheme to promote short-term mobility has also come under threat because of reductions in the budget of the European Union (Osborn, 2012).

In the time since *Student Mobilities, Migration and the Internationalization of Higher Education* was first published, we have nevertheless witnessed the *growth* of new initiatives within international higher education. Offshore campuses have continued to expand in number (Geddie, 2012), dual degrees are becoming more common, and international work placements are now being offered as part of undergraduate degree courses (Deakin, forthcoming). The initiative that has provoked the most discussion and debate is, however, the trend in Massive Open

Online Courses (MOOCs). These courses are free of charge, with a business-model that defines success as (world-wide) enrolments in the tens of thousands of individuals. Policymakers, educationalists and other higher education stakeholders have explored the implications of such courses for pedagogy, the financing of higher education and the long-term viability of the traditional university model (e.g. Marginson, 2012). Nevertheless, as Olds (2012) notes, within these debates, territorial dimensions usually remain unexplored. Viewing such developments through a more explicitly geographical lens (such as that adopted in *Student Mobilities, Migration and the Internationalization of Higher Education*) would, he argues, alert us to the likely spatial inequalities in access to such courses – particularly since Internet access continues to be limited in specific parts of the globe. It would also enable us to interrogate further the content of the courses that are available through such online providers and the implications for pedagogy. Indeed, as Olds argues, to date, few have questioned the relevance of US-provided courses for students located elsewhere (the majority of MOOCs are delivered by US universities, although a number of UK higher education institutions (HEIs) are now beginning to get involved). The same could be said for the thousands of transnational programmes (TNEs) offered worldwide, whose course content rarely 'travels' unproblematically (Leung and Waters, forthcoming). Rather, the content of many higher education courses reflects the particular social, political and economic relations of the state from which they emanate; thus, MOOCs face particular challenges in providing material that is relevant to students beyond the borders of the US. Moreover, to date, there appears to be little attempt within such courses to engage students with territorially-specific issues or needs (Olds, 2012).

The close links between international student mobility and immigration, in many parts of the world, have also been brought into sharp relief over the past two years. Within England, for example, changes to the student visa system and the policing of higher education by the UK Border Agency has led to a decline in inward migration from some countries (Mavroudi and Warren, 2013). As a result of such measures, a tension has emerged at the level of public policy in several countries (and particularly the US and UK) between, on the one hand, a desire to restrict inward student migration (as a means of responding to public pressure to reduce immigration) and, on the other hand, national and institutional initiatives to increase the number of international students (to increase fee revenue and diversify student populations) (King and Raghuram, 2013).

Issues pertaining to equality and inequality were an important focus of the original version of *Student Mobilities, Migration and the Internationalization of Higher Education* and continue to be highly relevant to academic analyses of both international higher education generally and student mobility more specifically. While policy discourse in this area has rarely addressed issues of equality with respect to socioeconomic class, there has been some change in relation to this over recent years. Most notably, within the UK, the educational charity, The Sutton Trust, has launched a new initiative to encourage more students from less privileged backgrounds to think about studying in the US, which includes a fully-funded summer school at Yale University. It appears that some schools in the UK are also encouraging their students to consider pursuing a degree abroad. While this has been something elite private schools have done for several years, some state schools are now actively promoting overseas universities as well (Brooks, 2012). In her work on Erasmus work placements, Deakin (2013) has been keen to suggest practical measures to encourage less 'likely' candidates to take up these international opportunities. It has also been argued by Waters and Leung (2012) that, in some specific locations, international higher education can, in itself, help to 'widen participation'. Their analysis of transnational education in Hong Kong, provided largely although not exclusively by British higher education institutions, suggests that while such education does not offer the same advantages as would studying in the UK, it does help to open up higher education opportunities to those not able to gain access to domestic courses.

Within the academic community, more attention has been paid recently to theorizing international student mobility and, in particular, to challenging 'the misperception that student mobility is an unproblematic transient phenomenon' (Findlay et al., 2012, p.128). Specific contributions in this area include a recognition that decisions about mobility for higher education always entangle both social and pedagogic concerns (Geddie, 2013). In very few cases are such decisions solely about gaining formal knowledge from leading universities; gaining access to other socially and culturally constructed knowledges is also very important (Findlay et al., 2012). Recent research has also sought to understand student mobility through the lens of class structures, arguing that many decisions are driven by a desire to secure access to transnational elites – and that the 'distinction' achieved by studying abroad for a degree can help to facilitate such access (Findlay et al., 2012). An alternative theoretical lens is offered by Raghuram

(2013), who has argued for an emphasis on the 'spatialities of knowledge' in analysing international student mobility. This, she suggests, helps to foreground the way in which 'student migrants become agents in configuring the constitution, power and sustainability of knowledge and knowledge institutions' (p.150).

Recent work has emphasized the complexity of student motives for embarking on a course of study abroad; it has also highlighted important variations across time and space. For example, Kang and Abelmann (2011)'s analysis of media discourses, within South Korea, about Pre-College Study Abroad, indicates that the meaning attached to such mobility has changed considerably over the past decade. Kang and Abelmann argue that moving abroad for pre-college study was initially understood as a separate field of activity, which offered the promise of human development. However, they suggest that as a result of the huge expansion in such activity in the 2000s and an increasing pressure on parents to globalize their children, mobility has now become 'domesticated'. By this, they mean that study abroad has come to be seen as an extension of the competitive and highly stratified domestic education market in which success relies on students' pre-existing character, the level of parental assets that can be drawn upon, and the preparation that is undertaken within the home.

Although it is important to recognize both the temporal shifts possible within individual nation-states (as outlined by Kang and Abelmann), and the changing dynamics in the wider global higher education market, evidenced for example by the growth of MOOCs, there remain important elements of continuity. The arguments advanced in *Student Mobilities, Migration and the Internationalization of Higher Education* when it was first published – particularly in relation to the importance of paying close attention to the geographies of student mobility and the inter-relationships between student mobility and education policy and practice – remain equally relevant today.

Rachel Brooks and Johanna Waters
February 2013

## References

Brooks, R. (2012) 'The new tuition fees regime is radically transforming patterns of student mobility within Higher Education', *British Politics and Policy at LSE*. Available online at: http://blogs.lse.ac.uk/politicsandpolicy/archives/28470 (Accessed 8 February 2013).

Deakin, H. (2013) 'How and why we should encourage undergraduate geography students to participate in the Erasmus programme', *Journal of Geography in Higher Education* (Advance online publication).

Deakin, H. (forthcoming) 'The drivers to Erasmus work placement mobility for UK students', *Children's Geographies*.

Findlay, A., King, R., Smith, F., Geddes, A. and Skeldon, R. (2012) 'World class? An investigation of globalisation, difference and international student mobility', *Transactions of the Institute of British Geographers*, 37, 118–131.

Geddie, K. (2012) 'International branch campuses: Developments in the United Arab Emirates', in Brooks, R., Fuller, A. and Waters, J. (eds) *Changing Spaces of Education: New Perspectives on the Nature of Learning*. London: Routledge.

Geddie, K. (2013) 'The transnational ties that bind: Relationship considerations for graduating international science and engineering research students', *Population, Space and Place*, 19, 2, 196–208.

Kang, J. and Abelmann, N. (2011) 'The domestication of South Korean precollege study abroad in the first decade of the millennium', *Journal of Korean Studies*, 16, 1, 89–118.

King, R. and Raghuram, P. (2013) 'International student migration: Mapping the field and new research agendas', *Population, Space and Place*, 19, 127–137.

Leung, M. and J. Waters (forthcoming) 'British degrees made in Hong Kong: An enquiry into the role of space and place in transnational education', *Asia Pacific Education Review*.

Lewis, N. (2011) 'Political projects and micro-practices of globalising education: Building an international education industry in New Zealand', *Globalisation, Societies and Education*, 9, 2, 225–246.

Marginson, S. (2012) 'Yes, MOOC is the global higher education game changer', *University World News*, 12 August 2012. Available online at: http://www.universityworldnews.com/article.php?story=2012080915084470&query=MOOCs (Accessed 8 February 2013).

Mavroudi, E. and Warren, A. (2013) 'Highly skilled migration and the negotiation of immigration policy: Non-EEA postgraduate students and academic staff at English universities', *Geoforum*, 44, 261–270.

Olds, K. (2012) 'On the territorial dimensions of MOOCs', *Inside Higher Education*. Available online at: http://www.insidehighered.com/blogs/global-highered/territorial-dimensions-moocs (Accessed 8 February 2013).

Osborn, A. (2012) 'Erasmus funds for students cleared at last moment', *University World News*, 14 December 2012. Available online at: http://www.universityworldnews.com/article.php?story=20121214151256632&query=erasmus (Accessed 8 February 2013).

Raghuram, P. (2013) 'Theorising the spaces of student migration', *Population, Space and Place*, 19, 138–154.

Sharma, Y. (2012) 'US branch campus demise is a cautionary tale for Asian ambitions', *University World News*, Issue 248. Available online at: http://www.universityworldnews.com/article.php?story=20121116104624469 (Accessed 15 February 2013).

Waters, J. and Brooks, R. (2011) 'International/transnational spaces of education', *Globalisation, Societies and Education*, 9, 1, 155–160.

Waters, J. and Leung, M. (2012) '"To have a degree is to be normal": Young people and transnational higher education in Hong Kong', *Sociological Research Online*, 17 (3).

# 1
# Introduction

In January 2010, the UK's *The Sunday Times* newspaper published an article entitled 'Why British students are flocking to America'. It began with the following invitation to its readers:

> Imagine a dinner party in west London. The wine is flowing and so is the conversation. A successful baby-boomer father turns to the woman on his left and boasts 'Chloe's at Oxford, you know'. But she merely raises an eyebrow. Oxbridge is so common these days. 'Henry's at Yale,' she replies coolly. In the silence that follows the envy is palpable as the man, who is used to feeling superior, realises he's missed a trick. This is the nightmare scenario propelling today's pushy parents to go one step further for their school-leaving children. The bar has been raised. The best British universities no longer carry enough cachet to impress. (Hunt-Grabbe, 2010)

Although the article presents a rather simplistic analysis of the factors that influence a decision to move abroad for higher education (HE) (as well as a rather caricatured portrait of a metropolitan middle-class), it does highlight some of the ways in which patterns of student mobility are changing. No longer are Anglophone countries such as the UK, US and Australia concerned solely with the inward migration of students; the benefits that can accrue – to universities, businesses and national economies, as well as to mobile students themselves – by stimulating the outward mobility of their own citizens has also been recognized. This is evident through the accounts given by those considering studying abroad (documented in *The Sunday Times* article mentioned above), and also through the policies that have been put in place by various Western governments to encourage exchange schemes and stimulate international partnerships between higher education institutions (HEIs). Recent years have also witnessed change in those countries which have traditionally been the main senders of overseas students. While nations such as China and India continue to send significant numbers of students abroad, they have also invested heavily in their own tertiary education systems in an explicit attempt to increase their attractiveness to the international student market. Indeed, the internationalization of higher education has come to occupy an important place on the agenda of policymakers across the world. In line with this developing policy focus, there is a growing academic literature on the internationalization of higher education. However, with some notable exceptions (for example, King and Ruiz-Gelices, 2003; Murphy-Lejeune, 2002; Waters, 2008), students' own perspectives – on their motivations, objectives and experiences – are sorely lacking. *Student Mobilities, Migration and the Internationalization of Higher Education* is intended to address this gap. Its strong empirical focus, drawing on case studies of mobile students from the UK, mainland Europe and East Asia, helps to develop an in-depth understanding of both the commonalities and differences in the experiences of students from different parts of the world who choose to move abroad to pursue a higher education.

This chapter introduces some of the key themes which are developed in more depth in subsequent parts of the book. Firstly, it explores the link between neo-liberalism, 'globalization' and education. Although international education is seen by some scholars as a direct manifestation of globalization, as Matthews and Sidhu (2005) note, this interpretation ignores the long history of international education and tends to focus solely on its economic drivers. Nevertheless, the relationship between education, globalization and neo-liberalism is important – in terms of understanding policy imperatives in this area as well as the perspectives and motivations of individual students. The chapter then focusses more specifically on 'student mobilities', making links to the increasing influence across the social sciences of what has been termed the 'mobilities paradigm' and to recent calls for more research to explore the heterogeneity of different groups of skilled migrants – including international students (Favell et al., 2008). The chapter then introduces briefly a number of key concepts which provide the theoretical underpinnings of *Student Mobilities, Migration and the Internationalization of Higher Education*, before outlining the overall structure of the book and the focus of individual chapters.

## Neo-liberalism, 'globalization' and education

Neo-liberalism, as Peck and Tickell (2006) note, is a distinctive political and economic philosophy that first emerged in the 1970s, 'dedicated to the extension of market (and market-like) forms of governance, rule and control across – tendentially at least – all spheres of social life' (p.28). Peck and Tickell also suggest that, despite the transnational nature of many manifestations of neo-liberalism, it has deep roots in local political economies and should be understood as a politically-grounded project with significant spatial variations. They argue that it has its own geography, 'with its centres of discursive production (in places like Washington D.C., New York City and London), its ideological heartlands (like the US and the UK), its constantly shifting frontiers of extension and mediation (such as South Africa, Eastern Europe, Japan and Latin America) and its sites of active contestation and resistance (...Seattle, Genoa, Cuba...)' (Tickell and Peck, 2003, p.164). Developing this analysis, they maintain that neo-liberalism should not be thought of as a specific 'end state' but, rather, 'a continuously realised *process*' (p.165, emphasis in original).

Within the academic literature, neo-liberalism is often conflated with globalization; 'globalization' is frequently assumed to mean the increasing dominance of market mechanisms worldwide:

Neo-liberal politicians will often invoke globalization, as a signifier of powerful and in many respects unstoppable market forces, in order to advance the case for government sell-offs and privatisation, fiscal austerity, financial and labour market deregulation, trade liberalization, welfare cutbacks and so forth. Simultaneously, critics of these policies and opponents of free-market globalization will often pointedly label all such phenomena as evidence of a creeping neo-liberal (or sometimes American) hegemony. What the former are trying to depoliticise the latter seek to repoliticise – and the use of the label 'neoliberal' suits the latter because it is they who wish to underline the political origins and character of the programme. (ibid., p.164)

However, in this chapter we argue that it is important to keep the two terms analytically distinct. The emergence of a neo-liberal orthodoxy is only one of many possible forms of 'globalization'. We also suggest that the term 'globalization' should itself be problematized. While much of the research that we draw upon throughout this book

– particularly from the discipline of education – takes the increasingly 'global' nature of contemporary society as axiomatic, we show how this straightforward analysis is not shared by all. Indeed, there are important contestations about 'globalization as empirical fact' (i.e. the extent to which recent changes in communications, transport, the economy and other cross-border flows represent anything profoundly new) as well as about its ideological underpinnings. We now explore some of these debates in more detail.

As the large literature across the social sciences attests, globalization is a highly contested concept, describing empirical changes – to economic activity, politics and culture – but also suggesting particular conceptual tools to make sense of contemporary society. Indeed, Popkewitz and Rizvi (2009) note that: 'One of the major intellectual tensions has to do with globalization as a reality to deal with, a way of thinking about an ideological construction, and/or as something about the in-between "spaces" of institutional relations and knowledge systems' (p.9). In an attempt to understand some of these tensions, Fitzpatrick (2001) outlines four main positions taken by social and political theorists in relation to globalization debates. He terms these 'sponsors', 'sceptics', 'doubters' and 'hecklers' (see also Held and McGrew, 2005). In his analysis, both 'sponsors' and 'sceptics' understand globalization as a real and significant phenomenon, which has brought about considerable changes to economic, social and political activity across the world. Sponsors, Fitzpatrick suggests, are typically located on the right of the political spectrum and welcome the changes they see as intimately linked to globalization, understanding them as the first stage of a post-Communist era when democratic liberalism becomes the norm (for example, Fukuyama, 1992). Sceptics, in contrast, are much more ambivalent about the results of globalization, and warn that the unrestrained spread of global capitalism is likely to result in increased inequalities and instabilities (see, for example, Castells (1996) and Giddens (1999)). The 'doubters' occupy a different position in the debate: they deny that globalization is an appropriate description for contemporary social, political and economic change. Scholars such as Hirst and Thompson (1996), for example, argue that there are more continuities with the past than discontinuities, and that large-scale global changes have been occurring since at least the 1880s. Thus, global interconnectedness through trade, investment and tourism is seen as an important feature of the past, as well as the present. Finally, the 'hecklers' (of which Fitzpatrick argues Pierre Bourdieu (1998) is a good example) understand globalization as a myth promoted by those who have most to gain from the spread of global capitalism. In this analysis, globalization is invoked primarily as a means of neutralizing criticism that would otherwise be directed at the state.

An alternative analytical framework for exploring these contestations has been developed by Rizvi and Lingard (2010). Drawing on some of the tensions between the perspectives outlined above, they argue that it is possible to understand globalization in at least three main ways: firstly, as an empirical fact that describes profound shifts taking place around the world; secondly, as an ideology that masks various expressions of power and specific political interests; and thirdly, as a 'social imaginary' that expresses the sense people have of their own identity and its fit with the world around them. (The differences between globalization as empirical fact and globalization as discursive system have also been highlighted by a number of other writers: see, for example, Olssen, 2006.) Empirical understandings typically emphasize the ways in which technological developments in transport, communications and data processing have facilitated the 'compression' of time and space (Harvey, 1989). Capitalism, it is argued, has taken full advantage of these developments: cross-border flows of capital have increased significantly in speed; new transnational modes of production have developed, based on more flexible organizational forms; markets have been able to extend their reach considerably; and new transnational companies have emerged as powerful players on the world stage (Jarvis, 2000; Olssen, 2006; Rizvi and Lingard, 2010). While some have argued that such trends have fundamentally undermined the economic (and political) power of the nation-state, there is a growing body of work which suggests that, instead, nation-states have played a critical role in ushering in these changes (Brown and Lauder, 2009; Green, 2006). Indeed, Rizvi and Lingard (2010) maintain that global capitalism requires 'strong, reliable nations which can influence and co-ordinate the behaviour of their citizens' (p.29).

Globalization can also be understood as an ideology. In developing this argument, Rizvi and Lingard (2010) claim that the strong ideological discourse which is associated with globalization:

...suggests that the globalization of the economy in particular is inevitable and irreversible. It implies moreover than nobody is in charge of globalization, and that it benefits everyone. It is possible to contest each of these claims, but as ideological assertions they are often assumed, rather than put forward as claims to be tested or debated. (p.33)

They contend that, at one level, globalization refers to a range of 'loosely connected ideas designed to describe new forms of political-economic governance based on extension of market relationships globally' (p.31). However, they go on to argue that there is no necessary reason why these ideas have become so closely associated with neo-liberalism – and concomitant preferences for a minimal state, privatization and deregulation. Indeed, in line with the 'heckler' position in Fitzpatrick's typology, outlined above, they maintain that neo-liberalism is only one way of interpreting globalization – but one which 'is designed to steer a particular formation of the subjective or phenomenological awareness of people' (p.32). This is an argument pursued in similar forms by others. Sklair (2010), for example, contends that globalization could have led to very different forms of political organization with considerably greater emancipatory potential. He suggests that the advances in information and communications technology (ICTs) could have been used much more effectively to co-ordinate anti-capitalist activity. Alternative ideological perspectives can be seen within education, as well. Indeed, Ozga and Lingard (2007) suggest that globalizing pressures can present progressive challenges to restrictive notions of national citizenship. They note that while the creation of mass schooling in the 19th century was linked to the 'imagined community' of the nation, 'new technologies challenge such spaces of containment and at the same time constitute possibilities for alternative forms of cosmopolitan citizenship linked to an emergent post-national order' (p.70).

Finally, Rizvi and Lingard (2010) point to the importance of the 'social imaginary'. A social imaginary is, they argue, based on 'the common understandings that make everyday practices possible' (p.34). It is largely implicit and carries normative notions about how society should work. They argue that while there are different, competing social imaginaries, which interpret global interconnectedness in different ways, as a result of global power dynamics some imaginaries become privileged over others. In many ways echoing their arguments outlined above about the dominance of neo-liberal ideology, they suggest that a neo-liberal social imaginary has also gained ascendance. This has happened, they contend, not through a single process but as a consequence of 'a range of historically specific and interrelated processes which include: the global circulation of ideas and ideologies; international conventions and consensus that steer education policies in a particular direction; cooperation and competition inherent, for example, in the practices of international trade in education; [and] formal bilateral and multilateral contracts between system which offer a high degree of coercion' (p.42).

Both typologies outlined above – Fitzpatrick's and Rizvi and Lingard's – provide useful analytical purchase on the various ways in which globalization has been understood in the education literature. There are certainly some scholars who have argued that, in contemporary society, education policy and practice have both been profoundly changed by globalizing pressures. Kenway (1992), for example, has suggested that the process of learning has undergone a fundamental change – as, under neoliberal conditions, it has been commodified and uncoupled from its traditional institutional location. Moreover, Usher and Edwards (1994) have argued that globalization has tended to undermine the modernist goals of national education as a unified project and, as result, education can no longer control or be controlled. Indeed, some scholars have contended that the state's capacity to control education has been significantly limited by the growth of both international organizations (such as the OECD) and transnational companies (Ball, 2007). Ozga and Lingard (2007) suggest that one consequence of this questioning of the nation-state as the 'natural' scale of politics and policy has been the emergence of alternative interpretive frames – some of which draw on more localized traditions and values. They cite the example of Scotland which, they argue, as a result of devolution, has had greater freedom to promote its own distinct educational values. Nevertheless, this analysis is not shared by all. As intimated above, many writers contend that the demise of the nation-state has been overstated and that national governments retain considerable influence – in shaping education policy within their own borders, as well as upon the nature of globalization itself (Olssen, 2006). Green (2006) argues that most governments still see education as an important vehicle for nation-building and shaping national identities. National curricula still place considerable emphasis on national languages and cultures and while national education systems have become more porous, they still attempt to serve national ends. This is an important theme in relation to student mobility policy and is explored in more depth in Chapter 2.

## Student mobilities

The technological advancements discussed above, which have made communication, transport and data processing faster, quicker and easier, have had a significant impact on people's inclination and ability to move. Although there is a well-established history of migration across long distances, more people are now moving than ever before. In 2005, there were 191 million international migrants compared with 155 million in 1990 and only 81 million two decades earlier, in 1970 (Castles and Miller, 2009). Mobility is stimulated by the increasingly global and interdependent nature of many political and economic systems, but also by the 'social imaginaries' of individuals – their 'consumer desire and subjective awareness of global opportunities' (Rizvi, 2009, p.269).

Rizvi (2009) argues that these changes have significant implications for educational research and present specific challenges to the researcher:

> With deterritorialisation, pluralisation and hybridisation of cultures, the idea of a geographically bounded object and field of research has become hard to sustain. Educational research must therefore pay attention to the transnational spaces which are constituted by new relationalities that are necessarily non-linear, complex, open-ended and evolving. (p.287)

The increasing interest of social scientists in 'movement' is evidenced by the emergence of what Urry (2007) terms the 'mobilities paradigm'. This, he argues, 'enables the "social world" to be theorised as a wide array of economic, social and political practices, infrastructures and ideologies that all involve, entail or curtail various kinds of movement of peoples, or ideas, or information, or objects' (p.18). He contends that by exploring different kinds of movement, we can understand better the ways in which the world beyond the self is sensed and experienced.

Researchers who have focussed specifically on young people have argued that, in contemporary society, mobility can have a significant impact on identity formation. Indeed, Dolby and Rizvi (2008) maintain that an increasingly large number of young men and women develop their identities within the context of global mobility, seeing themselves as neither tourists nor immigrants, but occupying an entirely new cultural space. Although they note that we should 'be cautious about generalising from this post-modern valorisation of mobility and transnational dwelling' (ibid., p.3), they go on to argue that even those who move relatively little geographical distance are still profoundly affected by the mobility of others; such young people 'are undoubtedly caught up in the continual circulation of global culture, through the media, movies, fashion, the Internet – their identities are now inextricably linked to the currents of modernity that flow across the world at the speed of a mouse click' (ibid., p.5). They, like their peers, become caught up in the global consumer-media culture, which both integrates and segregates young people (Kenway and Bullen, 2008). In their discussion of those young people who *are* geographically mobile, Dolby and Rizvi (2008) distinguish between: those who move throughout the world with ease – typically those of dual nationality; those who move under more constrained circumstances – to escape political repression or because their parents are seeking better employment opportunities; and those within 'the growing category of youth movement which is still largely uncharted' – young people who move for educational purposes and, in doing so, create new networks and circuits of identity (p.5). It is this third and relatively neglected group that provides the focus for *Student Mobilities, Migration and the Internationalization of Higher Education*.

While this book furthers our understanding of the motivations and experiences of those young people who move to pursue an education abroad, it also articulates with debates on skilled migration more broadly. There is now a large literature on labour mobility but, as Favell et al. (2008) note, while there have been some studies of the 'transnational capitalist class' (Sklair, 2001) and the emergence of new, highly mobile global elites (Elliott and Urry, 2010), the hetereogeneity of this highly skilled group is rarely explored. Moreover, some groups, which are often subsumed under this label – such as students, nurses and technical workers – cannot really be considered 'elites' (Favell et al., 2008). The biggest single area of research on skilled migrants has focused on concerns about a 'brain drain' – the movement of talent from developing countries to developed nations. However, this concept has been largely undermined over recent years, as alternative terms such as 'brain gain' and 'brain circulation' have gained currency. Indeed, the premise which underpinned much concern about brain drain – that it is the most talented people within a country who are the most likely to move – has been widely discredited. There is now substantial evidence that in relation to movement for higher education: increasing numbers of Asian students are choosing to remain in Asia; those who do study overseas are more likely to return home after they have completed their degrees; and Western countries are currently devoting considerable resources to opening up new educational facilities within many Asian and Middle Eastern countries which have traditionally sent large numbers of students abroad (Favell et al., 2008).

Although the primary focus of this book is *international* student mobility, research has pointed to the importance of exploring educational mobility at the national and even the local level. In his analysis of secondary school choice in England and Wales, Taylor (2002) argues that to understand this process fully, attention must be paid to the factors that determine pupil mobility including, for example, spatial constraints on travelling arrangements to school. Similarly, research by Ball et al. (1995) on the secondary sector has shown that, within a market-driven system, different 'circuits' of schools emerge, which intersect, in quite complex ways, with social class and cultural capital. They identify three main circuits of school (local, community, comprehensive schools; cosmopolitan, elite maintained schools; and local independent schools) and argue that different class fractions tend to choose within one circuit only. They go on to suggest that spatial factors are important, with different classes having different abilities to overcome what Harvey (1989, p.211) has called 'the friction of distance'.

Similar arguments have been made in relation to the higher education sector within the UK. Data on university admissions have emphasized the different geographies of HE choice, with high achievers from more privileged backgrounds choosing within national markets of high status HEIs, while their peers engage with regional markets of less prestigious institutions. Clayton et al. (2009) argue that a focus on mobility is critical to understanding patterns of participation in higher education: spatial considerations play an important role in students' decision-making and are inextricably linked to social position. While the middle-class students in their sample were happy to move away from home to pursue their degree, those from working-class backgrounds had markedly different attitudes. Indeed, Clayton et al. (2009) maintain that 'investing in the familiar' (by attending a local university, finding a 'similar' student body to one's friends at home and/or making frequent trips back home) can be seen 'as a form of social capital in order to alleviate the dangers with what has been recognised as a financially, socially and culturally risky transition' (p.157). In their analysis, the geographies of both home and university offer spatial resources 'critical to the ongoing re-constitution of student identities' (ibid., p.157). Social class is an important variable in all three studies mentioned above, affecting propensity to move as well as the extent to which space is used as a resource. Nevertheless, one of the main criticisms of the 'mobilities paradigm' is its relative neglect of structural constraints (Favell et al., 2008). While this book draws on many of the insights provided by new work from across the social sciences on mobility (particularly in Chapter 6), close attention is paid throughout to the ways in which opportunities for and experiences of studying abroad are inflected by social structures including social class and gender.

## Key conceptual ideas

Although *Student Mobilities, Migration and the Internationalization of Higher Education* has a strong empirical focus and seeks to explore the experiences of students as they move across the globe in pursuit of a higher education, the book is also informed by a number of important theoretical debates. These emanate from the disciplines of education, sociology and geography and help to maintain a strong inter-disciplinary focus. Below, we introduce some of the key concepts which are addressed in a number of later chapters. These are: discourses around 'employability' and the relationship between overseas study and labour market advantage; the role of student mobility in reproducing social advantage within families; the construction of 'cosmopolitan' identities; and the fertility of adopting geographical perspectives in the analysis of educational processes.

## Employability

A common theme within the academic literature on higher education in many countries of the world is the congested nature of the graduate labour market and the increasingly protracted character of transitions from university into work (Brown and Hesketh, 2004). Researchers have highlighted the lengths to which many students now go, in response to this congestion, to 'distinguish themselves' from other graduates: paying increased attention to the status of the university (Reay et al., 2005); engaging in a range of work-relevant extra-curricular activities (Brooks, 2007b; Brown and Hesketh, 2004); and, on completion of a first degree, pursuing postgraduate qualifications (Brooks and Everett, 2009). Studies that have focussed on the strategies of Asian students, specifically, have also pointed to the important place of studying abroad as a further strategy in this pursuit of distinction (Ong, 1999; Bodycott, 2009; Singh and Doherty, 2008). There is substantial evidence that, in certain countries at least, an overseas qualification does often lead to substantial labour market rewards. Rizvi (2000), for example, has argued that Malaysian employers attach a particularly high status to overseas qualifications and, thus, the primary objective of many Malaysian students who move to Australia for university is to obtain a well-recognized qualification that will enable them to secure a good job on their return home. An overseas education suggests *more* than simply a different form of academic qualification, however – it provides overseas experience/exposure that is highly valued by employers, as well as by graduates themselves. For example, Waters' (2007) work on Hong Kong nationals who move abroad for degree-level study has shown clearly the advantages that accrue on their return home. Indeed, she argues that as well as the various useful attributes and abilities that are developed during a period abroad, the common culture of their education 'provides the foundation for an exclusive and "elite" group identity' (Waters, 2007, p.478). An overseas education may also open up specific opportunities within a *global* labour market. Brown and Tannock (2009) point to the paradox that while higher education has expanded in many parts of the world over the past decade, producing more graduates for domestic labour markets, a 'global war for talent' has developed between the most prestigious companies worldwide, opening up a global market for skills. In this growing market, internationally-recognized qualifications assume an important role:

> The all purpose lubricant of the (allegedly) frictionless world of elite global mobility is human capital, in which the 'human' part is measured in terms of internationally recognised qualifications and quantifiable talent and is every bit as universal and inalienable as human rights. (Favell et al., 2008, p.16)

To date, however, the majority of work on the labour market rewards of overseas study has been conducted on students who move from the 'East' (and, in particular, south-east Asia) to the 'West'. We know relatively little about the way in which concerns about future 'employability' feed into the decision-making processes of those students who move *from* Western countries to pursue a higher education abroad and the extent to which there are commonalities or differences between those students who move from China, Malaysia and other parts of south east Asia, and their Western peers. By focusing on students who move from various countries within Europe, as well as their mobile counterparts from other parts of the world, *Student Mobilities, Migration and the Internationalization of Higher Education* makes an important contribution to developing a fuller understanding of the relationship between student migration and labour market participation worldwide.

### Education, class and social reproduction

Within the UK, there is now a large literature on the ways in which policies aimed to promote consumer 'choice' in education have been played out. The 1988 Education Reform Act and the 1992 Further and Higher Education Act introduced a raft of measures aimed at increasing choice within compulsory schooling and the post-compulsory sector, respectively. Since then, although changes in government have resulted in some modifications to the means by which parental/student preferences are expressed and taken account of, 'choice' has remained a central plank of education policy under subsequent administrations (Brooks, 2007a). Debates have ensued regarding the potentially exclusionary nature of choice; research has suggested, for example, that middle-class families are far more likely to exercise choice (through the acquisition and consumption of information on the relative merits of different schools/ HEIs as well as the complex mechanisms of school selection), than are their working-class counterparts (Ball, 2003). They are also far more likely to approach education strategically, reflecting the desire for valuable cultural capital (Brown, 1990). Similar findings have emerged from other Anglophone countries, which have adopted largely market-based education policies, including the US and New Zealand (Chubb and Moe, 1997; Lauder and Hughes, 1999). While studies of students who move overseas to pursue a higher education have generally not been framed within this particular choice-based policy discourse, they do nevertheless tend to reveal very similar calculations and strategic decisions. At the heart of both UK research on educational decision-making and that which has focussed on mobile students in other parts of the world, is the desire on the part of many middle-class families to accumulate cultural capital (Bourdieu, 1986) and ensure social reproduction through their engagement with the educational market, whether this is conceived of in national or international terms.

As we will discuss in later chapters, for many students, a decision to move overseas for education is taken by the whole family, and is frequently seen as a family project. Ong (1999) has shown how, for those living in Hong Kong, sending a child abroad for his or her education is often a first step towards securing citizenship of another country and thus gaining access to new economic opportunities. Here, the child's education is understood as opening up opportunities for the whole family. A slightly different perspective is offered in the work of Beck and Beck-Gernsheim (1995) who argue that parenting in contemporary society is no longer based on an unconditional acceptance of the child as it is; instead the child becomes a 'project', the focus of parental effort. Here, the focus of effort is on securing advantage for the child him- or herself, rather than other family members. Nevertheless, it is similarly strategic in nature. Indeed, in outlining similar child-focussed 'projects' in their research amongst middle-class families in London, Vincent and Ball (2006) suggest that the strategic way in which middle-class parents make decisions for their children is both an enactment of class relations and an act of reproduction, 'focussing on the future and equipping the child with the social and educational resources deemed necessary by families within particular social groups' (p.167). Drawing on this literature, *Student Mobilities, Migration and the Internationalization of Higher Education* explores the extent to which students' choices are increasingly made within the context of an international education market and exercised by travel overseas, and whether overseas study should be considered a largely middle-class (and thus relatively exclusive) pursuit.

## Cosmopolitan identities

Cosmopolitanism can be understood, broadly, as openness towards peoples, places and experiences from different cultures (Hannerz, 1996). Theorists of contemporary society have suggested that the increasingly interconnected nature of the world offers possibilities for the development of various new forms of cosmopolitanism (Fine, 2007; Parekh, 2003; Venn, 2002). Beck (2002), for example, has outlined what he calls the process of 'cosmopolitanization'. This refers to 'internal globalization' whereby 'issues of global concern are becoming part of the everyday local experiences and the "moral life-worlds" of the people' (p.17) and stands in contrast to a national perspective:

> The national perspective is a monologic imagination, which excludes the otherness of the other. The cosmopolitan perspective is an alternative imagination, an imagination of alternative ways of life and rationalities, which include the otherness of the other. It puts the negotiation of contradictory cultural experiences into the centre of activities.... (p.18)

Here, encountering and negotiating 'difference' is seen as a creative and productive exercise, facilitated by the changes wrought by globalization. Turner (2002) also sees cosmopolitanism in positive terms. Indeed, he puts forward the notion of 'cosmopolitan virtue', which combines a respect for other cultures and an ironic, yet patriotic, stance towards one's own. He argues that the ability to respect others requires a certain distance from one's own culture, and yet this ironic distance may only be possible once one already has an emotional commitment to a specific place.

While theorization of cosmopolitanism may be flourishing, the empirical base for such work is not always clear. Drawing on research which sought to explore the development of globally oriented subjectivities, Matthews and Sidhu (2005) argue that 'agential forms of citizenship, cosmopolitanism and global consciousness are a source of optimistic inspiration, but they are not automatically initiated by processes of internationalization and globalization' (p.49). Similar debates ensue with respect to international education, more specifically. Texts intended to promote student mobility are replete with claims about the inter-cultural learning, global outlook and understanding of 'difference' often inculcated by a period of overseas-study. For example, the green paper published by the European Commission in 2009, entitled *Promoting the Learning Mobility of Young People* (CEC, 2009), argues that studying abroad can 'help combat the risks of isolationism, protectionism and xenophobia which arise in times of economic crisis' (p.2). Similarly, in its guide to promoting outward student mobility written for UK HEIs, the Council for Industry and Higher Education maintains that 'a period of time experiencing a different culture improves students' cultural awareness, helps them broaden their horizons and develop an inter-national or even global outlook' (Fielden, 2007, p.12). The develop-ment of such 'cosmopolitan' attitudes is held to benefit the individuals concerned as well as the organizations that are likely to recruit them and the wider society in which they live.

There is some evidence to suggest that a period studying abroad does often bring about a change in outlook (Hayden et al., 2000; Madge et al., 2009). On the basis of their research with students from China who studied in Australia, Singh et al. (2007) contend that: "through trans-national mobility, international students imagine, conceive and experience being insiders and outsiders on both their places of origin and destinations. In doing so, they contribute to the production of a distinctive cosmopolitan space' (p.196). Similarly, Murphy-Lejeune (2002) suggests that mobile students become 'new strangers' who:

> question the notion of borders and the meaning of home. Their travels have no final destination and, whether physical or virtual, space opens up for them...Places are just locations, where one can work, live and love....Home becomes one's language and friends, a house one carries around as a portable commodity. (p.234)

However, a rather larger body of literature suggests that, in many cases, educational mobility does not have this effect. Various studies from different parts of the world have pointed to the ways in which overseas students often do not integrate well with their domestic counterparts (Ehrenreich, 2008; Fincher and Shaw, 2009) and may, in some cases, be subject to racism and other forms of discrimination (Collins, 2010). Where cultural mixing does occur it is often within the confines of an 'international student community' (Tsoukalas, 2008). Research has also highlighted the dominance of English as the chosen language of communication of students in such communities, even when residing in a non-Anglophone nation (Caudery et al., 2008). Work such as this raises significant questions about the extent to which overseas students encounter 'difference' and thus the opportunities available to them for developing a more cosmopolitan perspective in the ways suggested above.

Mitchell's (2003) work on changes to compulsory education in schools across the world also problematizes the nature of cosmopolitanism in contemporary society. She argues that within multicultural education there has been a shift away from 'person-centred education for all, or the creation of the tolerant "multicultural self" towards a more individuated, mobile and highly tracked, skills-based education, or the creation of the "strategic cosmopolitan"' (p.387). In contrast to the multicultural self, she contends that the strategic cosmopolitan is not motivated by 'ideals of national unity in diversity' (p.388) but by the need to compete in a global marketplace and to remain constantly attuned to the changing demands of the economic environment; they are the 'nodal agents' in the worldwide spread of capitalism. We return to some of these more critical understandings of cosmopolitanism in later sections of the book.

### Geographical perspectives on education

A geographical sensibility can enrich our understanding of education in several ways: through an emphasis on *place* and *context* influencing academic outcomes; by exploring the role of spatial *mobility* in education; through an examination of the importance of *'educational spaces'*; and by drawing on ideas from *'spatial theory'*.

For many years, geographers have highlighted the importance of geographical context in facilitating an understanding of educational processes. Experiences of education are embedded in specific places and times, as several key works by geographers have demonstrated (Bondi and Matthews, 1988; Gibson and Asthana, 1998a, 1998b, 2000; Herbert, 2000; Warrington, 2005). In particular, the relationship between education and social deprivation/exclusion has been widely addressed, with scholars arguing that academic attainment is often not a reflection of personal achievement or failure, but can be determined by structural factors beyond an individual's control. These structural factors lie squarely in the neighbourhood or locality (the notion of 'neighbourhood effects' is frequently invoked). Building on these ideas, *Student Mobilities, Migration and the Internationalization of Higher*

*Education* reflects more recent attempts by geographers and others to move beyond the locality when examining educational access and 'success', to incorporate *transnational* space, drawing upon a large body of work emanating from geography, sociology and social anthropology on 'transnationalism' (Brooks and Waters, 2009a; Collins, 2008; Hanson Thiem, 2008; King and Ruiz-Gelices, 2003; Waters, 2006).

A geographical perspective on education also makes explicit the relationship between access to education, social class and *spatial mobility* (Ball, 2003; Ball et al., 1995; Butler, 2003; Taylor, 2002; Warrington, 2005). In relation to the debate in the UK and elsewhere around middle-class choice and education, it has become increasingly clear that 'choice' necessitates resources linked to mobility. This book takes the unusual approach of focussing on the relationship between educational choice, class and *international* mobility. It seeks to contribute to an emergent literature addressing the links between migration and education in light of recent trends in overseas study and the consolidation of an international market in higher education (Butcher, 2004; Findlay and King, 2010; King and Ruiz-Gelices, 2003; Lewis, 2005). Other explicitly geographical work on mobility and education has included an examination of the transnational circulation of knowledge and academic mobility (Ackers, 2010; Jöns, 2009; Morano-Foadi, 2005; Williams, 2006).

There has also been a recent focus on 'educational spaces', defined by Gulson and Symes (2007, p.8) as 'spaces specifically designed with the process of teaching and learning in mind'. This acknowledges the fact that the spaces in which education and learning take place are undergoing almost continual transformation, expansion and development (Ackers, 2010; Dillabough et al., 2007; Edwards and Usher, 2008; Holloway et al., 2010; Kraftl, 2006). Advances in technology (particularly the growth of ICTs) and in access to technology, and the emergence of a knowledge-based economy (KBE) necessitate an understanding of the *plurality* of spaces (such as homes, workplaces, international space and cyberspace) within which learning can and does take place, as well as diverse definitions of contemporary 'education' (occurring, for example, at 'non-traditional' stages in the life course or in non-academic contexts) (Ackers, 2010).

Finally, we can see the influence of 'spatial theory' on educational research (Edwards and Usher, 2008; Gulson and Symes, 2007). Here we prefer to focus on what Gulson and Symes (2007) term 'spatial concerns' as these, we would argue, represent a more accurate depiction of the contribution of 'spatial theories' to understanding social processes around education. In their edited collection on *Spatial Theories of Education*, 'spatial concerns' include 'scale, mobility and identity' (p.12) and 'geographies of exclusion' (p.11). These issues are examined, to varying degrees, in this book in relation, specifically, to student mobilities.

## Structure of the book

The first section of *Student Mobilities, Migration and the Internationalization of Higher Education* seeks to provide an introduction to some of the key debates which underpin the book. While this chapter (Chapter 1) has outlined both the significance and multi-faceted nature of contemporary student migration, Chapter 2 proceeds to address the important policy contexts of student mobilities, approaching this through an analysis of different policies at international, regional and national scales. It argues that while some scholars have contended that the internationalization of education should be understood as primarily a response to top-down globalizing pressures, individual nations retain considerable decision-making powers, and respond to the wider environment in different ways. Indeed, we suggest that there are complex articulations between global influences and the priorities of particular nations and regions. In this chapter, we also argue that, in understanding the drivers of international student policies, we need to look beyond the economic sphere: political, social and cultural factors all extend considerable influence over the formation of policy.

The second section of the book is concerned with providing geographically diverse, in-depth case-study examples of some of the issues raised in the introductory section, drawing on substantive research. Chapters 3, 4 and 5 focus on students from East Asia, Mainland Europe and the UK, respectively. Chapter 3 examines recent work on the transnational mobility of students from East Asia as they seek more valuable 'cultural capital' overseas. As a region, East Asia is the most significant source of international students globally, with China at the forefront of this mobility (British Council, 2004). For middle-class Chinese families, the accumulation of cultural capital frequently includes the practice of sending children overseas for education. An overseas (particularly 'Western', English-speaking) education is an essential part of what Mitchell (1997) has described as the 'self-fashioning' of Chinese elites, providing *embodied* cultural capital, inculcating children into the mores of a cosmopolitan middle-class lifestyle (Mitchell, 1997; Ong and Nonini, 1997). It also represents a valuable set of credentials that are generally recognized and rewarded by employers in the home society. This chapter focusses on recent research on highly mobile students from China, Malaysia, Hong Kong, South Korea, Singapore and Japan. It highlights: the important links between overseas study and immigration for many East Asian students; the significance of educational mobility as a 'family project'; and the embodied nature of international educational mobility.

Chapter 4 focusses on the experiences of mobile students within mainland Europe. In contrast to the experiences of their East Asian peers, European students tend to move for relatively short periods of time, usually between six months and a year (Findlay et al., 2006). Much of this movement has been facilitated by the European Union's (EU) Erasmus programme, which provides funding for students to spend part of their degree programme at an institution in another EU member state. Drawing on some of the themes introduced in Chapter 2, this chapter considers the extent to which student mobility in mainland Europe is allied to broader economic and political imperatives, such as the inculcation of a particular European identity (King and Ruiz-Gelices, 2003), and the relationship between EU initiatives and national education policy. The chapter also explores: the uneven geography of student flows across the continent; changes to such flows over time; and the social characteristics of mobile students. Finally, it considers the impact of student movement on both the politics and economy of the region.

Chapter 5 draws on findings of several recent research projects examining the international mobility of students from the UK as they seek higher education overseas and subsequent employment. To date, most of the interest in international student mobility has focussed on young people moving from countries in East and Southeast Asia to the major student-receiving destinations in North America, Canada, Australia, New Zealand or the UK (e.g. Butcher, 2004; Collins, 2006). Whilst these students are seeking the valuable cultural capital attached to an English-speaking, Western education, the motivations for UK students who go abroad for their education are less clear. This chapter explores: the factors that inform the decision to study at overseas institutions; the social and familial context to the decision-making process; and the relationship between social class, gender and ethnicity and overseas study. It also considers the nature of the experiences UK students have both while studying abroad and on return to the UK to seek employment. Amongst other things, we demonstrate the privileged nature of UK students' experiences of studying abroad; the relevance of particular global 'circuits' of higher education; and the way in which overseas HE often provides a respectable 'alternative' to the most prestigious and desirable universities in the UK. The third section of the book highlights the main themes and issues to arise out of these case studies, drawing the examples together. Chapter 6 examines the emergent *geographies* of student mobilities, and aims to bring a distinctive geographical perspective to the forefront of discussion. It does this in three main ways. Firstly, it points to the important spatial disparities in the internationalization of higher education, and the uneven flows of students which result from this. Secondly, it highlights the power imbalances represented by this system, the 'winners' and 'losers' within international geographies of student mobility, and the importance of what Massey (2005) has termed 'contemporaneous plurality'. Finally, the chapter explores what the 'new mobilities' paradigm and the concept of transnationalism represented by the social sciences can offer an analysis of student migration. In particular, it suggests that greater emphasis needs to be placed on both the material and symbolic meanings of educational mobility.

Chapter 7 reflects more broadly upon the nature of higher education in a changing world. It draws upon the regional case studies presented in Chapters 3 to 5 to argue that while the internationalization of higher education is strongly linked to the wider policy context (discussed in detail in Chapter 2), it is also explained by other aspects of societal change. Firstly, we explore the increasing importance of travel within young people's lives, the links between travel and higher education and the resources offered by overseas experiences for 'identity construction' within late modern society (Conradson and Latham, 2005). Secondly, we consider the relationship between international higher education and other types of migration, focusing specifically on the acquisition of citizenship and/or permanent residency of another country. We then go on to explore the ways in which international higher education may be affected by the changing nature of the graduate labour market and, as a result of the emergence of 'mass' higher education systems in many parts of the world, the increased competition for professional and managerial jobs. Finally, we focus on some of the pedagogical and social issues that are brought into sharp relief by significant increases in student migration. We consider the impact on knowledge creation and transfer, and on the inter-cultural experiences of both mobile and immobile students. To some extent, these changes can be seen as broadly positive: ushering in a more international curriculum in many subject areas in HEIs across the world; increasing the diversity of student bodies; facilitating cross-national friendships; and encouraging a more cosmopolitan outlook amongst those who choose to study overseas (and, perhaps, amongst those they come into contact with). It is also the case that, for some students, increasing opportunities for mobility have allowed them to secure better financial support and/or pay lower fees abroad than if they had remained within their own country. However, this chapter also points to the ways in which increasing student mobility may be serving to exacerbate inequalities – between both individuals and regions.

Chapter 8, the conclusion, draws together key themes from the previous seven chapters, outlines the key intellectual contributions made by the book and suggests fruitful future directions for research and policy in this area. It begins by highlighting the increasing importance of student mobility – to regional bodies, national governments and individual institutions – and exploring the ways in which strategies for internationalization have changed over the past decade. Drawing on the preceding chapters of the book and, in particular, the case study chapters, it then identifies three key themes. Firstly, it considers the different *scales* from which issues related to student migration can be approached, from the personal and familial to the national and transnational, and the different insights that each level of analysis can provide. Secondly, it examines some of the conceptual concerns that cross-cut these different scales of analysis, focussing specifically on the uneven geographies of student mobility. Thirdly, it attempts to bring together academic scholarship and more practically-orientated practitioner debates to identify some important policy implications. Here, we suggest some ways in which supranational organizations, national governments and individual institutions could respond to the various inequalities we have highlighted throughout the book. We end with some final remarks on the internationalization of higher education and point to the pressing need for further research in this area – not least to explore the ways in which the advantage that accrues from international mobility can be made more accessible to all students, and not just those from the most privileged backgrounds.

# 2
# Policy Context

## Introduction

It is frequently asserted within the academic literature that education policy-making has undergone a fundamental change over recent decades. This argument has two particular strands: firstly, that policy is no longer determined at the level of the nation-state, but by a number of highly influential transnational organizations; and, secondly, that economic imperatives have come to outweigh all others. This is articulated clearly in a recent paper by Montsios (2009), who contends that 'we are experiencing not only the transnationalisation of education policymaking but also the full submission of education to the pursuits of the global economy' (p.471). In this analysis, the 'internationalization' of HE (including the increasing mobility of students in pursuit of a degree) is seen as a direct consequence of these changes. Indeed, Cantwell and Maldonado-Maldonado (2009) claim that 'a general consensus has emerged whereby globalization is understood as an inevitable, downward pressing social, economic and political force and internationalization is the process of institutions responding to globalization' (p.289). In contrast, however, in this chapter we argue that while the changes brought about by both the growing international neo-liberal consensus and the increasing influence of international organizations are significant, individual nations retain considerable decision-making powers and can (and do) respond to the wider environment in different ways; indeed, there are complex articulations between global influences and the priorities of particular nations and regions. We also suggest that, in seeking to understand the imperatives that drive 'internationalization' in general and student mobility in particular, we have to look beyond merely the economic sphere. Political, social and cultural factors are also important, and exert considerable influence on policy-making.

In developing this argument, we begin by considering the wider international context – specifically, the role of international organizations in the structuring of education policy and the impact of a dominant, worldwide neo-liberal agenda. We then go on to explore the ways in which this agenda is mediated, first, by the region – by drawing on the example of the European Union – and, secondly, by the individual nation-state. We show how economic and political (and, in some cases, cultural) factors are important in structuring both regional and national responses to global pressures and the ways in which student mobility is understood and facilitated. As we noted in Chapter 1, the terms 'globalization' and 'neo-liberalism' are often used interchangeably in the literature. We have suggested that this can be problematic – as it can imply, erroneously in our view, that there are no other possible forms that globalization can or could take. However, in the discussion that follows the majority of references to 'globalization' in the work we cite is to the specific neo-liberal variant.

## The international context

### The role of international organizations

The World Bank plays a key role in what has been viewed by some as the increasing globalization of education policy. In 2009, it was the biggest external loan provider for educational programmes, which were implemented in about 85 countries across the globe (Montsios, 2009). Its influence was particularly apparent during the 1990s, mainly in developing countries. During this decade, the amounts lent by the World Bank – largely through its 'Structural Adjustment Policies' – for the purposes of education, constituted 27 per cent of all global external finance on education and 40 per cent of the total aid provided for education by international organizations (ibid.). As has been well-documented in the academic literature, all its funding is provided on terms which directly or indirectly define specific policy agendas that individual countries are expected to follow. These are informed by neo-liberal imperatives and, typically, are aimed at reducing national deficits through cuts in public spending, abolishing restrictions in global trade and opening national markets to capital flows. As Rizvi and Lingard (2010) note, Structural Adjustment Policies:

> Served to institutionalise everywhere the neo-liberal notion that governments were highly inefficient in promoting growth, and even in addressing the problems of social inequalities. [They] promoted

the ideology that only markets could solve the intractable problems facing societies. Markets thus defined the limits of national policies, by exerting an unprecedented amount of influence in shaping policies and in allocating funds for social and educational programmes. The policy role of nation-states was thus redefined as a facilitator of markets rather than an instrument that steered them or mediated their effects. (p.40)

In relation to education, specifically, the World Bank has tended to promote: decentralized school management, a 'free choice' of school for parents and pupils, greater involvement by the private sector, performance-related pay and the monitoring and evaluation of results (Montsios, 2009). While many such initiatives have been aimed primarily at the compulsory sector of education, they have had significant impact on the tertiary sector, too. In particular, they have helped to promote a standardized form of education in many developing countries that have been the recipients of World Bank loans, and encouraged them to see higher education as an arena in which they are required to compete against other nations.

While the World Bank's policies have sought to abolish restrictions in trade within developing countries, the World Trade Organization has led efforts to lessen restrictions on trade in services more generally through its General Agreement on Trade in Services (GATS) which came into force in 1995, as a result of the Uruguay Round negotiations. This agreement aims to prevent two forms of discrimination – between incumbents and new entrants to a market, and between domestic and foreign service providers – and is based on the assumption that competition will result in improved services as providers strive to meet consumers' needs more effectively (McBurnie and Ziguras, 2001). It specifies a range of conditions under which global trade in education is to be pursued (such as transparency of rules, liberalization of markets and the development of rules for solving disputes), and countries that join the GATS process are required to make a commitment to the ongoing liberalization of trade through periodic negotiations. Underpinning the agreement is an understanding of education as a commodified service and a specific ideological position, which institutionalizes 'a particular way of looking at international education, defined in terms of the efficiency of global markets in education rather than in terms of international education's more general political, social and cultural purposes' (Rizvi and Lingard, 2010, p.171).

The United Nations Educational, Scientific and Cultural Organization (UNESCO) is also influential in this field, and is the only United Nations agency with a mandate in higher education. Its first 'World Conference on Higher Education' was held in Paris in 1998 and, as Waters (2008) notes, helped to promote internationalism through its pronouncement of a 'World Declaration' on HE. In more practical terms, it led to the establishment of two networks that have generated research and policy debate on issues related to globalization and HE: the UNESCO Forum on Higher Education, Research and Knowledge and the Global University Network for Innovation. In 2009, a second World Conference on Higher Education was held, which reaffirmed the organization's commitment to maintaining a global outlook and helping to facilitate both the mobility of students and cross-border education more generally. Indeed, in his opening address to the conference, Koïchiro Matsuura, Director-General of UNESCO, contended that:

> The role of international cooperation is imperative because no institution can function in isolation. Governments must work with national objectives in mind, to ensure access on the basis of merit and to promote quality standards and stimulate innovation and research. But they must do so with a global outlook. It is through sharing ideas and knowledge that our societies will become more prosperous and sustainable. (2009, p.14)

These sentiments were shared by Angel Gurría, Secretary-General of the Organization for Economic Co-operation and Development (OECD), in her address to the conference, claiming that 'For higher education, globalization is a natural condition that is to be embraced' (2009, p.5). Here, assumptions about the inevitable and largely unproblematic nature of globalizing pressures are evident.

The OECD is also an important player in its own right, in contributing to the emergence of a common global agenda within higher education. The organization's aim is to bring together the governments of countries around the world that are 'committed to democracy and the market economy' and 'provide a setting where governments compare policy experiences, seek answers to common problems, identify good practice and co-ordinate domestic and international policies' (OECD, 2009, p.2). Its economic orientation and focus on the development of human capital have both been well documented, with Montsios (2009) claiming that, within the terms of its analysis, 'all educational phases are viewed as contributing to productivity and therefore all types of educational provision...should be aligned to this purpose' (p.477). However, as Henry et al. (2001) and Rubenson (2008) observe, the

OECD's understanding of the relationship between education and the economy has changed over time. In the 1960s and 70s, for example, although the two were seen as closely intertwined, education was understood as the most important driver of greater future income equality. By the 1980s, however, the nature of the relationship was seen differently: education was no longer promoted as a common good but as an instrument in global competition, and concerns for equality of opportunity were replaced by calls for flexibility and responsiveness to the needs of the labour market (Rubenson, 2008). Equity came to be conceptualized in terms of market participation, rather than as something to be pursued in support of social democratic ideals.

The OECD's impact in sustaining this agenda is significant (Vickers, 1994). Through its regular benchmarking exercises (such as its annual *Education at a Glance* publication and its education 'Indicators'), international comparisons (the Programme for International Student Assessment (PISA), for example) and policy reviews and recommendations, it has exerted considerable influence on education policy in many developed countries. Indeed, most national governments not only take their country's performance in OECD assessments very seriously, but also have dedicated 'international divisions' within their bureaucracies, which deal with global educational indicators and comparative performance measures (Rizvi and Lingard, 2010).

OECD benchmarks have, it is argued, had an important impact on both standardizing many educational processes in countries across the globe and helping to develop a global education policy. However, it is not the only actor in this field: as noted above, UNESCO has also engaged in the measurement and monitoring of national education systems, for example. In relation to HE, specifically, a key influence over recent years has been the 'world rankings' of universities produced, firstly, by the Graduate School of Education in Shanghai Jiao Tong University (SJTU), China in 2003, and then, a year later, by the UK-based *Times Higher Education Supplement* (THES). These have since been published on an annual basis and have received considerable attention from the media, the HE community and national governments. The measures used by both rankings systems have been criticized for advantaging large English-speaking universities especially in the US and the UK and for tending to 'both reproduce and exacerbate the existing vertical differences in the higher education landscape' (Marginson and van der Wende, 2007, p.320). Moreover, the rankings give no recognition to the differing goals and missions of universities, nor are they sensitive to internal differentiation (e.g. that an institution may be relatively weak in one disciplinary area, but a world-leader in another). Nevertheless, their impact has been significant. In Germany, for example, the relatively poor performance of German universities and, specifically, concern that no German university was in the 'top ten' of either league table led to the 'Excellenzinitiative', established in 2005. This aimed to develop a more hierarchical HE system and a German 'Ivy League', through concentrating research funding in national 'centres of excellence' (Hazelkorn, 2009). Similarly, Japan's recent HE reforms, which have sought to replace the traditional public-private distinction with differentiation based on market-sensitive profiles has, in part, been a response to global rankings (ibid.) as have similar developments in China and South Korea (Baty, 2009b). Such responses have also been replicated at the regional scale: when the first international league tables appeared, the European Union was concerned that only ten European universities were located within the top 50, compared with 35 American institutions, and began to formulate plans for developing a European Institute of Technology to increase regional competitiveness. As Hazelkorn (2009) notes, the SJTU and THES rankings can be viewed as an artefact of globalization: they appear to order global knowledge and provide a framework through which the global economy and national positioning can be understood.

The increasing standardization of higher education, through such benchmarking and ranking exercises, provides a further way in which the private sector has been able to infiltrate public sector provision. English language testing services, for example, which have assumed an important place in facilitating international student mobility (from non-English speaking nations to the US, UK and Australia, in particular) provide considerable business for a small number of large companies. The main players in this field are the American 'Educational Testing Service' (ETS), the International English Language Testing Service (IELTS), which is jointly managed by British and Australian public-sector organizations, and the University of Cambridge's ESOL examinations. ETS provides the Test of English for International Communication (TOEIC) and the Graduate Record Examination (GRE), required for admission to many graduate schools in the US. Although officially a non-profit organization, it has been criticized for operating as a multinational monopoly and for competing with for-profit companies in selling materials to help students pass the very tests that it develops (Nordheimer and Frantz, 1997).

Such standardization can be seen as both a response to and a driver of international student mobility. The common currency of English-language tests, the conditions tied to World Bank loans, the OECD's educational indicators, the WTO's policies to promote free trade and the criteria used to put together global university rankings all contribute to the globalizing pressures felt by HE sectors across the world. They encourage universities to view themselves as in competition with institutions in other countries for talented students, and young people (albeit, in most cases, a highly privileged minority) to come to see themselves as choosers within an international marketplace. Moreover, such pressures have been accompanied by a distinct shift in the discourse of international education and student mobility. In the 1970s and 80s, the economic, political and cultural purposes of education all carried considerable weight within the dominant discourses of the OECD and UNESCO, and international education was seen as a means of furthering both co-operation between nations and the inter-cultural skills of individual students. In contrast, more recent understandings of international education have positioned it, instead, as an export industry, and as a matter of global *trade* rather than aid (Rizvi and Lingard, 2006).

Nevertheless, while noting the increasing global pressures on higher education systems over recent decades and the constraints imposed upon national policymaking (Kelly, 2009), it is important to recognize that the influence of these international organizations is spatially differentiated; it is not experienced in the same way in all parts of the globe. Firstly, different organizations have different spheres of influence. The World Bank has more influence on developing countries than other nations, for example; the OECD, in contrast, impacts primarily the Western world. They also exert their influence in different ways, with the World Bank relying on loans and other forms of financial support, and OECD on the generation and production of different types of data. Secondly, countries differ considerably in the extent to which they are able to resist global pressures (Yeates, 2002). This is an important argument that is developed in more detail later in the chapter.

### The global economic context

The relationship between education and the economy has always been significant. Looking as far back as the 19th century, the introduction of compulsory schooling in England, as a result of the 1870 Education Act, was predicated largely on economic grounds, to provide the educated labour required by industry to increase Britain's competitiveness with Germany and the US, as well as to provide leadership in national government and within the British empire (Page and Silburn, 1999). In some ways we can see broad continuity in contemporary society with the development of schooling systems being increasingly linked to capitalist expansion and national development in a global or transnational economic context (Waters, 2008). However, some scholars have argued that global economic pressures are now exerted more directly on *individual educational institutions* (especially those at the tertiary level) without being mediated by the nation-state (Marginson and van der Wende, 2007). Knight (2004) claims that, for the HE sector, 'it is usually at the individual, institutional level that the real process of internationalization is taking place' (p.6). While this particular argument is not shared by all (e.g. Deem, 2001) and is subject to critical scrutiny in later sections of this chapter, few scholars contest the more general contention about the importance of economic influences on contemporary higher education.

Indeed, although we will argue that, in understanding the pressures that drive student mobility and the wider processes of internationalization within HE, it is important to explore the role of both the region and the nation, recognition must also be given to the wider economic context in which universities are operating and young people are making decisions about where to study. This has been characterized by a shift from social democracy – in which the main form of social provision was through the state, and social welfare was accorded high importance as a means of addressing inequalities – to neo-liberalism – in which the market has become the main mechanism for the delivery of services, and social welfare is seen as merely a safety net. Although this is often seen as an inevitable consequence of globalization, Rizvi and Lingard (2010) highlight the ideological nature of such claims, arguing that 'these discourses are based on a politics of meaning that appear to seek to accommodate people and nations to a certain taken-for-grantedness about the ways the global economy operates and the manner in which culture, crises, resources and power formations must be filtered through their universal logic' (p.33).

Neo-liberal pressures can be seen to be exerting a two-way influence on student mobility: from the top-down, through the policies put in place and actions taken by national governments and individual tertiary institutions in different parts of the world; and from the bottom-up, largely through the decisions taken by young people as to where they will study. The two influences are, of course, closely linked: students' decision-making is strongly affected by the nature of the higher education systems in place across the globe. As noted above, central to the neo-liberal agenda is the belief that markets are much more efficient providers of services than public sector bodies, and that government expenditure on HE (as on other forms of social welfare) should be curtailed as much as possible. Thus, the last two decades of the 20th century witnessed a considerable reduction in state funding for HE in many parts of the world, and the emergence of a 'managed market', governed by the state using various market mechanisms (Kelly, 2009; Sidhu, 2006). As this coincided with an expansion in the number of places available in the tertiary sector, many institutions faced a crisis in their finances. In this context, international education was seen as a potential panacea, offering financially-stricken institutions a new source of revenue (Waters, 2008). In Australia, for example, federal government funding for universities declined by 30 per cent between 1995 and 2000. International students were pursued vigorously as a means of addressing this shortfall and, by 2003, cross-border student fees provided over 14 per cent of higher education revenues (Deumert et al., 2005). As many other Western countries were developing similar strategies, an aggressive global market developed with nation-states and individual universities deploying increasingly sophisticated branding and marketing techniques to entice students overseas (Sidhu, 2006). Recently, they have been joined by other non-Western countries, keen to gain a segment of the lucrative international student market. Such competitive pressures have been exacerbated by the international comparisons and various benchmarking exercises described above, which have exposed differences between both national systems and individual institutions. In response to this type of international market, some developing countries have attempted to restrict the number of students who pursue HE overseas (such as Malaysia). Others have, however, positively encouraged such migration, seeing it as a relatively cheap means of both responding to heightened domestic demand for tertiary education and increasing the skill level of the population as a whole.

Universities, themselves, have also been encouraged to act in more entrepreneurial ways within an increasingly marketized system. Indeed, Clark (1998) argues that in response to neo-liberal global pressures, all universities are being pushed into similar kinds of market-driven behaviour. Examples of this, he contends, include: taking on a wide range of entrepreneurial activity; diversifying the sources through which higher education is funded; strengthening the central management function of the institution; and persuading academic staff of the need for transformation and continual change. This last point is developed in more detail by Slaughter and Leslie (1997) in their work on *Academic Capitalism*. They argue that staff in HE institutions across the globe have come, increasingly, to adopt market-like behaviours as a result of the competitive environment which has grown up around them and changes to funding streams for academic research. In particular, they point to the decline in the availability of public funds and the growing necessity to bid for grants from private sector organizations and develop close links with multinational corporations. Although some scholars have been critical of the evidence base on which such claims have been made (e.g. Deem, 2001) and have pointed to the capacity for resisting neo-liberal pressures exhibited by some university staff (Archer, 2008), the increased focus on international education and the facilitation of student mobility can be seen, in part, as congruent with this agenda. International higher education has, it is argued, come to be viewed as a private good and commodity to be freely traded. In turn, this emphasis on free trade and movement between nations has stimulated the mobility of both university staff and students (Altbach and Knight, 2007). However, the way in which such influences are played out in particular countries and institutions varies considerably, as will be discussed in more detail later in the chapter.

These changes, wrought by neo-liberalism, have encouraged many young people and their families to see themselves as 'choosers' within an educational market. They have felt compelled to compete against others, to secure the 'best' education possible which will, many hope, smooth their path into the graduate labour market and well-remunerated professional employment. Such trends have been exacerbated by perceptions of 'credential inflation'. As we argued in Chapter 1, the increasing massification of HE across the globe has encouraged the view that a first degree is no longer sufficient to secure entry into well-paid professional employment. Studies from many countries have documented the ways in which young people (largely from middle-class backgrounds) and their parents have tried to secure new forms of 'distinction' within this shifting market. These have included: going on to higher levels of study (by enrolling for a master's degree, or some other form of postgraduate qualification); taking up internships, work experience and/or relevant extra-curricular activities; and gaining entry to high status universities (Brooks and Everett, 2009; Brown and Hesketh, 2004; Reay et al., 2005). In some parts of the world, moving overseas to pursue a higher education is an important component of such strategies. Indeed, in her analysis of migration between Hong Kong and Canada, Waters (2008) argues that:

> when faced with credential inflation, middle-class families in Hong Kong seek scarcity value through an overseas education. This bestows

greater value in the job market and serves to exacerbate the impact of credential inflation for locally educated graduates. (p.24)

As we noted in Chapter 1, the inclination and ability to 'choose' within educational markets differs significantly by social location (Brooks, 2005). Even within national markets, research has shown how different social groups have different capacities to overcome the 'friction of distance' (Harvey, 1989, p.211). In the UK, for example, data on university admissions have emphasized the different geographies of higher education choice, with high achievers from more privileged backgrounds choosing within *national* markets of high status HEIs, while their peers engage within *regional* markets of less prestigious institutions. Similar disparities are also played out within the international arena: those who move abroad for HE are typically from privileged backgrounds with considerable amounts of cultural, social and economic capital to draw upon (Brooks and Waters, 2009a; Findlay et al., 2006; Kenway and Fahey, 2007).

Alongside such arguments about the inequalities exacerbated by educational 'choice' policies are others which outline some of the disadvantages brought about by the increasing internationalization of HE. Some of these relate specifically to the provision of 'cross-border delivery' or 'commercial presence', where the student remains in his or her home country. These include: difficulties of regulating the content of courses offered by out-of-country institutions; damage to local universities and colleges by the incursion of foreign providers; the undermining of the values and priorities of the host county; and the potential exploitation of local academic staff by foreign employers (Altbach and Knight, 2007; McBurnie and Ziguras, 2001). Others focus more specifically on when students themselves are mobile, such as: the potential for local students to be 'shut out' of some courses by the presence of more lucrative overseas students; concerns that lower standards are required of overseas students at some institutions, when compared with domestic applicants; and the growth of bogus qualifications from private colleges (Waters, 2008). Pedagogical concerns have also been raised, such as the privileging of Western bodies of knowledge and modes of analysis among overseas students in universities in the US, UK and Australia (Kenway and Fahey, 2007; Sidhu, 2006) and the lack of space made available to international students in these countries to challenge the dominant culture of Western academia (Robinson-Pant, 2009) (see Chapter 7 for a more detailed discussion of these themes).

Nevertheless, it is important to recognize that, while the influence of the global economic context and the ascendancy of neo-liberalism, in particular, help to explain the increasing significance attached to international student mobility by many nation-states and HEIs, they should not obscure the important political motives that also underpin policies to facilitate student migration. Sidhu (2006) points to various ways in which the political agendas of both international organizations and individual countries have had an important influence on the way in student migration has been configured in particular parts of the world. For example, Malaysia's affirmative action programme, initiated in 1971, which sought to reserve domestic university places for ethnic Malays led to a significant outflow of students from other ethnic groups (particularly Chinese and Indian) to destinations such as the UK, Australia and the US. Moreover, Sidhu suggests that political imperatives also underpin the way in which overseas students are chosen by receiving countries. Indeed, she claims that particular groups are excluded through the visa-screening process operated by many Western nations and that, 'in the overwhelming majority of instances, it is "First World" identity markers that differentiate the desirable from the undesirable student' (p.24).

## Regional contexts

While we would argue that political imperatives are often as important as economic factors in driving global policy in relation to international education, generally, and student mobility, in particular, we suggest that similar motivations are at play at the *regional* level. Certainly, this has been the case historically. The Colombo Plan, for example, was an aid plan for the Asia-Pacific region established by Commonwealth countries in 1950. Alongside the provision of technical help and financial assistance, it offered scholarships for students in developing Asia-Pacific countries to study at a First World university (Oakman, 2005). Although its primary aim was to provide economic support and help establish local elites, it was also 'linked to the strategic interests of the developed countries within the broader politics of the Cold War' (Rizvi and Lingard, 2010, p.168), namely to slow down the spread and appeal of Communism. Political objectives are also evident in contemporary regional policies to stimulate educational mobility. Moreover, by focussing on the regional level, we demonstrate some of the ways in which global pressures are mediated by more local concerns. Indeed, in the next part of the chapter we illustrate this argument by drawing on a case study of the European Union and its HE policies from the 1970s until the present day.

## The European Union and educational mobility

As we note in Chapter 4, it has been argued that the EU's policies to promote educational mobility have been the most successful part of its entire social policy programme to date (Papatsiba, 2006; Recchi, 2006). These policies are predicated on three discrete yet interlinked objectives: to help to develop the EU economically, by furthering the inter-cultural competences of young people and their capacity and willingness to live and work in other European countries; to promote the cultural identity of the region, by fostering a distinct 'European' identity amongst young people; and to develop a political elite, committed to the goals of further European integration. It is, however, evident that the precise policy objectives that have underpinned student mobility programmes, as well as the EU's stance towards international education more widely, have not remained static over time. They have shifted significantly since the creation of the European Union in the 1950s. In charting these changes, we draw heavily on Susan Robertson's (2009) insightful delineation of three distinct but overlapping policy trajectories in her analysis of the evolution of European higher education.

Robertson argues that Europe's approach to internationalizing HE has become more complex over time as the European Commission and other key European actors have responded to pressure within regional and global economies, some of which have been discussed above. The first policy trajectory she identifies as 'Crossing National Boundaries'. Within this phase of policy development (from 1955 until 1992), HE was viewed primarily as a mechanism for the creation of the region of Europe and the development of its elites. Robertson contends that 'culturally, the concern was to create a European citizen with a European sensibility and sense of responsibility to a bigger political entity – Europe' (p.69); politically, it was to provide the new intelligentsia for European government; and economically, it was to provide a pool of graduates for a single European labour market. While various initiatives are associated with this trajectory, such as the creation of the European University Institute in Florence, Italy, in 1971 and encouragement for universities across the region to work more closely together, the most important policy development was the establishment of the Erasmus scheme in 1987, to facilitate short-term exchanges between higher education students. This was politically expedient as it allowed the European Commission to promote a strongly European agenda, while doing little in any direct sense to undermine the sovereignty of the individual member states. Despite failing to attract the number of students that was hoped for initially, the Erasmus scheme has been an important driving force in student mobility across the continent and is discussed in considerably more detail in Chapter 4.

The second policy trajectory identified by Robertson is what she terms 'Creating the New Europe and Europe of Knowledge Through Blurring National Boundaries'. This shift in higher education policy was marked by the Maastricht Treaty (signed in 1992) which gave the EU a more direct role in education and was a response to broader trends, namely the global transition from Keynesianism to neo-liberalism. Within this changing international environment, it was thought that in order to be competitive, Europe had to restructure along market lines. This gave rise to a number of significant policy developments, all of which aimed to promote economic growth within the region and make a substantial contribution to developing European human capital. Foremost among these were the commitment to develop a 'European Research Area' and a 'European Higher Education Area' (EHEA) via the Bologna Process established in 1999. Central to both is the promotion of academic mobility. The mobility of students (and also researchers and other staff) was seen as an important means of putting into practice a unified higher education area, with a common qualification framework and comparable quality assurance criteria and methodologies. Moreover, the EHEA was seen as a key marketing tool to attract students from other parts of the world, and to increase the appeal of Europe as a destination country for educationally mobile young people. Nevertheless, as Robertson recognizes, despite the large number of countries that have signed up to the Bologna Process (47 as of January 2011), the level of engagement with the policy has not been consistent across the continent. Neither does Bologna offer equal rewards to all; indeed, the increased mobility both within Europe and to Europe from other regions is likely to benefit the most affluent countries with more prestigious education systems, thus entrenching further the uneven geography of student migration.

Despite the enduring nature of many of assumptions made during this second policy phase, Robertson suggests that, since 2003, we have witnessed a third, distinct trajectory – which she calls 'Destination Europe: the EHEA as Lure'. This, she claims, signals a more explicitly globalizing strategy, aiming to 'legitimate the EC [European Commission] as a state-like actor' (p.78) and provide a more solid springboard for competition with the US. In this policy phase we have seen the emergence of initiatives such as the 'transfer' of the Bologna process to other parts of the world, through the 'Tuning[1]' and 'Asia-Link[2]' projects, and the creation of an active European HE market and industry. It is important to note that, in this third policy trajectory as in the previous two, student mobility retains a central role. Indeed, the 'Erasmus Mundus' programme, established in 2004, aims to encourage the mobility of students and academic staff between EU and non-EU universities through funding scholarships for individuals and partnerships between institutions. It has been seen as part of a wider marketing strategy for the European Higher Education Area. One of the Erasmus Mundus funding streams is dedicated specifically to projects to promote European higher education worldwide. Underpinning this activity is a clear concern that Europe has relatively little presence in the global market for international students.

Robertson's analysis is important in emphasizing, firstly, the salience of political and cultural objectives, in addition to the economic and, secondly, the distinctiveness of Europe as a region and mediator of global pressures. The significance of regional disparities is also noted by Marginson (2007) who argues that, unlike the 'Americanisation' of higher education, which shows few signs of being a 'top-down' political project, the 'Europeanisation' of HE, articulated partly through facilitating the mobility of students and staff, is a much more managed process, aiming at deliberate convergence. He acknowledges that some recent changes have been driven by 'internationalization' – i.e. negotiating closer collaboration between sovereign states. However, they have also been underpinned by the process of 'globalization', through the creation of pan-European systems and spaces with the potential to modify the role of nation-states (p.310).

While the European and American models remain distinct, there is some evidence that Europe's focus on developing the region is causing other parts of the world to re-think their own strategies to compete for international students. Olds (2007b), for example, suggests that the emergence of a more integrated European HE system has encouraged Australia, in particular, to push for greater collaboration between countries and institutions within the Asia-Pacific region. He argues that this has been prompted by concerns that, otherwise, Asian students may increasingly choose a European destination over Australia. However, other Asian countries have also seen some merit in developing stronger regional coherence: the ten countries of the Association of South-East Asian Nations have committed themselves to establishing a common space for HE in south-east Asia by 2015.

## National and local contexts

As we have noted above, it is our contention that the nation-state remains a key player in the drive towards internationalization. Knight

(2004), for example, outlines five specific national-level rationales which often underpin involvement in initiatives to promote internationalization and student mobility: developing human resources (e.g. through recruiting and retaining the brightest overseas students, and preparing well domestic students for participation on the international stage); establishing strategic alliances with other countries for geo-political and/or economic benefit; generating commercial trade (through the provision of various transnational educational services); nation-building; and developing social and cultural life, through recruiting a more diverse student population. These, she suggests, are common to many countries across the globe. It is also the case that, despite the frequent deployment of the discourse of 'an inevitable and unstoppable globalization' which gives governments and universities few choices (Sidhu, 2006, p.123), when we explore national policies in more detail, we find considerable disparities in responses to global pressures. These are considered below.

During the 1990s, many political theorists argued that the nation-state had lost its authority. This analysis was underpinned by the assumption that global economic pressures were placing severe constraints on the autonomy of national governments, while international bodies were usurping many of their powers. More recently, however, and particularly since the al-Quaeda terrorist attacks on the US on 11th September 2001, this view has been reassessed. As Rizvi and Lingard (2010) note: 'against a new discourse of security, it has become clear that many powerful states, such as the United States, have reasserted their authority; and that national policy authority is indispensable in coordinating and controlling global mobility, interactions and institutions' (p.29). They argue that the rise of international terrorism has drawn attention to the importance of strong nation-states by virtue of their capacity to influence the behaviour of their citizens while ensuring that the social conditions are in place to facilitate capital accumulation. In relation to policy more specifically, while the state is no longer necessarily the fundamental unit of world order as a result of the emergence of new policy actors (from the private and voluntary sectors) and global and regional networks, it retains an important role in both policy co-ordination and in the development and delivery of programmes. Indeed, in the sections that follow, by drawing on examples of differences in national approaches to student mobility and other aspects of the internationalization of HE, we argue that the state has become an important mediator of both global and regional influences. Specific political, economic, historical and/or cultural factors influential at the national level help to determine how particular countries respond to some of the global imperatives we have outlined above.

## The nation-state and international organizations

Although we have suggested above that international organizations have played an important role in developing a global market for HE, nation-states have been able to retain some autonomy in the face of such globalizing pressures. For example, Marginson and Rhoades (2002) point to the reciprocal influences on the World Bank and other international agencies that are exerted by some nation states and through the agency of some education professionals 'who individually and collectively fashion a discourse and pursue research agendas that offer ideas, data, legitimacy and challenge to the World Bank' (p.297). It is, however, important to note the considerable differences between countries in their capacity to resist global pressures: while China may be able to resist World Bank policies by virtue of its 'powerful, historically shaped indigenous institutional structures' (ibid., p.296), developing countries, which typically have a much less well-developed infrastructure, occupy a more vulnerable position.

Research on the way in which the World Trade Organization's General Agreement on Trades and Services operates has also highlighted the enduring influence of the nation-state. In their case studies of higher education in the Czech Republic and the Netherlands, Vlk et al. (2008) suggest that although the steering capacity of the nation-state has become more complex and less obvious than in the past, it is still the most important player in the policymaking arena; power is exercised through the formulation of national policies and decisions about whether or not to sign up to regional and international initiatives. Moreover, despite the high profile given to GATS within both policy debates and the academic literature, it is important to note that all countries that are members of the OECD have chosen to retain firm control of the national character of the HE system under their jurisdiction (Green, 2003) and analysis of World Trade Organization negotiations reveals a strong national-interest bias (Marginson and van der Wende, 2007). Indeed, Green (2003) contends that, even in the contemporary world, human skills remain relatively immobile and national. Thus, governments 'increasingly see them as state resources to be deployed in the battle for comparative advantage in the global market' (p.87) and are unlikely to want to give up their prerogative in relation to the development of education policy. Similarly, at a regional level, Susan Robertson (2009) has suggested that progress towards achieving a European Higher Education Area may well be impeded by European member states keen to protect their own national interests and reluctant to cede any further decision-making powers in relation to education. This is evidenced by the fact that the European Commission has been obliged to advance its educational agenda through voluntary rather than regulatory means, namely the 'Open Method of Co-ordination' (Green, 2003).

## Diversity in national approaches

The enduring influence of the nation-state is also evident in comparisons of specific national responses to global pressures. Sidhu (2006) points to considerable differences between the US, on the one hand, and Australia and the UK, on the other, in their reasons for wanting to develop international education and attract overseas students. In Australia and the UK, she argues, the international student is seen primarily as an object of trade, as someone who makes a valuable contribution to export income. In both countries, strenuous efforts to increase the number of international students within domestic universities followed a reduction in public sector expenditure during the 1990s. The significant decrease in state funding to Australian universities has been described earlier in the chapter, and similar trends have been seen in the UK. In both countries there are also important national political imperatives at play. Sidhu (2006) suggests that UK educational mobility policy is driven, not only by the desire to derive revenue from overseas students and thus ensure that its universities are internationally competitive, but also to develop and retain influence overseas. Indeed, she contends that within the marketing reports on overseas students 'the old colonial narrative of consuming other geographies is telling' (p.138). Her analysis of Australian motives is similar, suggesting that both political and economic objectives underpin international recruitment:

A discourse of national interest has been influential in shaping power-knowledge relations within international education. Various institutional reforms have been undertaken in the interest of national competitiveness to develop an education export industry. At the same time, an older colonial text, premised on Australia as an educator of Asia and Asians, remains in place, along with a national fear of being swamped by the other. (p.229)

In contrast, in the US, the overseas student is constructed rather differently: not as a source of additional revenue for a tightly-squeezed higher education sector, but as prized human capital. Such students are valued for: providing cheap academic labour within universities; maintaining enrolments in disciplines where domestic interest is waning (such as science and engineering); contributing to developing US enterprises; and upholding US interests overseas (Sidhu, 2006). This last point has assumed particular importance since the 2001 al-Quaeda terrorist attacks: international students are often regarded as members of a 'pliable elite class' with similar interests to the US (ibid., p.73), who can help to promote American values in other parts of the world on their return home. Such national differences are evident, not only in national policy statements, but also in the marketing campaigns which are targeted at overseas students. On the basis of her analysis of marketing material from a range of British institutions, including the British Council (the organization with overall responsibility for promoting British education overseas), Oxford Brookes University and the London School of Economics, Sidhu (2006) argues that economic imperatives are intertwined with icons of Empire:

> The student is imagined and constructed as an elite economic subject for whom an international education means acquiring a credential that has currency in the global economy. At the same time, an othering discourse is also at work, resurrecting a passive other who seeks tutelage from the West/North. (p.175)

Similar differences emerge with respect to the priorities and motivations of 'sending' countries. As noted above, affirmative action policies in Malaysia which have favoured Bumiputras (ethnic Malays) have led many ethnically Chinese students to seek higher education abroad, while the economic growth experienced by countries such as India and China over recent years has led to an increase in demand for prestigious overseas education from the expanding middle-classes (Rizvi and Lingard, 2010).

The importance of national interest in determining student mobility policies is also evident in Olds' (2007a) account of the development of a 'Global Education Hub' in Singapore. Since the late 1990s, this Pacific Asian city-state has been making significant efforts to develop a knowledge-based economy, through shifting the base of its economic activity and by presenting itself – within academic, industry and media circles – as a cosmopolitan and creative space (ibid., p.960). Education has assumed a key role in this process, 'being perceived as a vehicle to diversify the economy, spur on restructuring in indigenous institutions of higher education, while also re-branding Singapore as a hub of the global KBE' (p.964). Financial and other incentives have been used to attract a large number of prestigious Western universities to set up linkages with Singapore, including joint teaching and research programmes, student and staff exchanges and the establishment of offshore campuses. Institutions represented in this way include Massachusetts Institute of Technology, Stanford University, Cornell University, INSEAD and the Australian National University. Similar imperatives appear to underpin Mauritius' attempts to establish itself as a 'cyber-island' and regional hub by attracting ICT firms from India and Western countries. A key feature of its plans for development is a 'knowledge centre' in which over fifty foreign universities and professional bodies offer local programmes (Gribble, 2008).

National policy can also shift considerably over time, indicative of some degree of agency on the part of the nation-state. The UK provides an interesting example of this. In recent years, the British government's position on the internationalization of education has found formal expression through two specific initiatives. The 'Prime Minister's Initiative on International Education' ran from 1999 to 2004 with the aim of increasing the number of non-EU international university-level students in the UK by 75 000 by 2005, and encouraging collaboration between universities, colleges, government and other bodies to promote UK education abroad. This was followed by a second such initiative (commonly referred to as 'PMI 2'), which was launched in 2006 to run for five years. Although this was also motivated by a strong desire to increase the number of international students (at university level) coming to the UK and secure the UK's place as 'a leader of international education', more importance was placed on reciprocity between countries and institutions, acknowledging that British students and HE staff can themselves benefit significantly from the opportunity to study and/or work abroad. This shift in emphasis was evident in Prime Minister Tony Blair's speech of April 2006 (DfES, 2006), when he launched the second phase of his initiative, and also in the work that was commissioned subsequently. This has included a good practice guide on student mobility (Fielden, 2007) intended to help HEIs to prepare for greater outward (international) mobility by their students. Explicit in this work is a recognition that a period of study abroad can offer important benefits to both the individual and wider society through the acquisition of a more cosmopolitan outlook and the development of inter-cultural skills.

Student mobility policy is often intimately bound up with immigration policy which also differs from nation to nation, and changes over time. As will be discussed in more detail in Chapter 7, in the early 21$^{st}$ century, Australia made it increasingly easy for international students to secure permanent residency at the end of their studies (Baas, 2006). Here, stimulating inward student mobility was understood partially as a response to shortages of skilled workers within the labour market. In contrast, the US and UK both introduced more stringent processes for granting student visas – following concerns about potential terrorists entering the country after the attacks on the US of 11th September 2001 and, in the UK in particular, the growth of 'bogus colleges' (House of Commons, 2009; Norman, 2010).

## Regulation and student rights

Different national approaches to international education and educational mobility are also played out in the different ways in which countries choose to regulate such provision. A comparison of regulatory policies in three South East Asian countries (Hong Kong, Malaysia and Australia) was conducted by McBurnie and Ziguras (2001). In Hong Kong, the key goal of legislation at the time of their research was consumer protection: courses needed to be 'registered' or to have gained exemption from regulation through partnership with a Hong Kong institution but, in general, regulation relied on the assumption that an institution's home country had appropriate quality assurance mechanisms in place. There was, therefore, no attempt to regulate directly the quality of transnational education that took place; this was left largely to market mechanisms. In Malaysia, however, relevant legislation was driven by the aim of advancing specific nationalist goals (such as building local infrastructure, reducing the outflow of students and preserving particular values). Thus, strict regulation was put in place to ensure that higher education met what the government perceived to be the cultural and economic needs of the country. Specifically, formal approval was required to establish an educational institution, and also for each individual course that was run. Australia's regulatory system was underpinned by a further set of concerns, namely to protect both its local system of higher education and the reputation of Australian higher education within the global marketplace. This led to measures including: standard entry requirements for new providers (with the aim of protecting existing institutions); a quality assurance system (to maintain the credibility of Australian HE in an increasingly competitive market); and requirements of greater accountability from all providers (McBurnie and Ziguras, 2001).

National disparities in regulatory frameworks are matched by similar differences in the rights accorded to mobile students in various parts of the world (Deumert et al., 2005). As Deumert et al. note, while there are plenty of international policies that aim to encourage students to move to pursue higher education abroad, there are no such policies that seek to protect them during such stays. Instead, students' rights differ significantly between countries. For example, while New Zealand introduced a 'Code of Practice for the Pastoral Care of Cross-Border Students' in 2004 (see Lewis, 2005), its neighbour, Australia, had no formal means of offering significant pastoral care to mobile students. Moreover, national governments are under no particular pressure to address this issue as international students are not citizens of the host country and, for sending countries, they have moved outside their jurisdiction. Deumert et al. go on to suggest that the absence of global policy in this area 'results in the failure of social and economic institutions to recognize the multiple vulnerabilities of international students, constructing them mainly as consumers rather than individuals with a variety of social and economic rights' (Deumert et al., 2005, p.330).

## The importance of the local

Finally, there is some evidence to suggest that it is not only nation-states that are important mediators of global influence. Local authorities and individual HEIs can both also operate a similar role (Knight, 2004; Marginson and Rhoades, 2002). For example, over recent years the Japanese government has taken steps to promote internationalization across the HE sector and, specifically, to encourage inward migration of overseas students to help fill a shortage of highly skilled workers. In 2008, a 'Plan for 300 000 Exchange or International Students' by 2020 was published by the Council on Economic and Fiscal Policy – a significant increase on the 118 000 such students enrolled in Japanese universities in 2006 – while, the previous year, the Prime Minister's Office had argued explicitly for further internationalization of HE to enhance the global competitiveness of Japanese society (Yonezawa et al., 2009). However, on the basis of a survey conducted by Yonezawa et al., it appears that relatively few academics and students were committed to the government's agenda. Indeed, the authors note that 'the current policy emphasis on the international competitiveness of research and human relations alone...is not sufficient to accelerate the internationalization of higher education in Japan' (p.140). A similar degree of resistance to global pressures has been documented in some American states. While, taken as a whole, the US plays an important role in both encouraging and facilitating student mobility, there are some notable local disparities. For example, Marginson and Rhoades (2002) note that in some American states there is pressure to limit the proportion of out-of-state students and international students, in particular, who attend public universities – on the grounds that state taxes should be used to fund education for state residents only.

## Conclusion

The movement of students across the world in pursuit of a higher education is strongly affected by education policies, and also by policies in other areas, including employment and immigration. This relationship is, however, reciprocal: although much student movement is influenced by relevant policy, it also informs and stimulates it, for example as individual nations and universities seek to increase their attractiveness to potentially mobile students. In this chapter, we have sought to explore the complexity of policy in this area and assess its main drivers. In contrast to some of the claims about the 'globalization' of education policy, we have argued that while there are a range of international actors who exert considerable influence in this territory (for example, the World Bank and OECD) and a pervasive neo-liberal orthodoxy, the nation-state continues to play an important role in policy-making. This influence is evidenced through the significant diversity in national approaches to student mobility and the ways in which national governments themselves contribute to the shaping of international organizations. We have also suggested that it is important not to overlook the way in which policy is made and/or resisted at other scales. Indeed, we have argued that focusing on the regional level is of crucial importance in understanding recent drivers of student migration within Europe, while local imperatives (from particular geographical areas and/or institutions) can also influence significantly both the formulation and implementation of policy in different parts of the world. As a corrective to accounts which foreground the economic drivers of student mobility, this chapter has also emphasized the importance of political and cultural influences on policy – influences which are at play at all of the levels of policy-making discussed above, from the global to the local. These themes provide an important background to the actual practices of mobility in different parts of the world. It is to these case studies that we now turn, focussing firstly on migration by students from East Asia.

# 3
# Mobility of East Asian Students

## Introduction

Although increasingly discussed in terms of globalization, as the chapters in this book attest, the reality of international education is geographically highly uneven and far from global in scope and reach. In this respect, Asia – and particularly East Asia – has a disproportionately important role to play in global mobility patterns. The majority of all international students originate from Asia and most of these come from a relatively small number of countries – China, Malaysia, Hong Kong, South Korea and Singapore. Although the figures surrounding international flows of students are contested and inconclusive (based on differing, country-specific methods of reporting), they point to one clear fact – that East Asia is the most important source of international students globally (British Council, 2004 – although see Bone, 2010; OECD, 2007; OECD, 2009). One country presently dominates demand for international student places – the People's Republic of China – with its substantial and growing unmet domestic demand for higher education, and a seemingly insatiable desire for 'Western' experiences and credentials. This chapter intentionally focusses on the people who lie behind the numbers and statistics pertaining to international education and the mobility of students. It draws together various qualitative empirical studies of East Asian students abroad,[1] to consider their personal and social motives for, and experiences of, international education and mobility. In what follows, we examine some specific themes that have emerged out of a study of the contemporary academic literature on East Asian student mobility. Whilst the literature brings to light some distinct *differences* between the mobility of students from East Asia and those from Europe and the UK (discussed in Chapter 4 and 5), it also suggests some emerging and enduring similarities between international students more broadly. We begin this chapter, however, with a brief discussion of the most significant contextual factors, within which contemporary East Asian student mobility is embedded.

## Contextualizing and embedding mobility: structural factors

The international mobility of students from East Asia over the last 30 or so years corresponds to a number of socio-economic and political changes in the region. These include the rapid growth of a new middle-class in the so-called 'Asian Tigers' and Japan, the augmentation of knowledge-based economies (making higher education an ostensible 'necessity'), geo-political instability, and China's dramatic economic development. A remarkable transformation of the Asia-Pacific regional economy occurred from the mid-1960s onwards, particularly in Taiwan, Singapore, Hong Kong and South Korea (Dicken, 2003). With economic growth, the class structure of these East Asian societies was transformed and a new middle-class of capitalists and professionals emerged (Robison and Goodman, 1996). As has been shown in subsequent research, this new middle-class was extremely geographically 'mobile', resulting in large trans-Pacific population flows from East Asia to the US, Canada, Australia and New Zealand from the mid-1980s onwards (Castles and Miller, 1993). Similarly, in the People's Republic of China, phenomenal economic growth over the last two decades has resulted in a burgeoning class of wealthy individuals with the inclination and necessary resources to send their children abroad for education. As Chew (2010, p.95) has written: 'Bearing in mind that half of China's population is below the age of 25 and that undergraduate applications to Peking University in the past few years have over a million applicants for very limited places [...] structural mechanisms are in place for the rise in [overseas education]'. Consequently, China is now the largest source country of international students globally (Bodycott, 2009). Xiang and Shen (2009) have examined the link between international education and the *production* of social-class inequalities in mainland China, and identify three 'stages' in students' outward mobility. The first, from the late 1970s to the mid-1980s, involved state-sponsored individuals who were, upon their return, assigned to important positions in government and state-owned business (see Qian Ning, 2002, for an in-depth examination of this stage of outward mobility). The second stage, from the mid-1980s to the mid-1990s, involved large numbers of (wealthy) students going abroad for language education – in other words, they were able to purchase 'valuable' credentials. Most recently, the wish to attend particular, prestigious Western universities has taken hold, although only the wealthiest and best connected individuals can achieve this (Xiang and Shen, 2009). This latter stage in the development of educational mobility out of China corresponds directly to discussions in Chapter 5 on UK students abroad, and the more general discussion of geographies of student mobilities in Chapter 6. Here, we highlight 'the importance of "global circuits" of tertiary institutions...[throwing] into sharp relief the global framework within which a small minority of highly privileged young men and women are making their university choices' (Brooks and Waters, 2009a, p.1009).

Throughout East Asia, other developments have occurred that have made an overseas education a particularly attractive option. These include the consolidation of knowledge-based economies and the related importance of academic credentials for bolstering employment prospects. Within the region, access to tertiary education has grown over the last two to three decades, leading, some argue, to 'credential inflation' or 'diploma disease', and making overseas qualifications an attractive and 'rarer' alternative (Xiang and Shen, 2009). However, expansion has also served to exacerbate competition for access to the most prestigious local universities – the 'fierce competition' to which Seth (2002) refers in relation to South Korea. Higher education, at a local university, is the ultimate goal of most families, and yet a relatively small percentage of the population are able to achieve this. To take the example of Hong Kong, at the beginning of the 1980s, only 2 per cent of students of aged 17–20 had access to higher education, increasing to 8 per cent by 1990 and 18 per cent by 2007 (Education Bureau, 2007). Whilst this represents a remarkable expansion, it is still a significantly lower percentage than for many other countries (for example, around 45 per cent in the UK), indicating the 'fierceness' of the competition for university places in some countries within East Asia. In other countries, however, such as Japan and South Korea, a much higher percentage of school-leavers can access higher education 'domestically'. In these circumstances, *differentiation between* local institutions becomes important, and generally an overseas education (at a renowned international institution) is only sought when the option of studying at the most prestigious local institutions has been foreclosed.

Whilst this provides some context for mobility, it does not sufficiently explain why so many students from the region are choosing to go overseas. To answer this question, we have to turn to qualitative research on the motivations and strategies of individuals and their families in relation to education. Research on student mobilities tends to be divided into work on larger scale student flows and corresponding international, national, regional and institutional policy on the one hand, and in-depth, qualitative empirical research focusing on the experiences of individual students on the other. In this chapter, we pay greatest attention to the second of these, and a review of this literature would suggest that there are two primary issues of relevance here: first, the importance of a university degree; and second, the desire for an English-medium Western education. These will be discussed below. First, however, a distinction needs to be drawn between 'international students' and 'educational immigration'.

## International students versus 'educational immigration'

The majority of debates around international student mobility (and, indeed, most of the examples given in this book) concern individuals holding 'student visas' or 'study permits' and focus on education at the tertiary level. In later chapters, we also discuss free movement between EU countries, where a student visa is not required. However, not all individuals who move overseas for education travel in these conventional ways. There is another type of mobility that is surprisingly common amongst students from East Asia, known as 'educational immigration' (Butcher, 2004) and although *higher education* is the *ultimate* goal, individuals will often relocate overseas before the end of secondary education, completing the final years of high school abroad. They will then transition into university education overseas. This has been particularly well documented for students from Hong Kong, Taiwan and South Korea (Lee and Koo, 2006; Waters, 2008). To illustrate this, the following was reported in a Chinese-language newspaper published in Canada: 'In Hong Kong and Taiwan [...] youngsters may not be allowed to graduate if their results are poor. Here in Canada, as long as one goes to school, one will sooner or later graduate' (Ke, 1998, cited in Waters, 2008, p.115). This perception – that it is relatively easy to graduate from high school and thereby transition into university abroad – has been significant in driving educational migration from East Asia. There is a very real sense that it is impossible to 'fail' in the 'West', whereas failure is rife 'at home' as the following quotations from interviews with students from Hong Kong in Canada illustrate:

> Evan is reluctant to admit to failure, although he implies as much. He gave a typical response to the question of why his family had immi-

grated to Canada: 'Because they [his parents] think that in Canada the education system is better than in Hong Kong.' When pushed to elaborate on his parents' thinking he admitted: 'I think that the main purpose of the migration was that me and my brother didn't study well in Hong Kong, and there was a lot of stress and the standard was very high in Hong Kong. But in Canada, the general level of education...a large proportion of students can get into the universities [...]'. Another interviewee here indicates the negative repercussions of failing in the local system and remaining in Hong Kong: [...] 'Most people have exam anxiety and they will just fail the exam. They just can't go on to the next level. That's why the Hong Kong education system is so depressing, compared to Canada's education system, which is more like, if you don't do well in the provincial exam you can try again next year, or in May. You can try it three times in a year. But in Hong Kong you can only try it once a year and you can only try it twice. If you fail it more than that you just...You just get a low job or your self esteem will just go down so badly.' (Waters, 2008, pp.134–135)

For these reasons, students and their parents will pursue educational immigration before the student fails secondary education in Hong Kong.

Returning to this distinction between educational immigration and international student migration: Murphy-Lejeune (2008) describes 'marked differences between' categories of mobile student. She writes:

a...distinction must be made between *permanent residents* and *internationally mobile students*. The first category is defined by two main criteria, location of second-level qualification and permanent residence of the parents. For example, in France, permanent residents account for about 20 per cent of 'foreign' students...most of them may have grown up and been educated in France, even if they may not have acquired French citizenship...The second category of students are...defined as students who leave their country or territory of origin and move to another for the purpose of studying. (Murphy-Lejeune, 2008, p.20, emphasis in original)

Recently, however, research has emerged suggesting that this distinction is not as clear as it might seem. Ley (2010, p.208) quotes an interviewee from Taiwan, who moved his family to Vancouver, Canada, three years after his son had entered Canada on a student visa. The Taiwanese father said: '"My son came to study as an international student. He has been

here for five years. I came to visit him. He liked Canada very much so we decided to apply for entry."' In many cases, then, 'immigration' of the whole family begins with the mobility of an individual student. Waters (2008, p.137) describes the 'sound and rational [economic] logic' underpinning many Hong Kong families' decision to relocate the entire household overseas, where education is the primary objective. One of her interviewees told her:

> Because international students have to pay three times more than what the local students have to pay [...]. If you are an immigrant like, maybe for example an investment immigrant, you have to invest money...But when you do the calculations it is still cheaper – much cheaper – than to go there and study as an international student. So maybe some families make that decision based on the kids' future. Some families, for example my friend, they will stay there until the son or the daughter has finished their education and then they will move back to Hong Kong and continue their life, working. So you can see that it's an investment. It's an investment in a financial way. (Waters, 2008, p.137)

Thus, the distinction between international students and 'immigrant' students is rarely clear-cut. In this case, an unambiguous financial strategy underpins this family's decision to migrate for their children's education – it is seen as 'cheaper' to invest money in the Canadian economy ($500 000 under the 'investor' immigrant stream, returnable without interest after three years) than it is to pay 'full' international student tuition fees for two children over four or five years. This is a theme that has emerged in several studies of East Asian student mobility (e.g. Li et al., 1996). Butcher (2004) has examined educational immigration to Auckland and writes: 'not only is New Zealand one of the cheapest providers of English language education in the world, it is even cheaper if the student migrates to New Zealand and thus avoids paying full fees' (p.265). The fact is that many immigrant families are motivated to migrate overseas by concerns over their children's education. Those with permanent resident status will pay 'local' tuition fees. International students, in contrast, are likely to be charged 'full-fees', which are many times higher than the local rate. Statistics on international students, such as those produced by the OECD (2007, 2009), do *not* capture the seemingly large number of students who *immigrate* for education. The influence of education on global mobility patterns is therefore likely to be far higher than is usually thought.

## The family in educational mobilities

The importance of educational immigration for East Asian students raises another related theme that has emerged strongly in the literature on migration from this region – that is, the significance of *family*. Migration for education is rarely an individualistic pursuit, but enlists directly other household members. This can be seen in a number of ways. Firstly, as described above, East Asian student mobility often involves the migration and relocation of the *entire household* (parents, children, and sometimes although less usually grandparents too) (Kobayashi and Preston, 2007; Ley, 2010; Waters, 2005). This view contrasts starkly with the way in which we habitually conceive of international students – as footloose and, importantly, highly independent beings (see, also, argument made in Chapter 5). East Asian students, particularly those who have immigrated for education, are conversely seen as variously tied to and embedded within their family context. Another important point to be made here with regards to East Asian student mobility concerns the *age* of students. Most research on international students is concerned with those moving for tertiary-level education. However, in the context of East Asia, mobility at a far younger age is common, and a small body of work has recently emerged, examining this trend (Huang and Yeoh, 2005; Kim, 2010; Lee and Koo, 2006). Young children (at primary or secondary level) are usually relocated with a view to accessing higher education abroad too, although this is not always the case.[2] They do this as part of a family migration.

The recent literature on migration for education has described various emergent household formations related to this mobility. 'Wild geese' or *kirogi* families originate principally from South Korea. A simple definition of *kirogi* families is 'families that are separated between two countries for the purpose of children's education abroad' (Lee and Koo, 2006, p.533). The emergence of these families coincides with what has been termed the 'early study abroad' trend in South Korea. There are other features of *kirogi* families of note: they tend (just like tertiary-level international students) to seek education in a fairly limited number of overseas countries – the USA being by far the most popular destination of Koreans, followed by Canada, Australia and New Zealand (Lee and Koo, 2006). However, as Kim (2010) has observed, very recently a market in English-medium education has opened up *within* East Asia, in countries such as Singapore (Huang and Yeoh, 2005), leading to an increase in educational immigration *within* the region. Another characteristic of *kirogi* families is that children are invariably accompanied overseas by their mothers, whilst their fathers remain in South Korea to work. This type of education migration is highly gendered in nature.

Another type of arrangement, with many features that are similar to the *kirogi* family, is found amongst migrant households from Hong Kong, Taiwan, and more recently mainland China. These are the 'astronaut' families and 'parachute' or 'satellite' kids (Bohr and Tse, 2009; Ho, 2002; Kobayashi and Preston, 2007; Lam et al., 2002; Man, 1995; Orellana et al., 2001; Teo, 2007; Waters, 2002, 2003, 2008; Zhou, 1998). Unlike the 'wild geese' of South Korea, where a mother and child will travel abroad, in astronaut households the *whole family* emigrates, initially, overseas. After a short while, the father will return to East Asia to work. The reasons for migration, research has shown, are often multifaceted[3] but almost always encompass an overriding concern with children's education (Kobayashi and Preston, 2007; Waters, 2002). Like the *kirogi* families, astronaut households involve the separation of husbands and wives, and fathers and children for prolonged periods – usually between two and sixth months at a time. They reveal similarly gendered patterns – only in exceptional cases (see Waters, 2010) do fathers remain behind to take care of the children whilst mothers return to Asia to work. Astronaut households are usually relatively affluent and the parents are well-educated; most immigrate as 'business migrants' (often 'investors') or 'skilled workers' (Ley, 2010). It also involves migration to a relatively small number of countries – again the USA is a popular (although not *as* popular) destination, with Canada, Australia and New Zealand proving equally attractive locations. Unlike the 'wild geese', however, the children in astronaut households are usually older (at least of secondary age). It has been found that the family is most likely to relocate when the oldest child reaches the age of 14 or 15 – just prior to sitting the HKCEE (Hong Kong Certificate of Education Examination) in Hong Kong, or the high school and college entrance examinations in South Korea, which will, down the line, determine university entrance (Waters, 2008).

Whist this literature tends to stress the 'mother's sacrifice' for their children's education, in a relatively small yet significant number of cases, mothers will 'abandon' their children too, after deciding to join their husbands in the country of origin. These are the 'parachute' or 'satellite' kids (Orellana et al., 2001; Pe-Pua et al., 1996; Waters, 2003; Zhou, 1998) who often live overseas alone, without daily adult supervision. Qualitative research has portrayed the lives of satellite children from Taiwan, Hong Kong and South Korea, who immigrated to North America or Australia in the 1990s. Different studies of 'satellite' children reveal remarkably similar arrangements – siblings usually live together in a large house bought for them by their parents, in an affluent neighbourhood (in Southern California, for example, or in Vancouver, British Columbia) (Waters, 2003; Zhou, 1998). They have access to a bank account out of which they pay the household bills. Many have a cleaner visit once a week. In the case-study presented by Orellana et al. (2001), Korean children stayed with relatives or boarded with Korean American families in the Californian suburbs, but other research has shown that many children live alone without adult supervision (Waters, 2003; Zhou, 1998). Interestingly, given the educational drivers, one of the biggest 'social problems' associated with satellite kids is absenteeism from school and failure to complete academic assignments (Waters, 2003; Zhou, 1998).

Other pertinent examples are found in the work of Xiang and Shen (2009), who highlight a growing trend in the migration of 'little overseas students' (*xiao liuxuesheng*) from mainland China. Then there is also a small amount of work on 'study mothers', referring to a particular scheme, found in Singapore, called the 'Long Term Social Visit Pass', available to a 'Female Social Visitor whose Child/Grandchild is studying in Singapore on a Student's Pass' (Huang and Yeoh, 2005, p.386). Research has also examined migrant mothers and children from China and Korea in Singapore (Chew, 2010; Huang and Yeoh, 2005). By focussing only upon mobility for tertiary or higher education, some researchers have missed the substantial migration of children and parents, which can occur well before then, yet with similar educational goals in mind.

Education, therefore, is fundamentally a 'family project', imbued with familial expectations and goals, affecting students at all levels (primary, secondary and tertiary) (Sin, 2009; Waters, 2005). Sin (2009, p.293) argues that educational 'success', for Malaysian university students, tends to be 'framed around ideas of familial duties and responsibilities' and the need to reproduce *the family's* status and lifestyle. Students' choice of degree subjects is therefore far less directed by 'enjoyment', but rather has constantly to have strategic 'career goals' in mind (Sin, 2009). In Sin's (2009, p.293) study, one student participant, in particular, would have preferred 'to become either a chef or a musician' but instead chose a subject suited to 'the practicalities of labour demand'. Similarly, Waters (2003) has found that even though Chinese immigrant students often wanted to pursue personal interests in the arts or humanities at university, they were forced to bend to the wishes of their parents, who preferred more obviously vocational subjects (such as engineering, medicine, or other science-based degree programmes). Students also feel obliged to follow the requests of their parents because, invariably, family provides the main source of funding and income (British Council, 2004; Rizvi, 2000; Sin, 2009). One study by China's National Bureau of Statistics in 2001, cited by Bodycott (2009), concluded that more than 60 per cent of Chinese families invested one third of their total household income on their children's education. Sin (2006, p.253) draws on her research on Malaysian students in Australia to illustrate the weighty influence of parents over the lives of East Asian students:

> Siew Lui relies on her parents to finance the tuition fees and living expenses during her study in Australia. Since they would be paying for her overseas education, Siew Lui's parents had the ultimate say in the choice of study destination and academic programs. As a result, she had to forgo her personal interest in architecture to study economics and accounting, which were thought to be 'more practical' by her parents. Siew Lui's move to Australia was deliberately planned by her parents who wanted her to obtain permanent residence and to incorporate successfully into the Australian labour market. She was not happy with her parents' choice of degree programs for her, but nevertheless, felt obliged to follow her parents' wishes.

These findings (and, indeed, others revealed in Chapter 5), contrast with prevalent portrayals of international students, whose decision-making around their education is presented as relatively individualistic, even when family members are consulted (see Brooks and Waters, 2009a; Findlay and King, 2010; Waters and Brooks, 2010a). More generally, this book argues that many international students draw upon significant social capital (friends and family) at different stages in the migration-education-transition to work process. Discussions of East Asian migrants make especially strong reference to social capital in relation to wider discourses of 'filial piety' and Confucianism, stressing communal responsibilities and concerns taking priority over individual goals and objectives (Waters, 2003). Bodycott (2009, p.267) has discussed these ideas in relation to mainland Chinese international students, writing: 'confronting or disagreeing with parents can be seen as a sign of disrespect....In Chinese culture, the family plays an integral role in the process of career decision making.' East Asian transnational students, it would seem, have to confront a contradictory mix of 'tradition' and 'hyper-modernity' in their experiences of mobilities and international education. The gender dimensions of this are explored in relation to international students from Japan, below.

## Transnationalism

> [D]uring the last two decades of the twentieth century, a new form of transnationalism arose, driven by a perception that international migration is in the best interests of children, especially with respect to education. Livelihoods remain at the source, not the destination. In the twenty-first century, geographically dispersed families have made transnational practices an integral part of their lives. (Kobayashi and Preston, 2007, pp. 151–152)

In this quotation, Kobayashi and Preston (2007) suggest a close association between international migration, children's education, and transnationalism. Indeed, the majority of recent writing on the mobility practices of international students has, both explicitly and implicitly, made reference to the concept of transnationalism (Gargano, 2009) and has described these students as inherently 'transnational' (Collins, 2008). Writes Waters (2007): 'Like expatriates, the "overseas-educated" are also cosmopolitan and habitually transnational. They are fluent in at least two languages and have frequently lived overseas, consequently claiming an intimate understanding of more than one culture (Hannerz, 1996). Significantly, they also possess a strong sense of group identity that functions as valuable "social capital" in the work environment' (p.478). 'Transnationalism' is commonly defined as the process by which migrants actively maintain a variety of ties (political, social, economic and emotional) to more than one country simultaneously (Basch et al., 1994). As noted in detail above, recent scholarship on East Asian migration depicts the spatial dispersal of households; some family members continue to live and work in Asia as others reside in North America, Australia or New Zealand (e.g. Kobayashi and Preston, 2007; Ley, 2010; Waters, 2002). Many such families possess dual (or even triple) citizenship, caricatured in Ong's (1999) description of the Hong Kong-Chinese 'multiple-passport holder' who claims to feel at home anywhere, as long as it is near an airport. Transnational migration is inextricably linked to wider accumulation strategies, which include (usually centrally) the acquisition of education.

The transnationalism of East Asian students manifests itself in a number of different ways. Firstly, as suggested, many students are part of transnational families – households that are geographically 'split' between countries and sometimes also continents. In his typology of transnationalism, Vertovec (1999) calls this a transnational 'social morphology', indicating social relations that span international borders. This has been well documented in Canada, where an unknown number of immigrant families from Hong Kong, Taiwan, and more recently the People's Republic of China live in so-called 'astronaut' or 'wild geese' households, as discussed earlier. In all of these documented cases, the household is split and individuals' daily lives are effectively 'lived' in two places simultaneously – almost continuous contact (via telephone, fax, television and the internet) is maintained between the country of origin and destination. Many of the children in these families will have acquired two or more passports by the time they leave full-time education, and will often embody the kinds of cosmopolitan traits depicted by Ong (1999) in her book *Flexible Citizenship*.

This brings us to a second important aspect of the 'transnationalism' of East Asian students – its *embodied* nature. By virtue of the fact that they have often lived in at least two countries for a period of time, students will accrue various traits and characteristics – such as language, comportment, style of dress, sense of humour – which mark them out as different from their non-migrating peers (Ong, 1999). Sin (2006) describes this well in an account of the experiences of Malaysian students in Australia. These students assumed that 'exposure to a Western environment', as necessitated by an international education, 'would refine their speech and manners, thus granting them social prestige in Malaysia' (Sin, 2006, p.255). Here, transnational experiences are embodied in the individual and can be seen as a form of *cultural capital* (Bourdieu, 1986). This aspect of international students' experiences is explored in more detail below.

A small number of studies point to a more invidious side to international students' 'embodiment'. Participants in Matthews and Sidhu's (2005) study (which focussed largely on individuals from China, Korea, Indonesia, Thailand, Japan, Hong Kong and Taiwan in an Australian school) described themselves as 'visible' targets of racial abuse, where international students were frequently picked on and ostracized. Perhaps less obviously racist, but nevertheless damaging, was the way in which 'teachers struggled to pronounce the surnames of several international students' (Matthews and Sidhu, 2005, p.59). In the context of New Zealand, Collins (2006, p.217) has examined media representations of North East Asian students in Auckland, and uncovers 'a singular racial identity that is known by stereotypical economic, cultural and social characteristics.' Such representations 'serve to essentialise the difference and distance between the dominant population' and international students, with harmful social effects (Collins, 2006, p.221). A further, recent paper by Park (2010) explores the intersection of race and gender in British Columbia, Canada, in response to six attacks on East Asian female international students in 2002. These attacks, she argues, were inherently racist and resulted, in part, from a 'gendered orientalist script...of Asian cultural and moral inferiority' (Park, 2010, p.349). It is notable, however, how few academic studies have focussed on racism in relation to international students, despite some recent high profile media stories, particularly around attacks on Indian students in Australia (Baas, 2006).

Continuing the theme of 'embodiment', East Asian students' embodied transnational experiences are also revealed through their consumption practices. Collins (2008) discusses the 'culinary consumption choices' of South Korean international students. His research presents a seemingly contradictory picture – on the one hand, students regularly frequent Korean restaurants in their country of study and cook Korean foods at home. At the same time, they are seen habitually to socialize in 'global franchises' such as Starbucks. This latter practice (patronizing Starbucks) is in fact, Collins argues, part of students' 'reconnecting' with home, as Starbucks has become 'localised in South Korea and has subsequently been re-globalised through the journeys students have made to Auckland and the practices they engage in here' (Collins, 2008, p.166 – see also Collins, 2010, for a discussion of the 'embodied' transnationalisms of South Korean international students).

Linked to their consumption practices, international students are also actively involved in the '(re)construction of place or locality', making reference here to Vertovec's (1999) 'typology' of transnationalism (see also Collins, 2004, 2008). Collins (2004) describes how South Korean students have changed the landscapes of Auckland's inner city. The number of international students in Auckland alone is approaching 50 000, and the majority of these are from East Asian countries (Collins, 2004). In addition to demographic and economic impacts, Collins writes, 'international students have also been associated with a socio-spatial transformation in the inner city of Auckland' (2004, p.53). Parts of the city are now 'filled' with places selling Korean merchandise (shoes, bags and clothes). There is a Chinese supermarket and bookshop, a Korean hairdressing salon and a Japanese cafe. An 'Asian' food court has appeared and it is reported that Auckland's apartment blocks increasingly resemble those in Hong Kong and Tokyo. In their work on international students in Melbourne, Australia, Fincher and Shaw (2009) describe how developers are producing apartment blocks for students with particular perceived 'cultural tastes' in mind. One local developer reportedly said; 'the people who move into them know what they are moving into and a lot of them are from high rise cultures. So you have lots of kids coming from Hong Kong and Singapore and Kuala Lumpur and so on and...a lot of them are out of exactly those types of buildings' (cited in Fincher and Costello, 2003, p.174). Perhaps inadvertently, the development of particular apartment blocks for certain 'types' of international student has resulted, Fincher and Shaw (2009) argue, in the segregation of transnational students in central Melbourne, with detrimental effects.

One final point to make with regards to the 'transnationalism' of East Asian students concerns their subsequent mobility, on completion of their education. According to Ong (1999, p.89), migrants from Hong Kong (including students) 'seek the kinds of symbolic capital that have international recognition and value...especially in the transnational spaces where the itineraries of travelling businessmen and professionals intersect with those of local residents'. This notion of 'transnational spaces' raised in relation to 'businessmen' and 'professionals' is significant and chimes with the motives and objectives of mobile students (Waters, 2007). Waters (2007) has described how international education operates in the creation of what Leslie Sklair (2001) termed a 'transnational capitalist class' – an 'exclusive' group of transnational professionals, whose 'commonalities' are formed in and through experiences of international education. She writes:

Sklair's (2001) concept of a 'transnational capitalist class' (TNCC) asserts the pivotal role of cosmopolitan professionals in both initiating and directing globalization. According to Sklair, the TNCC comprises four sub-groups: 'corporate executives', 'globalizing professionals', 'globalizing bureaucrats and politicians', and 'consumerist elites'. Together they constitute a 'new class...[pursuing] people and resources all over the world in its insatiable desire for private profit and eternal accumulation' (p.4). Members of this group are seen to possess similar lifestyles, patterns of consumption and, importantly, *educational histories*...They have 'outward-oriented global rather than inward-oriented local perspectives on most economic, political, and culture-ideology issues' (p.20), whilst collegiality is cultivated through 'an institutional network of schools, clubs, [or] resorts' (p.13). Although Sklair gives far too little attention to the role of education in the creation of the TNCC, he does mention the potential importance of American business schools in inculcating a 'transnational...outlook' amongst international executives. (p.479)

In this paper, Waters (2007) proceeds to argue that Western-educated locals are a crucial and yet neglected faction of the TNCC, operating in key, strategic positions within international financial centres throughout East and Southeast Asia. Overseas-educated graduates have the advantage of embodying various cosmopolitan traits, of being tied into particular transnational social networks, *and* of having a good understanding of the local market. The 'overseas-educated', she argues, 'constitute an *exclusive club*, formed through similar experiences of education and migration, which bestows various tangible privileges upon its members' (p.480).

Thus, international education is often seen by students as a ticket to future international mobility enabled by their inherent 'cosmopolitanism' – they have the ability and drive to take their credentials 'anywhere'. A rather different picture, however, is painted by Li et al. (1996), who compared the 'migration intentions' of Hong Kong students, one group studying in Hong Kong and the other in the UK. They found that 80 per cent of total respondents intended to return to/remain in Hong Kong following graduation from university – thus living in the UK (and pursuing an 'international' education) would seem to have had little influence on the propensity of these students to be 'transnational'. Other studies of ostensibly 'internationally mobile' students have similarly suggested rather limited subsequent mobility – the majority of students in Waters' (2008) study of Hong Kong immigrants in Canada *returned to Hong Kong* following their graduation, to seek work in the local labour market. For some, this had always been their intention, and a degree from a Canadian university was simply seen as a means to this end (as opposed to a spring board towards a cosmopolitan and transnational existence). In relation to mainland China, Xiang and Shen (2009, p.520) discuss the extent to which the Chinese state is attempting to 'attract [overseas] graduates back to China': by the end of 2007 nearly 320 000 had returned (Xiang and Shen, 2009). The authors chart a whole host of 'generous offers' to returning overseas graduates, including financial incentives ('golden hellos'), free office facilities, housing and seed funds for research (Xiang and Shen, 2009). These findings contrast, to a certain extent, with pervasive discourses surrounding 'hyper-mobile', spatially 'flexible' and elite transnational migrants. They suggest a transnationalism of sorts, but a circumscribed transnationalism, which would appear to be in some ways more aligned with the old fashioned notion of 'return migration'.

Ong (1999, p.19) provides perhaps the most famous depiction of this, writing about:

> the flexible practices, strategies, and disciplines associated with transnational capitalism...the new modes of subject making and the new kinds of valorised subjectivity. Among transnational Chinese subjects,

those most able to benefit from their participation in global capitalism celebrate flexibility and mobility.

This 'celebration' of mobility has been challenged, more recently, by geographers uncovering the realities of transnationalism for many individuals and their families – including the strains that physical separation place upon marital and parent-child relationships (Waters, 2002; Waters, 2010) and experiences of business failure and loss of self-esteem amongst 'successful' entrepreneurs (Ley, 2010; Ley and Kobayashi, 2005). It is perhaps worth reflecting, then, upon the extent to which international or immigrant students can be considered *truly* transnational, if we take transnational to indicate some sort of cosmopolitan and footloose existence. International students are tied to place in various ways.

## The search for cultural capital

> *[T]wo species of capital* now give access to positions of power, define the structure of social space, and govern the life chances and trajectories of groups and individuals: economic capital and cultural capital. (Wacquant, 1996, p.x)

The desire for international (and particularly 'Western') credentials has been expounded by Ong (1999), who has written: 'For many ethnic Chinese in Hong Kong and Southeast Asia, [...] strategies of accumulation begin with the acquisition of a Western education...' (p.95). According to Ong (1999), an overseas education should be conceptualised in terms of various 'accumulation strategies' – the accumulation of cultural, social and, ultimately, economic capital. Academic credentials reflect the significance of accumulating cultural capital for aspiring East Asian elites. Other writers have pointed to important political and economic drivers to mobility (Ley, 2010; Li et al., 1996; Skeldon, 1994) – particularly concerns in Hong Kong and Taiwan about the influence of the People's Republic of China in the territories.

Attempts to understand the motivations of international students more generally have suggested the importance of cultural capital in its embodied and institutionalized aspects (Findlay and King, 2010; Waters, 2008). Cultural capital is one of several different forms of capital, according to Pierre Bourdieu, who has proffered the most systematic and developed account of the role of capital in the stratification of society and the reproduction of social status. Put simply, Bourdieu has argued that *access* to capital determines life-chances, and this tends to be self-perpetuating. According to Bourdieu (1986), capital can take three principal forms: economic capital, 'which is immediately and directly convertible into money and may be institutionalized in the form of property rights'; cultural capital, 'which is convertible, on certain conditions, into economic capital and may be institutionalized in the form of educational qualifications'; and social capital, 'made up of social obligations ("connections"), which is convertible, in certain conditions, into economic capital' (p.243). Here we are primarily concerned with the second of these – cultural capital. Cultural capital can be either 'institutionalized', 'embodied', or 'objectified' (Bourdieu, 1986). Institutionalized cultural capital is represented by formal academic qualifications or credentials and there is seen to be a clear link between possessing institutional cultural capital and successful employment outcomes.

East Asian students' institutionalized cultural capital is often characterized by an extremely narrow selection of academic subjects at university. As Rizvi (2000) notes, 'A large majority of Malaysian students in Australian universities are...enrolled in the faculties of management, commerce, or economics' (p.215). A very similar pattern was found by Waters (2008) in her study of Chinese immigrant students in Vancouver, Canada. Over 60 per cent of those interviewed had 'majored' in economics, commerce, or a science subject. There is clearly a practical, pragmatic element to this. Most would seem to be driven either by perceived employment imperatives, or, as discussed above, by the expectations of parents and other family members.

The acquisition of specific academic credentials is only one aspect of cultural capital, however. This form of capital also 'presupposes embodiment', involving a process of incorporation that 'implies a labor of inculcation and assimilation, [and] costs time, time which must be invested personally by the investor' (Bourdieu, 1986, p.244). Recent scholarship on the mobility of East Asian students has made reference to the deliberate and self-conscious fashioning of embodied competences, linking to the earlier discussion of embodied transnationalism. Students perceive themselves as 'body capital' that can be 'constantly improved to meet new and shifting criteria of symbolic power' (Ong, 1999, p.91). For middle-class families from East Asia, the accumulation of cultural capital frequently includes the practice of sending children overseas for education. An 'overseas education' offers more than a valuable academic credential, however. It is an essential part of what Mitchell (1997) has described as the 'self-fashioning' of Chinese elites; it provides *embodied* cultural capital, inculcating children into the mores of a cosmopolitan and 'hypermobile' middle-class lifestyle (Mitchell, 1997; Ong and Nonini, 1997).

A review of the literature on student mobilities out of East Asia points to one overwhelming concern, directly related to cultural capital, and that is the desire for fluency in English. This is particularly the case for South Koreans choosing the 'early study abroad' route, where it is deemed 'too late' to migrate overseas once children have started high school (Lee and Koo, 2006). Writing about 'study mothers' from Korea and China in Singapore, Phyllis Chew (2010) has termed this type of transnational mobility 'linguistic migration', leaving us in no doubt of the critical importance of language acquisition. She writes: 'Linguistic migration is a migration necessitated primarily in search of a "linguistic capital", relating usually to "premium" languages such as English, which is readily exchangeable in the market place for other kinds of capital. Such linguistic pursuits are seldom impulsive or random actions. On the contrary, they are well-planned and carefully calculated projects' (Chew, 2010, p.83). Park and Bae (2009) have also discussed the significance of English in driving migration for education, this time in terms of 'language ideologies', encompassing:

> the belief that good English skills are an indispensable requirement for success in the global economy, that early exposure to an English-speaking environment is necessary for successful acquisition of English, and the more general ideology that views Koreans in general as being unsuccessful in learning to speak English without the opportunity of living overseas...But the most important for our purposes is the belief that competence in English conducive to social mobility can only be obtained at specific geographical locations, namely the English speaking countries of the West...In other words, *jogi yuhak* [early study abroad] must be seen as driven by globally dominant ideologies of English that constitute highly specific views of language, place and social space. (Park and Bae, 2009, p.368)

Park and Bae (2009) raise several issues which necessitate further examination. The first is the link that is frequently drawn between English skills and 'employability'. English provides students with a 'positional advantage' in their home labour market (Brown and Hesketh, 2004). There is a strong belief that employers in Asia (within certain occupational sectors) will value highly competency in English. One young Canadian graduate from Hong Kong ('Natalie') now working in human resources, quoted in Waters (2008, pp.164–165), expressed the following widely held view:

> I guess that some of the managers or HR [human resources], they find that people that come back [to Hong Kong] from the outside countries are more outgoing and they have better communication

skills. They are not afraid of expressing themselves. These are the good qualities that they are looking for. They don't want to hire a fresh graduate where they cannot speak English in front of the clients, even to get some information. Sometimes they [local graduates] are a bit introverted – they think of a lot of things but they won't tell you. In a Western style, it's sort of like, you have to stand up for yourself and express yourself and things like that. And also when they conduct the interview they will test your English level, so some of the Hong Kong graduates were stuck. It's not that they don't know how to answer; it's that they don't know how to express themselves because they don't have the practising experience.

As Natalie here implies, competency in English equates to more than merely being able to 'get by' in the language. It is about expressing oneself in an outgoing and confident manner and displaying, as Ong (1999) has described, a 'Western comportment'. The *kirogi* fathers interviewed by Lee and Koo (2006, p.541) spoke of wanting their children to speak 'fluent English without any accent'. Educational migrants desire that their children be *immersed* in an English-speaking environment. Research on educational migration from Korea to Singapore has shown how mothers remain highly dissatisfied with children's progression when educated through the medium of English in a (predominately) *non-English-speaking*, public school environment (Park and Bae, 2009). The option of living, for several years, in a *Western* country is clearly not open to everyone. On the contrary, this indicates a degree of privilege and exclusivity, which in and of itself imparts value on the holder by the simple virtue of being different.

The importance of English hints at the enduring colonial legacy underpinning the development of international education (Madge et al., 2009; Rizvi, 2000). Sin (2009, p.290) writes:

Despite 50 years of independence from British rule, Malaysian society, particularly among its older generation, still experiences a mild form of colonial mentality, apparent in the uncritical tendency to make reference to and follow standards set by the former British imperial power...A British education is very attractive in this sense.

Rizvi (2000, p.222), in his own study of Malaysian international students in Australia, observes the fact that students 'had already been subjected to Western cultural pressures well before they came to Australia for education.' The general tendency for international students to move from 'East' to 'West' in search of education, and the prominence of the English language in students' discourses (the widespread desire for an English-medium education) is undeniably attributable to highly uneven (post)colonial relationships (Li et al., 1996; Madge et al., 2009; Matthews and Sidhu, 2005; Ong, 1999). Matthews and Sidhu (2005) have urged scholars studying international education to take an 'historical perspective' when it comes to understanding the dominance of the English language. There are, they argue, unavoidable links between 'international education, modernity, colonialism and imperialism' (Matthews and Sidhu, 2005, p.56). They claim:

> Early expressions of international education, education aid programmes, were inspired by the rationales of colonialism, which were intended to produce an acculturated, governing elite in the colonies who were anticipated to support Western interests. Imperialism's influence extended to the post-independent societies, which were steered towards a Westernised template of civicness, towards sameness rather than diversity. These links continue to have implications for the capacity of contemporary expressions of international education to author post-colonial forms of cosmopolitanism. (ibid.)

However, despite this, as Rizvi (2000, p.220) argues, 'the fear of unbridled Westernization' amongst international students is misplaced. Students confront simultaneously colonial histories, local idiosyncrasies, and the 'contemporary homogenizing experiences of "global media spaces"' (Rizvi, 2000, p.221). International students cannot help but become 'locally embedded' to a certain extent, whilst at the same time, as observed by Collins (2004), they actively recreate the overseas urban spaces that they inhabit, and make them their own. The widespread 'Westernisation' of international students is at best a grossly oversimplified representation of reality. Correspondingly, Matthews and Sidhu's (2005, p.60) Australian study has shown that international students:

> did not automatically defer to Western cultural preferences. Many Chinese students preferred Chinese pop music, movies and novels, whilst Korean, Vietnamese, Indonesian and Chinese students identified a marked preference for their ethnic cuisines. Indeed, their immersion in Western culture appeared to reinforce rather than subjugate these tastes.

Waters (2008), in her study of Hong Kong immigrant students in Canada, found that Cantonese-speaking individuals were as concerned with mastering Mandarin (Chinese) as they were with becoming fluent in English. They had, it seemed, one eye on future employment possibilities in Mainland China. In their study of educational migration in Singapore, Park and Bae (2009, p.376) have argued that, generally English is prioritized in educational migration from South Korea, so that 'the global economy seems to have the final word on the material value of languages'. However, they continue, 'smaller spaces for *alternative orders of the linguistic market* [are] opened up by the lived experiences of *jogi yuhak* [early study abroad] families' (Park and Bae, 2009, p.376, emphasis added). When the everyday lives of Korean families in Singapore were examined, far greater linguistic diversity (and *appreciation* of the value of linguistic diversity) emerged. This was exemplified by the use of '*Singlish*' by Korean children 'for fun'. In particular, they note, students attending local schools 'appeared, in general, to have a stronger awareness of the utility and creativity of Singlish, because compared to students attending international schools...they had far more opportunities to interact with Singlish speakers and to experience the variety's usefulness' (Park and Bae, 2009, p.374). As such, the apparent pervasiveness of English over and above every other language does not always hold in practice.

Furthermore, despite the rhetoric, a 'Western' education is not always the preferred option for many international students. Often it instead offers a useful 'way out' of a highly competitive, stressful domestic system and a 'guaranteed route' to university (Matthews and Sidhu, 2005; Waters, 2006; Waters and Leung, 2010). For the majority of students, a university degree is the ultimate goal (Waters, 2008) – the overseas nature of it is of secondary importance. This observation further undermines the notion of Western dominance in international education. In fact, many international students from East Asia report 'failing' or 'anticipating failure' in their local system, and going abroad provided a 'second shot' at academic success (Brooks and Waters, 2009a). In most cases, entry to a prestigious local university would have been the desired route into higher education, if only that opportunity had been available. And finally, as observed in Chapter 6 on the 'geographies of student mobility', there is an emergent *regional* dynamic to international education – parts of East and Southeast Asia are themselves *attracting* large numbers of international students from the wider Asian region (Singapore being a prime example of this trend). These new geographies further undermine a simplified narrative of 'Western' dominance in international education.

## Gender and international study

Very little has in fact been written about gender in relation to international students. There has been some work stressing the gendered division of labour within, for example, 'wild geese' or 'astronaut families', as described above (e.g. Kim, 2010; Pe-Pua et al., 1996). However, the gender of international students themselves is rarely taken into account.

Exceptions are found in a few studies – two of female Japanese students in the United States (Ono and Piper, 2004) and the UK (Habu, 2000), and one of East Asian students in Canada (Park, 2010). These offer a valuable alternative perspective on overseas education.

In relation to their research on Japanese international students, Ono and Piper (2004) note the high proportion of females in this group. This, they surmise, is a consequence of persisting gender inequalities within the Japanese employment system and the prevalence of 'traditional' lifestyles in Japan. Women are investing in higher education abroad as a way of circumventing systematic disadvantages in their home country. Many of the women interviewed for their research:

experienced the constraints imposed by social norms and expectations of *what a Japanese woman should and should not be*. Although such norms are changing, the notion of 'good wife and wise mother' still influences the behaviour and values of many Japanese women. (Ono and Piper, 2004, p.112, emphasis in original)

These stereotypical representations of women serve to repress women's educational ambitions – many men are seen to prefer 'less educated' females as potential wives. There is a strong sense that women can be 'overeducated', thereby threatening patriarchal structures. Consequently, surveys have shown that, in Japan, parents' educational aspirations for their sons and daughters differ considerably – university is still seen as something that boys (not girls) should aspire to (Ono and Piper, 2004). Japanese women feel that an overseas qualification will allow them to work for a foreign company at home, where the treatment of staff is assumed to be more egalitarian. As Ono and Piper (2004) have observed, most female Japanese international students return to Japan to work following their graduation, but opt to work in foreign-owned companies. It is pertinent to ask whether this is a feature unique (at least in East Asia) to contemporary Japanese society (no doubt such gender inequalities persist in other parts of the world).

Habu's (2000) study of Japanese women in British higher education in many ways paints a similar picture to Ono and Piper. Women are seen to be 'pushed' abroad for study by 'conservative social norms which constrain their lives and limit their job prospects' in Japan (Habu, 2004, p.43). However, Habu also suggests that it is not the prospect of 'economic' betterment that drives these women, but a search for personal fulfilment. The paper also examines women's experiences of the British higher education system, and describes them as 'mixed' – some are treated as 'cash-cows' – 'universities that make their paramount financial interest in overseas students abundantly clear by neglecting them once they arrive' (Habu, 2004, p.61). Others reported that their experiences of higher education in the UK were extremely 'valuable'. Park's (2010) study focusses on the perceived vulnerability of female students from South Korea in Canada, but importantly this vulnerability is created through the intersection of gendered and racialized discourses, which serve ultimately to undermine the power and independence of the female international student. These studies, which attempt to prioritize (rather than sideline) the importance of gender in their analysis, offer a useful corrective to 'gender-blind' studies of migration.

## Conclusion

Undeniably, students from East Asia have a hugely important role to play in the global migration system and are the backbone of the expansion and development of international education. They are also likely to continue in this role for some time to come. From the perspective of Western tertiary institutions, Asian students are a highly coveted prize, representing a substantial source of revenue for colleges and universities, not to mention cultivating an image of internationalism and cosmopolitanism on campus.

Whilst we do not wish to pre-empt the later chapters in this book, which consider student mobility within Europe as well as the international mobility of UK students, it is possible to elicit some characteristic features of East Asian student mobility, which mark it out as distinct. First, we distinguished between 'international student' mobility and 'educational immigration'. Many internationally mobile East Asian students, we argued, are also *immigrants*. International students are often measured and defined by the fact that they are in possession of a 'student visa' or 'study permit'. In contrast, many East Asian families have applied for 'permanent residency' overseas (particularly in countries such as New Zealand, Canada, Australia and the United States) and have emigrated. Qualitative research has revealed that very often 'children's education' is the primary motivating factor in this move (Kobayashi and Preston, 2007; Ley, 2010; Waters, 2008). Second, students from East Asia often migrate overseas at a relatively young age – they will attend secondary and sometimes even primary school abroad before transitioning to HE in that country. This necessitates that an adult member (invariably the children's mother) relocates overseas also. Such positioning results in a third distinctive feature of East Asian student mobility – the transnational household formations that occur. Frequently, the father/husband will remain at home whilst the mother and children move overseas. Sometimes (as is seen in the case of 'astronaut' households), the whole family will migrate abroad, only for the father to return to the country of origin shortly afterwards to work. Transnational families are thus an important feature of educational mobilities in the East Asian context.

There are also many similarities with other groups of international students. The importance of accumulating cultural capital would seem to apply to most international or immigrant students, regardless of their region of origin. Arguably, as we will see in Chapter 5, UK students may be distinctive in this regard. However, for the majority of student groups, the embodied nature of cultural capital is particularly important, as is the desire for fluency in the English language. A colonial legacy has meant that Western credentials hold particular appeal for East Asian students.

We have also observed, in this chapter, some areas where the literature has much less to say, and a dearth of work on the salience of gender would seem to exemplify this point. Over the last 15 or so years, the more general literature on population migration has shown a far greater degree of sensitivity to potential axes of difference *within* migrant groups (along lines such as gender, race, ethnicity and sexuality). However, the more specific literature on internationally mobile students that we have been concerned with here still has a long way to go in this regard.

# 4
# Mobility Within Mainland Europe

## Introduction

Unlike educational mobility in most other parts of the world, the movement of students within Europe tends to be for relatively short periods of time and is stimulated strongly by regional policy, made by the European Union. Although students do migrate under their own initiative and outside of formal programmes, the vast majority move under the auspices of the 'Erasmus' scheme, founded in 1987, which provides funding for students to spend part of their degree programme at an institution in another EU Member State. Indeed, it has been suggested that programmes to promote the mobility of students within Europe have been the most successful component of EU policy to date (Papatsiba, 2006; Recchi, 2006). Whether or not this is the case, it is certainly true that such initiatives have consumed considerable attention from policymakers since the mid-1980s and have been given renewed vigour since the late 1990s under the terms of the Bologna Process. This policy context is explored in the first part of the chapter. Drawing on some of the arguments made in Chapter 2, we consider the various schemes that have been put in place by the European Union to encourage student mobility, and the objectives which underpin them. In particular, we assess the extent to which student mobility is allied to broader economic and political imperatives, such as the inculcation of a particular pan-European identity, and the relationship between EU initiatives and national education policy. We then move on to consider the uneven geography of student mobility within mainland Europe. Here, we pay particular attention to the differences in student flows between countries and changes to patterns of mobility across the continent over time, and explore the reasons for some of these trends. The characteristics of the mobile student are the focus of the next section of the chapter. We explore the socio-economic status of such students, and the extent to which the accrual of 'capital' may be a significant driver of mobility. We also highlight the importance of previous experiences of travel, and significant gender differences in propensity to travel. In the final section of the chapter we focus on the impact of mobility programmes, assessing specifically their success in achieving the economic and political objectives upon which EU policy is predicated.

While this chapter focusses, almost exclusively, on the patterns and experiences of educational mobility *by Europeans* within mainland Europe, it is important to note that most foreign nationals in European countries are from outside the region. Indeed, of the 1.1 million foreign students enrolled in European tertiary institutions at the beginning of the 21$^{st}$ century, over half (54 per cent) were from non-European countries (Kelo et al., 2006). Of this number, 40 per cent were from Asia, 31 per cent from Africa, 8 per cent from Latin America and 6 per cent from northern America. This recruitment pattern is clearly likely to have considerable impact on, amongst other things, the position taken by national governments (in relation to the internationalization of HE), the marketing strategies of individual universities, and the experiences of international students (whether they come from Europe or not). Nevertheless, while Europeans remain a minority amongst the mobile students of Europe, to many EU policymakers, they have considerable political, cultural and economic importance. They thus constitute the main focus of this chapter.

## European mobility policy

Studies of student migration in Europe tend to draw a distinction between 'spontaneous' and 'organized' mobility. The former refers to students who make their own arrangements to travel to another country for study, typically for the whole of an undergraduate or postgraduate degree. In contrast, 'organized' mobility refers to the various bi-lateral or multi-lateral schemes by which students can pursue HE abroad. While spontaneous mobility is the dominant form of student migration in many parts of the world (see, for example, Chapter 3), within Europe it is the organized form that is more prevalent. In large part this can be explained by the key role played by EU policy in fostering mobility from the late 1980s onwards. Indeed, it has been argued that while spontaneous mobility for the whole of a degree was originally considered to be a possible focus for European initiatives, it was ultimately dropped as a goal in the face of objections from individual universities that were determined to retain control of their own admissions processes, and national governments that did not want to have to offer social assistance to students from other countries.

In analysing changing patterns of mobility across Europe over the past few decades, it is possible to identify three distinct stages of internationalization (Teichler, 2001; Wächter, 2003). The first of these lasted until the mid-1980s and was largely spontaneous and individual; thus, although free movement was, from its inception, one of the main goals of the European integration project, HEIs and national and regional bodies played no particular facilitative role during this time. The second stage (from the mid-1980s until 2002) was characterized by a significant shift towards organized mobility as a result of the Erasmus scheme (European Community Action Scheme for the Mobility of University Students), initiated in 1987, which brought universities across Europe into much closer contact. As part of the scheme, students are funded to study in another EU country for a period of between three months and a year, within a department recognized by the programme and which is part of an inter-institutional network. Emphasis is placed on 'curricular integration' between departments, and the home department is expected to recognize the academic achievements of students during their period abroad (Teichler, 1996). Ertl (2006) argues that, during this second period, mobility was used strategically by the EU to address the ambivalent position in which it found itself, in relation to education and training policy more generally:

> This ambivalence was characterised by the pressure for a more harmonised system on the one hand and the insistence of the Member States on national autonomy on the other. By promoting the mobility of European citizens, the EU increased the pressure for education and training systems that allow movement from one national context to another. (pp.13–14)

While the success of the Erasmus scheme in exerting this kind of pressure is rather unclear, most scholars nevertheless agree that its inauguration in 1987 was a defining moment in the internationalization of HE across the continent in terms of encouraging many more young people to spend time studying in another country and in privileging organized (and short-term) forms of mobility over the spontaneous (and, typically, longer-term) alternative (Maiworm, 2001).

The third stage (from 2002 onwards) was heralded by the signing of the Bologna Declaration in 2002 and is characterized by an explicit commitment to creating a European higher education space and to furthering mobility – amongst teachers, researchers and administrative staff as well as students (Prague Communiqué, 2002). The Bologna Process is not, however, restricted to members of the European Union, and encompasses 'the wider Europe, stretching from Azerbaijan to Iceland' (Birtwistle, 2007, p.182). At the time of writing there are a plethora of initiatives to aid academic mobility across the continent. These include: a new generation of EU programmes in education and training, with associated targets (Comenius, aimed at schools; Erasmus, for higher education; Leonardo da Vinci, for vocational training and Gruntvig, for adult education); various 'Framework Programmes' to integrate research and encourage researcher mobility; Marie Curie Actions, which finance mobility for science and technology researchers; and the 'Diploma Supplement', to promote recognition of higher education qualifications across Europe.

The European Union's policy on student mobility is underpinned by both economic and political objectives. The purported economic benefits – for both the region and the individual – are articulated particularly clearly. The goals of the Erasmus programme, for example, include: achieving a significant increase in the number of university students spending an integrated period of study in another Member State 'in order that the Community may draw upon an adequate pool of manpower with firsthand experiences of economic and social aspects of other Member States'; and developing a pool of graduates with experience of intra-Community co-operation 'thereby creating the basis upon which intensified co-operation in the economic and social sectors can develop at Community level' (CEC, 1989, pp.1–2).

Free movement has long been an important pillar of EU policy – the labour market counterpart to monetary union, and a means of responding to fluctuations in local employment markets – and the EU's attempts to foster mobility amongst students can be seen as part of this broader goal. Indeed, the movement of young people between European educational institutions is promoted 'as a device for the formation of a highly educated and mobile labour resource which sees the European Union as its potential labour market and which improves the economic competitiveness and hegemony of Europe on the global scene' (King, 2003, p.173). Although the free movement doctrine was initially developed as a means of encouraging working class migration from southern European countries to their northern counterparts, more recently it has been seen as an important tool for furthering the European 'knowledge economy' and enhancing Europe's competitiveness as a region on the international stage. Indeed, one of the main aims of the Bologna Process is to provide a response to the challenges of globalization by increasing the attractiveness of the European higher education system – with student mobility occupying a central place in this process.

At the individual level, studying in another European country is thought to foster a wide range of competences associated with labour market advantage, such as independence, resilience, autonomy, linguistic ability and inter-cultural skill, and to instil an interest in professional mobility. More generally, studying abroad is also seen as an important means of stimulating further learning, as the European Commission's White Paper on the Learning Society makes clear:

> Support for mobility also plays a part in encouraging the enhancement of knowledge. Geographical mobility broadens the individual's horizon, stimulates intellectual agility and raises the general level of learning. (CEC, 1995, p.34)

Alongside these economic aims, official discourses place considerable emphasis on the potential contribution of student mobility to achieving various political objectives. Studying in another European country is seen 'as a catalyst for the formation of a European identity necessary for the legitimation of European institutions and for the overall project of European integration' (King, 2003, pp.172–173). Kenway and Fahey (2007) claim that official EU documents tend to construct the mobile university subject as primarily a citizen of the 'world of Europe', largely emancipated from the constraints of national borders, who is free to take up a strong political attachment to Europe. It is also argued that the type of student mobility that the EU has aimed to facilitate focuses on the creation of a new type of 'European elite', comfortable at working across borders, fully committed to the project of closer European union, and with the competences, acquired through travel, to accelerate further European integration (King, 2003; Papatsiba, 2006). Developing this analysis, Recchi (2006) contends that through its wider policy statements it is clear that 'the EU tends to favour the way of life of mobile, well-resourced and well-educated Europeans, who have participated in Erasmus exchange programmes and developed a cosmopolitan outlook' (p.72). They are seen as the leaders of the future.

The political objectives that underpin student mobility policies are also evident in a number of other educational initiatives, dating back as far as the 1950s. These have included: a European Civics Campaign;

a guide for teachers entitled 'Introducing Europe to Senior Pupils' (published in 1966); and, in 1998, a Resolution to promote a 'European Dimension in Education' (Keating, 2009). As Keating (2009) notes, this Resolution 'firmly established the link between education and Community identity and belonging' (p.142) with its emphasis on inculcating a sense of European citizenship, increasing awareness of common socio-political issues and enhancing young people's knowledge of historical and cultural aspects of Europe (see also Papatsiba, 2006). Moreover, Stoer and Cortesao (2000) argue that the European Dimension involved above all 'conceptualising and developing Europe as a system of cultural representation...a "symbolic community", able to generate a sense of identity and allegiance' (p.258). The EU's belief that education provides the foundations for European citizenship finds particularly clear expression in the White Paper, 'Towards a Learning Society' (CEC, 1995), published in 1995. It states: 'By imparting a broad knowledge base to young people enabling them to both to pick their way through its complexity and to discuss its purpose, education lays the foundations of awareness and European citizenship' (p.14). Although Keating (2009) argues convincingly that the way in which citizenship has been conceptualized in EU policy has evolved over time (with a shift from an ethnocentric, 'national' model towards a post-national model), the use of education as a vehicle for promoting specific political objectives has remained largely constant.

Student mobility policies are also inextricably linked to the broader political imperative of encouraging mobility between European countries more generally, as a means of deepening European integration at a societal level. It has been argued that implicit in European policy is a belief that practices operate a strong influence on values (rather than vice versa) and, thus, that migratory experiences are likely to be the most effective means of bringing about 'collective identities based on acculturation and contacts occurring in the everyday life of another European country' (Recchi, 2006, p.73). Thus, the EU's 'Action Plan for Mobility' (CEC, 2002), for example, claims that those who take advantage of the rights of free movement, enshrined in the Maastricht Treaty (1992), come to appreciate the benefits of EU citizenship and endorse European unification more vigorously. Similarly, Directive 2004/38, which defines the right of free movement for EU citizens, is based on the assumption that the opportunity to settle permanently in another EU member state is likely to strengthen feelings of European Union citizenship. It has thus been seen as a key element in promoting social cohesion across the continent.

While few scholars deny the salience of the political and civic objectives that underpin the various initiatives to promote mobility across Europe, there is some debate about their relationship with the economic imperatives, discussed above. Some commentators have suggested that both sets of concerns are of equal importance within EU policy (for example, King, 2003). Others, however, have argued that the economic objectives are the main drivers of policy – pointing to the market mechanisms upon which the Erasmus scheme is based (Wielemans, 1991), the privileging of the 'economic' to secure the acceptance of student mobility programmes by the European commissioners (Papatsiba, 2006), and the centrality of the 'knowledge-based economy' discourse to many mobility policy texts (Kenway and Fahey, 2007).

Despite the claims that policies to promote student mobility are amongst the most successful aspects of EU activity to date, the relatively small number of participants on Erasmus and other similar schemes testifies to the rather limited nature of this 'success'. The EU's failure to reach even its own target for student mobility (discussed in more detail below) can be explained, partially, by the disinclination of Europeans more generally to move across country borders. However, it is also related to the endurance of strong national systems of education and training, and the historical reluctance of Member States to cede any significant power to Europe in these areas. Ertl (2006) contends that, to date, there have been three main periods of EU policy-making in relation to education and training: 'pre-Maastricht' (1957–1992), characterized by very limited intervention in the education systems of Member States; 'post-Maastricht' (1992–2007), characterized by greater intervention in training policy, but with explicit reference to 'non-harmonization' and subsidiarity with respect to general education; and 'post-Lisbon' (from 2007 onwards) with a much stronger focus on co-ordinating national processes of reform:

> The open method of co-ordination and its emphasis on assessment and quality control has undoubtedly added fresh momentum to EU policies in education and training. EU activities in the field affect more aspects of education and training than before, and are potentially more effective because they follow more ambitious aims and include measurable indicators and schedules. (Ertl, 2006, p.20)

Similar trends can be identified in relation to higher education, with the Sorbonne Declaration of 1998 committing signatories to 'the harmonisation of the architecture of the European higher education system' and paving the way for the Bologna Declaration the following year. However, despite the dramatic tone of such statements, standing in contrast to the scepticism about educational convergence evident in previous decades (Papatsiba, 2006), progress towards a harmonized system remains limited and strong, formal differences between education systems endure. Such differences have been shown to impede the mobility of HE staff (Musselin, 2004), and to have made the 'conversion' of qualifications from one system to another difficult (Paunescu, 2008; Philips, 2006).

## The geography of European mobility

Despite the strong policy emphasis on intra-European mobility, the overall number of students who move abroad for HE is relatively small. As Favell (2006) notes in relation to mobile Europeans generally, their lives 'are extraordinary precisely because it is not easy to opt out of the standard social trajectories offered to middle-class children in European nation-state societies. Thus, they remain, for all their numbers, the exception in a generally immobile Europe' (p.274). Indeed, while the EU is considered to be a world leader in generating regional mobility *possibilities* (through the legal enshrinement of freedom of movement), this institutional encouragement has not been accompanied by a dramatic rise in the number of Europeans actually moving within the continent. Indeed, there has been a decline in intra-European mobility since the early 1970s, when working class migration from southern Europe to more northern countries dried up (Favell et al., 2008). Favell et al. suggest that reasons for this decline may include: a notable reduction in cross-country differences in salaries; a deep-seated persistence of national identities and habits across Europe; and the general affluence of the region (noting that this is often associated with relative geographical stability). The movement of students has not shown any significant deviation from these trends. Despite the energy devoted to generating a European educational mobility programme and the relatively high profile of the various initiatives across the continent, the Erasmus scheme failed to attract the 10 per cent mobility (of all HE students within the EU) by 1992 that was an original aim of the programme; instead, the actual level was around 4 per cent. As King (2003) notes, given that under the Erasmus scheme young people are actually paid to migrate, the relatively low level of participation highlights the limitations of governmental (or indeed supra-national) control and incentive regimes.

In this section of the chapter we consider the geography of student mobility in Europe, drawing on the available statistical evidence.

However, it is important to recognize the very limited nature of this evidence base. The right of Europeans to move and reside freely in other European countries for temporary or intermittent stays, with no requirement to register, makes the collection of data on those who move to pursue education difficult. As has been pointed out by many scholars in this area, outside of the Erasmus programme there is a notable absence of any reliable data (e.g. Birtwistle, 2007), with much student migration 'invisible' and/or 'too volatile for the statistical eye' (Recchi, 2006, p.75). Although the European Union recently commissioned a study to rectify some of the gaps in the statistical data on student mobility (Kelo et al., 2006), the authors of this report note the scale of the problem in the introduction to their work. They claim that one of the most important findings of their study is that the available 'mobility statistics' do not, in most cases, report on mobility at all. Instead, they report on foreign students, using the foreign nationality of students as a measure of mobility. They go on to claim that only ten of the 32 European countries in their research collect data on genuine mobility (what they define as students moving across borders for the purposes of study) (Kelo et al., 2006, p.3). Other problems in compiling statistics on foreign students include: the heterogeneity of the group – with courses of varying content and length, and with different qualification requirements; the range of multi- and bi-lateral agreements that govern students' travel; the differing entitlements of such students from country-to-country; and the range of different administrative authorities responsible for counting their number (Salt, 2005).

In exploring patterns of mobility, it is important to distinguish between what has been termed 'diploma mobility' (i.e. the movement of those who wish to pursue the whole of an undergraduate or postgraduate degree, often outside of any formally-organized scheme), 'credit mobility' (i.e. movement to study *part* of a degree course in another European country, typically as part of an organized programme such as Erasmus) and other voluntary moves (Sussex Centre for Migration Research, 2004). While acknowledging the imperfections of the available data, Rivza and Teichler (2007) estimate that one out of about every 40 European students decides to study for the whole of a programme abroad ('diploma mobility'), typically in another European country, and note that this proportion has not increased significantly over the past two decades. Amongst these students, those from countries too small to offer a complete HE (such as Luxembourg and Lichtenstein) are over-represented, as are Greek students, because of the limited access to HE in their home country (Raikou and Karalis, 2007). A considerably higher number of European students (one in about every ten) spend a short period of time in another (usually European) country during their HE ('credit mobility'); and this proportion has increased markedly over the last 20 years. Almost all of the robust statistical data that are available relate to credit mobility and, in particular, the EU-sponsored Erasmus scheme. This is discussed in more detail below. First, though, we outline some general patterns which emerge from the wider data on student mobility.

It is notable that European students who wish to move outside their home country for HE tend to favour strongly other European countries. Indeed, 82 per cent of those enrolled abroad in 2002/03 remained within Europe (Lanzendorf, 2006). Outside Europe, only Australia and the US host considerable numbers of European students, while Germany and the UK are the most popular European countries for mobile European students, together hosting around 38 per cent of the total population. France and Spain are the next most popular countries, hosting 8 and 5 per cent of mobile students, respectively (ibid.). Austria and Denmark also receive a large number of foreign students relative to their size (Salt, 2005). Overall, however, mobility in Europe tends to be to a rather circumscribed group of countries; indeed, the ten most popular countries account for 95 per cent of the total number of students abroad (Lanzendorf, 2006).

The Erasmus scheme is the best-known student mobility programme in Europe and accounts for around one third of all mobile students in the continent (Sussex Centre for Migration Research, 2004). In 1987, the first year of the programme, 3000 students and 11 countries participated in the scheme. By the 2003/04 academic year, 135 586 students were taking part, drawn from 31 nations (Birtwistle, 2007), and most countries have seen a steady increase in mobility over recent years. However, despite the expansion of the European Union, the rate of growth in student numbers has slowed: from about 30 per cent on average until 1995–96 to less than 10 per cent in the following years (Maiworm, 2001). Moreover, the spread of mobile students has not been even, and clear disparities between countries can be observed (see Table 4.1). In general, there are net flows from less wealthy, southern European countries (including Italy, Greece, Portugal and Spain) to their wealthier, northern neighbours (particularly the UK and Ireland, but also Belgium, Denmark, France, the Netherlands and Sweden) (King, 2003). Although the balance between net inflows and outflows has decreased over time, the UK and Ireland remain significant outliers, taking in approximately twice the number of Erasmus students they send out (ibid.). Over the last decade of the 20th century there were a few changes to the overall pattern of exchanges in Europe: while

**Table 4.1**  Socrates/Erasmus Programme: Students by country of origin and destination, 1998/99 and 2002/03

| Country | 1998/99 | | 2002/03 | |
|---|---|---|---|---|
| | Outward | Inward | Outward | Inward |
| Austria | 2 705 | 2 196 | 3 312 | 2 834 |
| Belgium | 4 470 | 3 375 | 4 653 | 4 046 |
| Bulgaria | 0 | 0 | 612 | 67 |
| Cyprus | 35 | 14 | 91 | 64 |
| Czech Republic | 879 | 243 | 3 002 | 970 |
| Denmark | 1 751 | 1 945 | 1 847 | 2 883 |
| Estonia | 0 | 0 | 302 | 171 |
| Finland | 3 441 | 2 423 | 3 402 | 4 427 |
| France | 16 372 | 16 264 | 19 396 | 18 825 |
| Germany | 14 700 | 12 940 | 18 494 | 16 113 |
| Greece | 1 765 | 1 086 | 2 115 | 1 545 |
| Hungary | 856 | 277 | 1 830 | 853 |
| Iceland | 147 | 112 | 163 | 170 |
| Ireland | 1 504 | 2 907 | 1 627 | 3 472 |
| Italy | 10 868 | 6 890 | 15 217 | 10 973 |
| Latvia | 0 | 0 | 232 | 45 |
| Lichtenstein | 1 | 0 | 7 | 7 |
| Lithuania | 0 | 0 | 1 001 | 132 |
| Luxembourg | 23 | 12 | 33 | 13 |
| Malta | 0 | 0 | 72 | 202 |
| The Netherlands | 4 332 | 5 750 | 4 241 | 6 349 |
| Norway | 1 101 | 983 | 1 010 | 1 244 |
| Poland | 1 426 | 312 | 5 419 | 994 |
| Portugal | 2 179 | 1 754 | 3 171 | 3 279 |
| Romania | 1 250 | 116 | 2 701 | 355 |
| Slovenia | 0 | 0 | 422 | 129 |
| Slovakia | 59 | 20 | 654 | 131 |
| Sweden | 3 321 | 3 623 | 2 656 | 5 320 |
| United Kingdom | 10 005 | 21 261 | 7 957 | 16 987 |
| Total | 97 571 | 97 571 | 123 897 | 123 897 |

*Source*: European Commission, Directorate-General for Education and Culture, quoted in Wächter and Wuttig, 2006, p.164.

countries such as France, Germany and Italy demonstrated considerable stability in their student numbers, Scandinavian countries (Denmark, Finland and Sweden) and Iberia witnessed an increase in their net numbers, and some of the smaller countries (Austria, Belgium, Greece and Ireland) have seen a decline (ibid.). In the late 1990s, central and eastern European countries become eligible to participate in Erasmus schemes, and demand for the available scholarships has been very high – as a period abroad has been seen as an effective means of facilitating professional mobility (Rivza and Teichler, 2007). However, there has been less interest in studying in these countries from students in western Europe. Latvia provides a particularly good example of this: while 2385 Latvian students participated in Erasmus schemes between 1999/2000 and 2005/06, only 615 Erasmus students came from other countries to Latvia (ibid.). There are also some interesting disparities *within* European countries. For example, students attending universities in southern Italy are less likely to participate in Erasmus schemes than their peers studying in the northern half of the country (Cammelli et al., 2008). In other countries, differences by institution have been noted: around 40 per cent of eligible universities have signed 'institutional contracts' – but larger and more prestigious institutions are over-represented amongst this group (Sussex Centre for Migration Research, 2004; Teichler, 2004a).

To date, there has been relatively little work which has explored the reasons for these differential patterns, although King's (2003) research is a very useful exception. He considers whether economic factors (specifically, the relative wealth of countries, and the quality of their HE systems) can predict mobility patterns. Although there is a net flow from poorer (southern) European countries to their wealthier (northern) European neighbours, as noted above, there are also important anomalies: Finland and Germany are both wealthy countries with net outflows, while Ireland is less wealthy but has a net inflow of students (ibid.). The quality of the national HE system is no better a predictor: while some high-quality systems do indeed have net inflows (such as the UK and the Netherlands), Finland and Germany again do not fit the pattern, having both a relatively well-funded HE system but also net outflows of students. King goes on to consider whether language may be a more important influence on the geography of student mobility. He notes that the more widely the host country language is spoken, the larger the attraction to international students. This would help to explain why the UK and Ireland receive the greatest net inflows of students – as they both use the most widely-spoken European language, and UK students have a poor record of language-learning when compared to their peers in other European countries. King contends that this would also explain why Spain receives healthy inflows of students (as Spanish is the second most commonly spoken European language) and why some universities in countries with less common languages have started to offer courses taught in English (in the Netherlands, Sweden and Denmark, for example).

It is clear that geographical proximity and cultural similarity both have an important influence on choice of country (Lanzendorf, 2006). There is also some evidence (albeit largely anecdotal) to suggest that young Europeans may be becoming increasingly sensitive to fee differentials between countries. For example, reports in the British media have suggested that countries that charge low fees (such as the Netherlands) or no fees at all (such as Sweden) are becoming increasingly attractive to young people from countries with high tuition fees (Clark, 2006). It is also possible that more aggressive marketing on the part of some countries is affecting the choices of young Europeans. For example, the Swedish government has recently established a website dedicated to attracting overseas students: www.studyinsweden.se. However, further research is needed to explore in more detail the reasons why mobile students choose to study in particular countries.

## Characteristics of the mobile student

Despite the assumptions that are sometimes made about the very privileged backgrounds of those who are most 'mobile' within Europe, an historical analysis of mobility across the continent suggests that non-elite-based migration has been common. Indeed, Favell (2008) argues that 'the history of spatial mobility in Europe has in fact been intimately linked with the ambitions of the socially mobile, and therefore those ranked lower on the social scale' (p.83). In developing this argument, he points to the prevalence of worker migration from the countryside to cities across Europe during periods of industrialization and, more recently, white collar migration to more metropolitan centres. He goes on to claim that, in contemporary society, social mobility remains an important driver of intra-European migration. While 'global elites' and 'corporate movers' constitute important sub-groups of European migrants, Favell identifies two additional types of mover who, typically, do not share the same kind of privileged background: the 'Euro-families', who have seen their number increase markedly over recent years as travel opportunities have become cheaper and more widespread, and the 'social spiralists' who have taken advantage of the opportunities for free movement within Europe to compensate for a relative lack of cultural and social capital within their home nation:

> Europe is finally providing an alternative route for provincials who found the competitive route through the capital blocked – mono-polised as always by the same national elites, going to the same

schools and universities....The leap abroad can make all the difference in terms of trajectory, acceleration, lift off. (Favell, 2008, p.93)

To what extent can this analytical framework be applied to students who move to another European country to pursue their higher education? Firstly, there is some debate as to whether students should be seen as a sub-group of other types of migrant (such as the highly skilled) or whether they constitute a separate group of their own. Salt (2005) highlights their commonalities with highly-skilled European movers, particularly given their potential to enter the labour market of the host country on graduation. Similarly, Findlay et al. (2006) suggest that student exchanges between developed nations 'can be interpreted as training for professionals and managers destined for an international career in global corporations and other transnational organisation' (p.293). Others, however, have pointed to the significant differences between students and other migrant groups. Murphy-Lejeune (2008), for example, contends that: their 'privileged circumstances and attribute of youth' means that they 'can travel more lightly' (p.25) than other migrants; their migratory experience is less dramatic because of its temporary nature; and their detachment from their home culture is loosened rather than seriously tested because of their certainty that they will return home at the end of their course of study.

Secondly, there is some ambivalence in the literature as to the social characteristics of those who move abroad for their studies. There is now fairly clear evidence, derived from recent, large-scale surveys, that those who move as part of organized programmes such as the Erasmus scheme are typically from families with both experience of HE and average or higher than average incomes, and with parents employed in professional, executive or technical occupations (Cammelli et al., 2008; Krzaklewska, 2008; Olero and McCoshan, 2006). Indeed, Findlay et al. (2006) found that having a mother in professional or managerial employment was the strongest predictor of European mobility amongst the UK students they surveyed. They go on to claim that 'students from working class and non-white backgrounds stand much less chance of engaging in international student mobility because of the financial and linguistic constraints on the environment in which they are embedded and because of the socio-economic and mobility cultures from which they are drawn' (p.313). Such patterns, they argue, are exacerbated by the structure of the UK HE system: those institutions that are most likely to send students abroad are those seen as high status, typically attended by more socially-advantaged young people. Similar findings have emerged from research in Romania, Poland and Bulgaria: in all three countries, the financial position of one's parents was seen by students as an important selection criterion for mobility, and a lack of institutional support for mobility was evident (Paunescu, 2008). Drawing on this evidence about the socio-economic characteristics of many mobile students, Kenway and Fahey (2007) argue that 'the cosmopolitan Euro student traveller' (p.168) who has so far evolved as a result of EU higher education policy is no ordinary migrant but one who possesses considerable privileges in terms of both their education and social class. They go on to suggest that he or she has much in common with Bauman's 'tourist': one of the 'winners' of globalization, who is emancipated from the constraints of space as a result of the resources at his/her disposal and who is bound by few territorial responsibilities:

Educational tourists might in part be thought of as having spatial emancipation that allows them to accumulate the European educational credentials and experiences that further enhance their education and class privileges in the labour markets of Europe and beyond. (p.169)

This analysis of the mobile European student is not, however, shared by all. Indeed, in line with his more general argument about intra-European migration, Favell has argued that it is misleading to see student mobility primarily as a form of elite migration (Favell et al., 2006). He contends that those from highly privileged backgrounds often have routine access to international travel and experiences and so do not need to propel themselves individually on to the international stage through educational programmes such as Erasmus. Moreover, such mobility 'is not for the risk-averse or psychologically conservative and will not be chosen if they already have easier, elite-based success in their own countries' (p.9). A similar theme is pursued by Recchi (2006) who argues that student mobility within Europe appeals to lower middle-class individuals, in particular, 'as a shortcut to capital accumulation – be it economic or cultural capital, or a mix of the two' (p.76).

Irrespective of the precise social location of the individuals involved, there is certainly evidence to suggest that the accrual of 'capital' may be a significant driver of mobility. It is argued that young European students can be distinguished from other migrants by their 'qualitative investment in their futures' (Murphy-Lejeune, 2002, p.100) and that part of their motivation for seeking higher education abroad is a belief that the 'mobility capital' they are likely to amass as a result will help them to secure a much-prized international position. This kind of 'professional preparation' has typically ranked alongside academic progress, understanding of another country and linguistic competence when Erasmus students have been asked for the main reasons why they embarked on a period of study abroad (Maiworm, 2001; Teichler, 2004a), and shows remarkable consistency across Europe. In most accounts, 'career-oriented' motives (such as improving future employment prospects, achieving higher marks on return home, and developing intercultural skills) are combined with what Krzaklewska (2006) terms an 'experimental dimension' in which cultural and personal reasons for mobility (such as self-development, learning from new cultures and gaining new experiences) are emphasized. She suggests that this can be seen to reflect a certain ambivalence in the conceptualization of 'youth' itself in which an emphasis on having fun and experimenting with different identities exists alongside an equally strong emphasis on labour market preparation. This combination of motives is typical of what Rivza and Teichler (2007) have termed 'horizontal mobility' – migration to neighbouring countries where systems of HE are broadly similar and cultural differences are likely to be relatively small – and characterizes much 'integrated mobility' such as through the Erasmus programme.

In contrast, the mobility of those 'free movers' who migrate outside the confines of organized programmes tends to have more in common with what Rivza and Teichler call 'vertical mobility' – mobility which is undertaken in order to secure what students perceive to be a 'better' education. In many ways, this reflects some of the arguments made above about the uneven geography of intra-European mobility. For example, poor facilities for conducting empirical work in Portuguese universities have prompted some doctoral students to move abroad. Indeed, Araujo (2007) argues that for many of the doctoral students involved in her research, mobility was essential 'because the lack of equipment to do tests and other experiments in Portugal would have forced them to do a more theoretical thesis or take much more time to complete it' (p.395). Similarly, the Polish and Bulgarian science students who were involved in Guth and Gill's (2008) research had been keen to move abroad for their doctoral projects so that they could work in better-funded research centres with higher quality facilities. They were also attracted by the better financial support they believed they would receive abroad (though grants, studentships and part-time work).

A small number of studies have suggested that the mobility of some European students may be motivated, not by the desire to secure a *better* education elsewhere, but by the relative lack of suitable opportunities within their own country. For example, Raikou and Karalis (2007) claim that the restricted number of university places within Greece often motivates Greek nationals to move abroad for degree-level study. Similarly, Wiers-Jenssen (2008) argues that in Norway, those who fail to gain access to very competitive medical courses often choose to pursue a medical degree in another European country rather than follow an alternative course in a Norwegian institution. This has certain parallels with the British students (discussed in Chapter 5) who, after failing to secure a place at Oxford or Cambridge, chose to pursue an elite education overseas rather than enrol at what they perceived to be a 'lesser' British university (Brooks and Waters, 2009a).

Studies of European students have also pointed to the importance of previous experiences of travel as a predictor of propensity to study abroad (Teichler, 2004a). Murphy-Lejeune (2002), for example, notes that a majority of her respondents had travelled considerably prior to enrolling in a foreign university, and that their first trip had typically been at a young age through family holidays or language courses. She argues that such experiences are cumulative and have a significant impact upon the extent to which educational mobility is perceived as an attractive option. Indeed, she speculates whether there is a 'critical age' during which young people show greater inter-cultural flexibility than at other stages of the lifecourse. Similarly, Findlay et al. (2006) argue that the 'mobility cultures' within which young people grow up:

> increasingly shape the motivations, aspirations and behaviour of students, encouraging many to experience foreign places through travel and for study or work reasons. Such values are culturally derived. (pp.314–315)

While, in many cases, such mobility cultures may well be associated with a high socio-economic status, there are clearly other reasons why a young person may grow up in a family in which travel is frequent and an openness to other cultures is inculcated – for example, if one parent has family overseas. There are also significant gender differences in the make-up of the mobile student population: various evaluations of the Erasmus programme, for example, have shown that young women are generally over-represented, typically accounting for around 60 per cent of participating students (Maiworm, 2001; Olero and McCoshan, 2006; Teichler, 1996). While such studies have not discussed the reasons for this disparity by gender, it is possible that young women are using migration as a means of partially compensating for gender differences in the ease of accessing high status tertiary education (Leathwood and Read, 2009) or prestigious employment (Faggian et al., 2007), along the lines of the 'social spiralists' discussed above. Finally, the subject of study also has an impact on mobility – with language students much more likely to travel abroad for some of their higher education (although usually for only part of their degree programme) (Teichler, 2004a), followed by those pursuing courses in social science, business and law (Kelo et al., 2006).

## The impact of mobility

As was discussed above, European policies promoting student mobility have tended to be underpinned by two inter-linked sets of objectives: firstly, those with an economic focus, which centre on developing the capacity of individuals to work and communicate effectively across European borders and, secondly, those with an explicitly political orientation – to develop a European identity among young people across the continent and emphasize the shared cultural values upon which such an identity is based. The success of mobility programmes in achieving these two sets of objectives will first be discussed before moving on to consider some of the other effects of intra-European student movement.

Large-scale studies of former Erasmus students have suggested that studying abroad has no obvious advantage or disadvantage on subsequent labour market participation, although it may help to ease them into jobs that require an understanding of other countries (Teichler, 1996). However, while the evidence base is at present rather thin, there is some indication that there may be significant differences by country: King's (2003) research with UK students concludes that 'the official discourse that the year abroad provides students with tools that aid employability seems to be backed by survey findings' (p.170), while Bracht et al. (2006) note that the professional value of the Erasmus scheme is substantially higher for students from Eastern Europe than for many of their western counterparts. There is also some evidence that, amongst all students, a period of study abroad is associated with international mobility, international competences and international work tasks, even if it does not lead to direct career enhancement (Bracht et al., 2006). For example, a study of Italian graduates who had spent part of their HE in another European country demonstrated that they were more likely than their peers to be geographically mobile for job reasons. Indeed, five years after graduation 17.4 per cent of such graduates were working abroad, compared with only 3.5 per cent of other graduates (Cammelli et al., 2008). Moreover, many of the interviewees in Favell's (2008) study of 'Eurostars' (geographically mobile young Europeans) had got their first taste of travel abroad through an EU programme such as Erasmus or Socrates. This had then often led to further migration within Europe through a number of different paths: taking up further opportunities for study, pursuing new professional opportunities abroad, getting a taste for foreign countries 'or, of course, romance' (p.67).

Associated with the broader economic objectives of EU mobility policy are rather more specific 'educational' aims. At an individual level, these focus on accessing new knowledge, and developing new linguistic skills and inter-cultural competences (CEC, 2009), while at the regional level, mobility is seen as an instrument for the transfer of scientific knowledge (Kenway and Fahey, 2007). While large-scale surveys of Erasmus students suggest that most believe their academic progress during their time abroad is better than during a corresponding period at home (Maiworm, 2001; Teichler, 1996), it is not always clear that they benefit from the gains that they make. Indeed, both Ehrenreich's (2008) study of German language assistants who had spent time abroad as part of their HE and Paunescu's (2008) research with Romanian, Polish and Bulgarian students who had taken part in EU-sponsored mobility schemes indicate that there are considerable problems with integrating courses studied at a 'foreign' institution with the curriculum at home. The language students in Ehrenreich's research received little reward for their enhanced oral skills, as all the assessment in their German universities focussed exclusively on the written word, while those who took part in Paunescu's focus groups described many problems with demonstrating credit equivalence on their return home. Thus, for the students from eastern Europe involved in this study, Paunescu concludes that 'the educational value of mobility rests mainly in the extra-curricular, social and cultural contexts where it is placed' (p.193). A more wide-ranging analysis of the impact of student mobility on the practices of HEIs has arrived at a similar conclusion: that, despite the EU's hopes that confronted with the needs of mobile students, universities would bring into line their structures and teaching objectives, in practice such students have had little impact (Papatsiba, 2006). It also seems that as a result of the tendency of 'international' students to socialize with each other rather than the host community, linguistic gains can often be less than students were expecting. Indeed, fewer than half the language students in Ehrenreich's (2008) sample had spent most of their time abroad with native speakers.

Similar themes have been highlighted by studies which have focussed more explicitly on the extent to which different actors share the same understanding of student mobility. Caudery et al.'s (2008) analysis of the motivations of European exchange students at Scandinavian universities, for example, suggests that the goals of the students themselves were often out of line with those of both the host government and the EU. In contrast to the EU's promotion of multilingualism and its emphasis on mobility as a means of furthering the linguistic competencies and inter-cultural skills of young people, the majority of the students involved in the research were keen to use English as the language of communication and to mix with other international students rather than the local community. While Swedish and Danish universities seem happy to respond to student demand by offering more courses in English, Caudery et al. report concern at governmental level at 'possible domain loss' if Swedish and Danish are not used in academic contexts. Papatsiba (2006) argues that the different expectations of the various actors involved is one reason why mobility programmes have not had the 'harmonising' effect on European higher education that many in the EU had anticipated. Other reasons include: the relatively small number of mobile students (never reaching the 'critical mass' that may have prompted change) and the disparity between the enthusiasm of students, on the one hand, and the level of academic support, on the other. Papatsiba maintains that:

> Where academics' involvement in student mobility is not seen as a gratifying activity in terms of career progression, and where institutions are expected actively to contribute to the reinforcement of national or regional competitiveness while their educational missions are being challenged to foster both excellence and democracy, it can also be added that students' [high level of] satisfaction...and the emphasis on the personal dimension of mobility...has provided the ideal excuse for limited system-level change. (pp.104–5)

In relation to its political objectives, the available empirical evidence is not conclusive. Papatsiba's (2005) study of mobile French students suggests that 'if the topic of European integration constituted a "politically correct" motivation to support one's application for studies in Europe, it seldom constituted the object of an explicit awareness at the end of the stay' (p.181). Instead, he suggests that the cultural impact of mobility was experienced at an individual level rather than as a collective experience. Indeed, cultural difference 'was treated like a new situation that stretched individuals' limits and potential for adaptability rather than as an opportunity to learn how to understand a foreign symbolic system and to position themselves in it' (p.183).

There is also evidence to suggest that it is relatively uncommon for mobile students (particularly those on short-term exchanges) to develop their inter-cultural skills through interaction with the host community (e.g. Caudery et al., 2008; Murphy-Lejeune, 2002).

Tsoukalas' (2008) ethnographic study of Erasmus students in Stockholm and Athens shows how the young people on the programme socialized only with fellow Erasmus students and, as a result of their strong group identity and 'the unusual activities and emotional intensity of their common life' (p.136), developed few links with the local community. Neither, however, did they learn much about other cultures from within their Erasmus group. This, Tsoukalas, suggests was a result of: the difficulty for young people of standing as a 'fully fledged representative' of their country; their often poor language skills, which impeded communication between group members; and the loss of many traits of their home country as a consequence of living abroad. Instead, he claims that the students spent most of their time engaged in rather unfocussed activities such as socializing, partying and drinking coffee, and 'the fact that these activities take place in an international milieu does not automatically turn them into instances of cultural learning...consequently, the inter-cultural learning of the Erasmus students is in the end limited, passive and ultimately of quite low quality' (p.145).

However, studies from the UK (King and Ruiz-Gelices, 2003) and Greece (Raikou and Karalis, 2007) have come to rather different conclusions. They suggest that those who spend time abroad, under the auspices of an organized mobility programme, tend to be more favourably disposed to European integration, have more interest in European affairs and are more likely to see their identities as at least partly European than their peers who remain at home. Similarly, on the basis of her work with three groups of mobile students (language assistants, those on Erasmus programmes and participants in a French grand école international study programme), Murphy-Lejeune (2002) suggests that these students' experiences effect fundamental change, causing them to 'question the notion of borders and the meaning of home' (p.234). Moreover, Tsoukalas' study (2008), referred to above, while highlighting the relative absence of any learning about the host community during an Erasmus exchange, also points to the significant potential impact of a period abroad once students return home. The young people in his research did not sustain the close relationships with their fellow exchange students (that had characterized their time away) on their return. Instead, they developed less intense but more discerning and reflective forms of communication which, Tsoukalas argues, is more conducive to inter-cultural learning. These links, he suggests form 'bridges that connect disparate social circles with each other' and with the peoples of Europe (p.147). Indeed, as the encounters between these young people were no longer 'hi-jacked' by the strong group dynamic typical of Erasmus groups, they became 'the incarnation of a modern form of community and the bearers of a transnational, potentially European consciousness' (p.151).

Given the emphasis within European policy on the creation of a stronger European identity, it is instructive to consider the characteristics of the 'Europe' that is being created. Reflecting some of the arguments made above about the power imbalances implicit in the geography of student mobility, some scholars have argued that the movement of students (as well as HE staff) under the auspices of various European programmes has tended to reinforce norms of the 'old Europe'. In relation to European researchers, Kenway and Fahey (2007) argue that, although they are encouraged to conduct cross-national and cross-cultural research, this often amounts to little more than 'academic sight-seeing', in which the underlying aim is often to impose epistemological homogeneity, as knowledge is 'transferred' from central points of power in the European system to more marginal locations. Indeed, they contend that the figure of the cosmopolitan researcher:

> Is not about the links between travel and the transfer of trans-cendental knowledge but rather the links between travel and cultural transformation. It is about effecting a form of cultural de- and re-territorialisation. (Kenway and Fahey, 2007, p.32)

The geography of student mobility suggests that the physical flows of young people are often in the opposite direction from those of knowledge transfer (i.e. from more marginal countries to the UK, Germany and other more central countries). However, it could be argued that the direction of the *flow of ideas* remains the same, as those from poorer, more marginal countries come to study in the universities of their richer European neighbours, are assimilated into particular ways of knowledge creation, and then facilitate the spread of these approaches within their own country on their return home. Similar arguments have been made about policies which aim to inculcate a 'European identity' in other phases of the education system. In their discussion of the 'European Dimension in Education' (a policy, discussed above, which aimed to promote European citizenship through the school curriculum), Stoer and Cortesao (2000) maintain that the conceptualization of European identity that underpinned this initiative gave little recognition to the multicultural composition of contemporary Europe. They contend that 'to a large extent the ethno-cultural articulation of the European dimension in education feeds off the homogenous and monocultural dominance that is still so commonly felt in European societies and their educational institutions' (p.263).

In relation to the debates about the relationship between mobility for education and social advantage, outlined earlier in this chapter, it is important to consider the impact of a period of study abroad on the social and cultural capital of the students involved. It seems clear that, over recent decades, educational mobility has had a significant impact on the social position of those who take up such opportunities. For example, Murphy-Lejeune (2002) argues that the main difference between student travellers and their peers rests in the acquisition of 'mobility capital'. This, she states, 'is a sub-component of human capital, enabling individuals to enhance their skills because of the richness of experience gained by living abroad' (p.51). For Kenway and Fahey (2007), such experiences tend to reinforce existing inequalities, with the individualistic focus of EU policy tending to obscure 'the ways in which student mobility contributes to accumulation of international cultural and social capital for certain privileged social groups' (p.31). Recchi (2006) pursues a slightly different argument, however, suggesting that, while the practice of mobility is an increasingly important criterion of social distinction, and EU mobility policies could unwittingly further the growing cleavage between 'locals' and 'cosmopolitans', these do not map on to clear social differences; it is not necessarily social elites who benefit. However, it has also been argued that while studying abroad may have had important social benefits in the past, these are become increasingly less pronounced as such mobility becomes more commonplace. Rivza and Teichler (2007) have argued that the professional value of the Erasmus programme is declining 'because study in another country gradually loses its exceptionality as compared to general experiences of internationalization and globalization affecting the daily life of others' (p.473). And, indeed, this does seem to be borne out by the available data. A study of the professional value of the Erasmus scheme has indicated that its advantages have declined over time, with the benefits for recent cohorts demonstrably less than for previous ones (Bracht et al., 2006).

## Conclusion

Despite the long history of movement between universities in Europe (Musselin, 2004), student mobility remains a relatively under-researched area and has attracted little conceptual analysis (Papatsiba, 2006). Favell (2006) argues that this is a pervasive problem that relates to European studies more generally. Indeed, he suggests that while there is a plethora of 'top-down' policy studies of European integration, very few scholars have considered what it might mean to study Europeanization from below. And yet, he contends, analysis of: 'the experiences, attitudes and social trajectories of prototypical free-moving European citizens offers a tangible grounding by which we might be able to chart the actual effects of European integration on the ground' (Favell, 2006, p.26). There are certainly a number of important questions about student mobility in Europe that remain unanswered – for example, we know little about the impact of the variation in financial support for students on mobility patterns. Nevertheless, by drawing together themes from the extant research on student migration, in this chapter we have been able to explore the characteristics of those students who do choose to study in another European country and the extent to which such mobility has fulfilled some of the economic and political aims of the European Union, which have driven much policy in this area.

We have argued that despite the strong policy emphasis on encouraging intra-European mobility, the take-up of such opportunities has been relatively limited; participation in the various EU-sponsored mobility programmes has often fallen short of target. There are also important disparities in the geography of such migration – with students tending to show preferences for studying in wealthier, northern European countries rather than their poorer, southern counterparts, and for countries which teach in widely-spoken European languages. In exploring the characteristics of these students, we have pointed to an ambivalence in the literature. In common with studies of such students from other parts of the world (outlined in other chapters of this book), some scholars have argued that it is typically the most privileged who participate in mobility schemes. Others, however, have suggested that intra-European migration may offer an alternative route to capital accumulation to those from less advantaged backgrounds, who cannot be sure of success within their domestic context. In relation to the EU's aims of developing a pan-European labour force and inculcating a stronger European political identity among young people, the available evidence suggests that those who study abroad are more likely than their peers to work abroad after graduation. There is also evidence from some studies that those who take part in Erasmus and other mobility programmes, on return home, are more likely than their peers to see their identities as at least part European. However, again there seem to be geographical variations: while research amongst British and Greek students has highlighted such shifts, studies of mobile French students have not found evidence of similar changes. Finally, in this chapter, we have sought to examine critically some of the ways in which intra-European mobility may serve to exacerbate inequalities – between individuals and also between European nations – through: the social and cultural capital that is often accrued through mobility; the unequal flows between different geographical regions of Europe; and unequal power relations which often underpin processes of 'knowledge transfer'. We return to some of these themes in subsequent chapters.

# 5
# International Mobility of UK Students

## Introduction

In the context of wider debates around students' international mobility, this chapter discusses the findings of several recent studies examining the motivations and experiences of international students from the UK. As we have already noted, the majority of research papers published to date have focussed on individuals moving from countries in East and Southeast Asia to the major student-receiving destinations in the US, Canada, Australia, New Zealand or the UK (e.g. Butcher, 2004; Collins, 2006; Ong, 1999; Waters, 2008). The popularity of Anglophone destinations amongst the wider international student population reflects in large part the high value attached to an English-medium, 'Western' education – English is widely thought of as the language of international business and trade (Ong, 1999). The motivations and experiences of (English-speaking) students from the UK, seeking an international education, have until recently therefore been unclear. Furthermore, universities in the UK consistently top international league-tables and rankings (for example, the annual *Times Higher Education* World University Rankings), whilst Britain is second only to the United States as the most significant importer of international students worldwide (British Council, 2004). This begs the question: *Why*, then, do UK students choose to study abroad? In answer, this chapter draws on empirical findings from a small number of substantial studies[1] examining UK students' mobility, to consider: the factors that have informed the decision-making of international students from the UK; and the experiences of UK students overseas. More specifically, this chapter discusses the key social characteristics of individuals considering overseas study, the geography of their decision-making (i.e. where they chose to study), their motivations and aspirations, and their experiences of study and subsequent employment. In terms of motivations and aspirations, we discuss the relative importance of employability factors, life-style considerations, and the need to accumulate prestigious 'academic capital'. Under 'experiences', we discuss social and cultural interactions, emigration and the labour market.

We begin by providing some brief policy context to the international mobility of UK students (see Chapter 4 for a detailed discussion of European policy in relation to this), before considering the kinds of individuals who choose to study overseas – their social characteristics. The geography of study destinations is then discussed, before turning to examine students' motivations and experiences. In our analysis we will be considering two types of 'educational migration' as outlined in Chapter 4 – 'diploma mobility' (i.e. movement for the whole of a degree programme, usually unattached to a formal mobility scheme) and 'credit mobility' (i.e. overseas study as part of a degree course, such as Erasmus) (Sussex Centre for Migration Research, 2004). Available data suggest that, amongst UK students, credit mobility is more common than diploma mobility and, prior to the publication of Findlay and King's (2010) report, most statistical data on UK students overseas related to the former. Very recent evidence, however, would suggest that diploma mobility amongst UK students is not insignificant, and is growing in popularity – according to Findlay and King (2010), the total number now stands at 14 584.

## The policy context to UK student mobility

To date, the internationalization of education in the UK has been a rather one-sided process, involving the selling of 'Education UK' to overseas consumers (particularly through the work of the British Council) and the consequent 'importing' of thousands of students annually. Latest data from the Higher Education Statistics Agency (HESA) suggest that the total number of international students in the UK in 2009 was 515 570 (BBC News, 2009). There are clear financial incentives to attracting international students, and UK HEIs are investing heavily in implementing 'internationalization' strategies, as a number of recent policy reports (e.g. Fielden, 2007) and dedicated practitioner conferences attest. The UK has followed Australia with a successful attempt to centralize the planning of international education, through the British Council. The British Council is a non-profit organization, which operates as an executive non-departmental public body and is sponsored by the UK Foreign and Commonwealth Office. In a statement of its 'rationale and values', beliefs in the 'benefits of internationalism' were earnestly espoused (British Council, 2004). It has a multi-million pound annual turnover from the selling of services such as English language courses and examinations abroad, and plays a major role in attempting actively to 'recruit' overseas students to the 'Education UK' brand.

The movement of students *from* the UK has been altogether less frequent. The Erasmus programme, set up in 1987, initiated students' mobility within Europe. In 1999, the UK became a signatory to the 'Bologna Process' (see Chapter 4 for a detailed discussion of this), which aimed, amongst other things, to create a European Higher Education Area by 2010, by standardizing degree structures and enabling the transfer of credits through the European Credit Transfer System. Increased student mobility across the European Union was one of its main objectives and it has, on many measures, been a success (the Erasmus scheme has now been running for 22 years and has celebrated its two millionth student (Baty, 2009d)). However, compared to most other EU countries, the UK has sent relatively few students abroad (Sussex Centre for Migration Research, 2004). As Findlay et al. (2006) have observed, British students are generally 'reluctant Europeans', seen to be 'turning away from international mobility, especially to [Mainland] Europe' (p.291). Recently, however, there has been some evidence to suggest that the number of UK students participating in the Erasmus programme is increasing – going up from 7235 in 2006–2007 to 10 278 in 2007–2008 (Baty, 2009d).

The previous UK government gave more formal support to international education through the 'Prime Minister's Initiative on International Education' (PMI) (1999–2004), and the PMI 2, which was launched in April 2006. As noted in Chapter 2, the PMI 2 was a five year strategy (building on the first PMI) with the aim of securing the position of the UK as a 'leader in international education', with targets that include attracting an additional 70 000 international students to the UK and significantly growing the number of partnerships between the UK and other countries, both by 2011. Importantly, the PMI 2 also includes an acknowledgement of the benefits that can accrue from sending British students overseas for education. Other reports and publications, such as the Council for Industry and Higher Education's guide for universities (Fielden, 2007), aim to prepare UK students for outward international mobility and reflect this shift in thinking around student migration.

Despite this, UK students have not routinely been the subject of studies on international mobility, and, aside from piecemeal anecdotal evidence, knowledge of this group of young people has been limited. The *Times Higher Education Supplement* recently included a small feature on UK students overseas, suggesting that 'unprecedented numbers of British teenagers are considering shunning UK universities for US colleges in the hope of a broader, cheaper and more luxurious education' (Shepherd, 2006, no pagination). The Fulbright Commission, which funds UK students to study in the US, reported a significant increase in the number of enquiries from British students in recent years (Shepherd, 2006). In another media account, concerns over 'cost' and the relatively high tuition fees (particularly at Masters and PhD levels) faced by students in the UK were given as a reason why increasing numbers would seem to be interested in studying abroad. Countries such as Sweden and the Netherlands offer postgraduate tuition in the English language for a fraction of the cost of an equivalent UK-based course (Clark, 2006). More systematic studies of UK students' international mobility have clearly been needed; their role in global international population flows has been ignored.

To a certain extent, this gap in our knowledge has been filled by a number of recent studies on UK students overseas, which have included some quantitative estimates of the numbers of students involved. According to these figures, approximately 24 859 UK students are presently studying abroad (as part of the Erasmus programme or for a degree) (Baty, 2009d; Findlay and King, 2010). In what follows, we examine in detail the motivations and experiences of UK students overseas.

Studies of other international student groups suggest that they represent an 'elite': relatively wealthy, with good foreign language skills, a high degree of familial support, and a history of international mobility (Murphy-Lejeune, 2002; Favell, 2008; Waters, 2008). When it comes to degree course, institution and country of study, international students are commonly highly strategic – concerned primarily with 'employability' objectives (Baláž and Williams, 2004; Findlay et al., 2006; Waters, 2006). And the outcomes for international students are generally good; there would seem to exist a strong positive relationship between possessing an 'overseas' degree and labour market success (Waters, 2008). Recent studies of UK students are less assertive. On the one hand, many of the characteristics described for the broader global population of international students can be seen amongst these British young people. Most are undoubtedly from privileged backgrounds: parental occupations and education suggest a solidly middle-class upbringing. They possess significant amounts of cultural and social capital (Bourdieu, 1986). Such capital includes a high degree of parental support (material and emotional) and familial involvement in their education (Coleman, 1988). Some students are concerned with 'employability'; i.e. with securing their 'positional advantage' within a saturated graduate labour market (Arthur and Rousseau, 1996; Brown and Hesketh, 2004; Brown and Lauder, 2006) through the acquisition of international credentials. At the same time, however, some of the findings of these studies suggest that UK students may be rather 'exceptional', or at least unconventional. Whilst employability may be a primary concern for some young people, others place greater emphasis on the desire to 'travel, to 'have fun', to seek 'excitement', and to transform their lives in ways not obviously related to study and the acquisition of credentials. This paints a quite different picture of UK students overseas. Similarly, when it comes to the outcomes from overseas study, British students are far more ambivalent than international students more generally. Almost without exception, students enjoyed their time abroad. However, many report the labour market *disadvantages* that possessing foreign credentials may bring (Brooks et al., 2012). This has provided a short overview of the kinds of experiences reported in recent research on UK students overseas. In what follows, we explore these and other aspects in more detail.

## Who goes overseas for study? Students' characteristics

Recent studies of UK students' international mobility provide some information on their backgrounds and lifestyles. Perhaps unsurprisingly, it has been found that those who study (or seriously consider studying) overseas are economically and socially privileged (King and Ruiz-Gelices, 2003; Findlay et al., 2006; Brooks and Waters, 2009a; Brooks and Waters, 2009b; Waters and Brooks, 2010a). In their survey, King and Ruiz-Gelices (2003) found that individuals who opt for a 'Year-Abroad' (YA) during undergraduate studies were more likely to have professionally employed parents than non-YA students. The Sussex Centre for Migration Research (2004) report, which examined UK students on a range of mobility programmes, confirmed that over 52 per cent of student interviewees had fathers in 'professional or managerial occupations'. More than 54 per cent were also receiving a financial contribution towards their education from their parents. The most recent study of UK students overseas has found that young people with parents employed in 'professional and managerial' occupations were more likely to have applied to study abroad than were those with other occupational backgrounds (Findlay and King, 2010). These findings also showed that a higher proportion of students who came from homes where *both* parents had been educated to university level applied to study overseas, compared with students where neither parent had a university degree.

In terms of students' backgrounds, secondary schooling would also seem to be significant. Those young people who had attended top private or independent schools were far more likely to consider studying overseas than were state-school attendees (see also Brooks and Waters, 2009a). The findings of both Findlay and King (2010) and Brooks and Waters (2009a, b) suggest that independent-school pupils are given access to much more and a greater range of information on the possibility of studying abroad than are state-school students. Amongst those state-school students surveyed, only 11.5 per cent had received any information or help from their school, compared to 32 per cent of independent school pupils (Findlay and King, 2010). As Brooks and Waters (2009a) have observed, outreach officers from Ivy League colleges often visit top independent schools in an attempt to recruit students. Some (independent) schools also offer 'pre-SATs'[2] to students as a matter of course. Such a high level of institutional support undoubtedly leads to more applications for overseas study from independent school students, in comparison to their state school counterparts (where almost no institutional help was reported).

These recent studies of international mobility have yielded some rich qualitative data on students' backgrounds and lifestyles (Brooks and Waters, 2009a, b; Waters and Brooks, 2010a). These data indicate that international students from the UK have access to significant amounts of capital (social, cultural and economic), associated with middle- and upper-middle-class lifestyles (Bourdieu, 1986). Social and cultural capital include: parental support and involvement in education, familial expectations with regard to educational achievement and the amount of financial invested by the family (Coleman, 1988). Parents were almost always highly supportive, and would demonstrate this in material as well as less tangible ways, frequently offering to foot the bill for overseas study (Waters and Brooks, 2010a). School, peer and familial pressure to attend a 'good' university was widely apparent; the concept of 'habitus'[3] (Bourdieu, 1984) would seem to be particularly salient here, capturing the multiple dimensions of privilege coalescing to make international education a viable, imaginable 'choice' (Waters and Brooks, 2010a).

Related to the points drawn above, it is also clear that UK students' mobility is significantly embedded in social networks of friends and family. Current debates on transnational mobility are very often based on assumptions concerning the *individualized* nature of this movement. In Chapter 3, we went some way towards discrediting these assumptions, when we showed how, in the context of East Asia, educational migration is nearly always a family project and very often involves the relocation of entire households (and not the independent mobility of a 'footloose' student). Similarly, in relation to UK students, their dependence on social networks was clear, if perhaps more subtle in affect (Brooks and Waters, 2010). Amongst UK students, there is little evidence to suggest, in fact, that family exert a strong *direct* influence over the *decision* to study overseas. Rather, their influence is bound up with the students' habitus, within which it was considered 'normal' to travel (ibid.). Many students experienced travel related to their parents' work, and had lived abroad for a period as a child. Others had a parent who was born overseas, and many had relatives living abroad. More will be said of this below. Suffice it to say, here, that all of this exerted in less conspicuous but still significant ways the influence of social networks over the propensity to study overseas.

Although we can draw many commonalities amongst these students, then, differences *within* groups of British international students are also observable. Some distinction can be drawn between those who chose to study overseas for undergraduate and postgraduate qualifications (Brooks and Waters, 2009b). Postgraduate students tended to be more socially diverse; including a greater number of individuals from lower socio-economic groupings and with more varied educational histories (such as mature students). They are less likely to have come from 'wealthy' backgrounds and their parents have (on the whole) fewer formal qualifications. International undergraduates, in contrast, are generally younger (they have not taken a 'break' from education), are more likely to have attended private secondary schools, and have highly educated parents working in (or retired from) professional and managerial-level occupations (Brooks and Waters, 2009b). Yet, despite this apparent diversity, on the whole, UK international students are a privileged group, with access to extensive social and cultural capital, directly supporting their educational achievement.

We can say little of any significance about the gender of UK overseas students, although there would seem to be a difference in this regard between 'diploma' and 'credit'-types of mobility. With respect to the 'Year Abroad', King and Ruiz-Gelices (2003) found that women were far more likely than men to take this opportunity for travel and study (70 per cent of their sample were female). Linked Erasmus-HESA datasets, reported by Findlay et al. (2006), suggest that males are underrepresented in Erasmus flows. In contrast, the research by Brooks and Waters (2009b) sampled a fairly even split of males and females (48 and 37, respectively). These findings were mirrored by those in the Findlay and King (2010) report – slightly more females than males went overseas for study, but the difference was statistically insignificant. Similarly, we have little information on the ethnicity of these students. Erasmus-HESA matched datasets for 2002–2003, reported in Findlay et al. (2006), claim that 8 per cent of UK students who participated in Erasmus schemes are 'non-White', compared to 16 per cent of those who have not participated in such schemes. Brooks and Waters (2010) found that 22 of the 85 individuals interviewed for their project were from ethnic minority backgrounds, suggesting that ethnic minorities are relatively well represented amongst UK students overseas. Findlay and King's report (2010), however, found no statistical significance when it comes to the ethnicity of students. It is therefore hard to draw strong conclusions from this.

Some information on the academic ability of students seeking overseas study is provided by Findlay and King (2010). Taking into account both GCSE results and predicted A level grades, they found a statistically significant relationship between academic ability and the propensity to study abroad. They succinctly conclude on this point: 'The academic cream of the English school system are those most interested in international study' (Findlay and King, 2010, p.22). Furthermore, as suggested above, students' biographies indicated the importance of travel (as a child or young adult) – whether on family or school trips, as part of a 'gap year' or as a 'year abroad' within an undergraduate degree programme (Brooks and Waters, 2009a; Brooks and Waters, 2010). Findlay et al. (2006, p.301) similarly reported:

> students who had lived or travelled abroad prior to entering HE, for example during a gap year between school and university, were more likely than others to engage in formal mobility during their time in tertiary education.

The significance of the 'gap year' comes out strongly across the datasets (Brooks and Waters, 2009a; Findlay and King, 2010; Sussex Centre for Migration Research, 2004) and is a prominent feature of many students' accounts. Favourable experiences when on a gap year prior to university (or on a foreign exchange programme during university) undoubtedly had an impact upon the decision to pursue education abroad. Experiences of travel were also, often, as noted above, related to the presence of family members abroad (Brooks and Waters, 2009a). Over one-third of the sample of 85 in Brooks and Waters' (2009a, b)

study had family members who lived overseas, and travel as a child was often closely associated to familial visits. They said of this:

> The vast majority of our sample, regardless of specific socio-economic background, had extensive experience of travel when younger, often led by their parents, but sometimes independently or with friends. Travel had instilled in them a desire to explore and actively to seek out alternative experiences... (Brooks and Waters, 2009b, p.202)

Overall, then, it has been possible to extract some quite distinctive characteristics of 'internationally mobile' UK students. On the whole, they are a privileged (well-educated, well-connected and well-supported) group.

## Where they go: geographies of UK students' mobility

As observed in earlier chapters, studies of the international mobility of students point to the overwhelming dominance of particular Anglophone countries in student preferences – namely the US, UK, Canada, Australia and New Zealand (British Council, 2004). International students are keenly aware of the cultural capital associated with university degrees from particular countries, as well as the strategic importance of learning in an English-speaking environment (Waters, 2006). Perhaps surprisingly, the choices of UK students mirror the geographical choices of international students more broadly. Language students aside, British young people display a strong preference for certain Anglophone countries, and for learning through the medium of English.

In their research, Brooks and Waters (2009a) found that of the 20 sixth-formers interviewed about possible overseas study, *all* were seriously considering the United States as a study destination. Only one other destination (France) was mentioned. The geographical characteristics of their sample are reproduced in Table 5.1.

As can be seen from the table, the United States plays a prominent role in the geographical imaginations of British sixth-form students. Whilst this does in many cases translate into actual travel, as the second and fourth column show, the destinations of students were in fact far more diverse. Nevertheless, this general preference for the US as a location for study, closely followed by Australia, is strongly reflected in the findings of other research (Sussex Centre for Migration Research, 2004). In their survey of sixth-formers, Findlay and King (2010) note that 51 per cent of all respondents were thinking of studying in the US,

**Table 5.1**   Respondents' countries of study (with most popular destinations highlighted)

| Country | *Number of respondents* | | | |
|---|---|---|---|---|
| | *Sixth-formers considering an UG degree overseas N=20* | *Those who had completed an UG degree overseas N=11* | *Undergraduates considering a PG degree overseas N=20* | *Those who had completed a PG degree overseas N=34* |
| **Australia** | 0 | 0 | 3 | 5 |
| **Belgium** | 0 | 0 | 0 | 2 |
| **Canada** | 0 | 2 | 1 | 9 |
| Finland | 0 | 0 | 0 | 1 |
| France | 1 | 1 | 1 | 1 |
| Germany | 0 | 0 | 1 | 1 |
| Hong Kong | 0 | 0 | 1 | 0 |
| Ireland | 0 | 1 | 0 | 0 |
| **Italy** | 0 | 0 | 0 | 6 |
| Japan | 0 | 1 | 0 | 0 |
| Netherlands | 0 | 0 | 3 | 0 |
| New Zealand | 0 | 0 | 1 | 0 |
| Singapore | 0 | 0 | 1 | 0 |
| South Africa | 0 | 1 | 0 | 2 |
| Sweden | 0 | 0 | 3 | 1 |
| Taiwan | 0 | 0 | 1 | 0 |
| **United States** | 20 | 5 | 15 | 8 |

NB Totals for the first and third columns sum to more than 20 as some respondents were seriously considering more than one country at the time of interview. The total for the fourth column does not sum to 34 as two respondents had studied at more than one overseas institution.

followed by 13 per cent opting for Australia. They also analysed secondary data from the UK and international agencies on UK students overseas. They note that there is currently no system for recording the number of students who leave the UK as part of 'diploma-mobility' and other statistical data available from international agencies on UK-domiciled students studying abroad are not definitive. However, the best possible estimates derived from an analysis of other available data led them to conclude that, for 2006–2007, the number of UK students abroad were as follows: 8438 in the US, 2282 in Ireland, 1783 in Australia, 1635 in France and 464 in Germany. They argue that:

> UK student diploma mobility has not followed a simple global trend across all destination countries, but is growing in some locations

and declining in others. In Ireland the trend has been clearly upwards...In the case of the United States, numbers appear to have increased over the first part of the present decade before levelling-off in recent years, while for Australia there is similar evidence of an initial increase rising to a peak in numbers in 2004. Since then there has been a small dip in numbers. Figures for France and Germany provide a different picture. In both cases decreases are apparent in terms of the overall numbers of enrolled UK citizen students... (Findlay and King, 2010, p.13)

There are multiple possible reasons for this bias towards particular study destinations. Waters and Brooks (2010b) have argued that film, television and other popular media have an important role to play in making certain overseas destinations both knowable and desirable to British students. This was particularly apparent in relation to the US – students had a strong preconceived idea of what it would be like to live and study there, mainly influenced by TV and Hollywood films. They were seeking 'difference', but also the kinds of 'familiarity' that frequent exposure by media can produce (Appadurai, 1996). Consequently, few students anticipated any sort of 'culture shock' from studying in the US. Many wanted to recreate a lifestyle through overseas study, 'as seen on TV' (Waters and Brooks, 2010b).

Language ability (or lack of it) is another important reason why UK students choose particular overseas destinations for their education (Sussex Centre for Migration Research, 2004). Indeed, British students' poor foreign language skills have been blamed for the relatively small number of UK students choosing to go overseas for (credit or diploma-type) study and also for the apparent recent 'shift' from European to Anglophone destination countries (Sussex Centre for Migration Research, 2004). The vast majority of 'diploma-mobility' involves study in English. Even when students choose particular European destinations, most commonly these courses deliver their education in English. Very few diploma-mobility students would seem to study in a 'foreign' language (Waters and Brooks, 2010b). Only two individuals in Brooks and Waters' (2009a) sample had studied in a language other than English. In contrast, credit-type mobility is dominated by 'language students' – i.e. those with good proficiency in a second language (Sussex Centre for Migration Research, 2004). Consequently, when we examine credit mobility only, we find that mobile students have a much higher rate of language proficiency, and that France is the most popular destination country (44 per cent in the Sussex survey).

The apparent preference for particular countries – and especially the United States – often relates to the desire, amongst many mobile students from the UK, to attend the most prestigious institutions, almost irrespective of which country these institutions are located in. As we have already noted, this student cohort is privileged, with access to social and cultural capital. These students aspire to achieve 'the best' academically, with a weight of parental and familial expectations on their shoulders, and this includes the need to study at highly esteemed institutions. We will discuss this issue further below in relation to Oxbridge entrance. In the eyes of UK students, many of the 'top' universities in the world are found in the US (i.e. Ivy League schools) – a perception borne out by international league tables of HEIs (such as the *Times Higher Education* QS World University Rankings and Shanghai Jiao Tong University Rankings – see discussion in Chapter 6). Findlay and King (2010) claim that: 'the USA fitted into a wider mobility trajectory that involved global mobility to achieve an international career' (p.39). Related to this, they found that the 'USA and Australia are also very different destinations in terms of the calibre of UK students enrolling to study at these destinations' (p.39). Their data suggest that the USA attracts the most academically capable of UK students.

There is some evidence, however, to suggest that UK students are moving to particular countries because they want to live there long term (see Brooks et al., 2012). This would seem to be especially true of Australia (Findlay and King, 2010). We discuss this aspect in more detail below. Some Scandinavian destination countries, such as Sweden, Norway and Denmark, are chosen by British students for primarily financial reasons. These countries do not currently charge tuition fees to international students. And a final point to make with regards to the geography of international student choices concerns the *relative* diversity of postgraduate destinations, compared to those chosen at undergraduate level (Brooks and Waters, 2009b). Reasons for this relative diversity include a greater emphasis placed on the specific pedagogic content of courses and, consequently, less concern with the cultural capital imbued by particular institutions.

## Overseas study: aspirations and motivations

In this section, we draw on the available data to discuss some of the reasons why UK students choose to study overseas; how this decision is closely tied to various personal and familial aspirations, as well as to more strategic objectives. As we have observed above, some of the most commonly cited reasons why students opt for overseas study (to improve their English-language abilities, for example, or to attend a prestigious 'Western' university) are unlikely to apply for students from the UK. Instead, the research suggests a number of other reasons why an overseas education may appeal to British students: concerns over 'employability' and gaining 'positional advantage' in a saturated graduate labour market; the desire to attend a globally prestigious university; the opportunity for travel, excitement and adventure; and the (longer-term) possibility of emigration. In what follows, we discuss these ideas in more detail.

In its research on credit-type movements (i.e. *within* a degree pro-gramme), the Sussex Centre for Migration Research (2004) describes a number of what it calls 'drivers of mobility'. These are given as: employer-led interest, enhanced career prospects, improved language competence, relevance to degree subject, personal development and professional dev-elopment. It also notes the *disincentives* for, or *inhibitors* of, overseas study. In a survey of 214 students, 22 per cent gave 'insufficient money' as the primary reason why they would not consider going abroad, followed by time away from a partner (20 per cent), language issues (14 per cent) and distance from the parental home (9 per cent) (Sussex Centre for Migration Research, 2004). We have more detail available on the motivations and aspirations of students undertaking diploma-mobility (i.e. going overseas for the whole of a degree). Here, in their survey of 560 UK nationals living and studying overseas, Findlay and King (2010) observed two overwhelm-ingly important factors driving the overseas mobility of British students: the 'search for a world class education' and the 'opportunity for a unique adventure' (p.31). We discuss these in turn below.

For some students, then, the decision to go abroad for education is clearly highly strategic, and motivated by a desire to 'be the best' acad-emically. This means that students will only consider studying at parti-cular, internationally renowned universities, discounting all others. The importance of specific HEIs for UK students strongly suggests the exist-ence of what have been termed 'global circuits of higher education' (Brooks and Waters, 2009a). This mirrors findings of research on the com-pulsory education sector (mentioned in Chapters 1 and 2), which have shown that, within a market-driven system, different 'circuits' of schools emerge (Ball et al., 1997), intersecting with social class and cultural capital (Brooks and Waters, 2009a). In short, research has shown how different 'class fractions' tend to choose within one particular circuit of schools – elite, independent or state. Rarely do individuals move *between* circuits. These arguments have been extended to higher education within the UK – Reay et al. (2005) suggest that while privately educated students will associate most strongly with elite universities such as Oxford and Cambridge, middle-class state-educated pupils tend to apply to redbrick institutions (i.e. higher education institutions founded prior to 1992), and those from working class backgrounds will opt for new universities (i.e. former polytechnics). There is also a relationship between the 'type' of institution preferred by different class fractions and their geography – high achievers from more privileged backgrounds tend to choose within national markets of high status HEIs, while their peers engage within regional markets of less prestigious institutions. Can the same be said for international higher education? Is going abroad a reality only for the highest achievers from the most privileged backgrounds? The data would suggest that, on the whole, this relationship between class and mobility holds true even at an *international* scale (Waters, 2006; Brooks and Waters, 2009a, b).

In their research on British young people considering studying overseas, Brooks and Waters (2009a) argue that a minority of highly privileged young people are making their HE decisions within global rather than national or regional circuits. Some considered that only an Ivy League university (such as Harvard, Yale or Princeton) would be good enough if they failed to gain a place at Oxbridge. At some schools, this was considered a 'usual' strategy, as the following interview quote reveals:

I think there were about, from my school, say five who went this year to America. A lot more apply and then...often don't take their place if they get into Oxford or Oxbridge...Like if I don't get into Oxbridge, then I'd like to go to America. (Student Interviewee, quoted in Brooks and Waters, 2009b, p.201)

Similarly, Findlay and King (2010) conclude that:

some of the by-products of the globalization of higher education, such as the emergence of a hierarchy of universities including an elite set of 'world class universities', are important in driving the international mobility of students, and that many students are aware of this social process. Perhaps it is not therefore surprising that the single most important driver of international student mobility...is the desire of those in the sample to attend what they consider to be a world class university. (p.31)

As Brooks and Waters (2009b) argue: 'Even a failure to secure a place at one elite institution did not lead to a shift "downwards" to less prestigious circuits, but merely a movement "sidewards" to a similarly-ranked institution in another country' (p.202). This latter point links to another, important related issue around the choices and decisions of UK students – for many British students, overseas study is a way of avoiding 'failure' at home and offers a 'second chance at "success"' (Brooks and Waters, 2009a; Findlay and King, 2010). For these students, failure to get into their first choice university in the UK resulted in an application to an overseas institution. It should be noted that in most cases, these were the most highly achieving, high aspiring students, burdened by significant parental expectations (Brooks and Waters, 2009a). They were students for whom Oxbridge was the only option in the UK, and an Ivy League institution in the US was the only acceptable alternative to Oxbridge. Interestingly, the geographical location of the overseas institution was almost incidental. What mattered, for these students, was the cultural capital implied by the status of the educational institution.

Although largely absent from some of the other research findings, Findlay et al. (2010) suggest that for a minority of students, studying abroad is seen as the first step in an international career. What is perhaps more interesting, however, is how *few* students discuss international career objectives – the vast majority, even in Findlay and King's (2010) study, wanted to return to the UK following graduation. A minority of students across the studies also mentioned the ultimate desire to live abroad after graduation, and saw international study as a way of achieving this (Brooks et al., 2012).

Amongst Findlay and King's (2010) sample of UK students, the desire for a unique, exciting experience was the second most-given reason for studying abroad. Indeed, Waters and Brooks (2010a) have stressed the frequent *absence* of overtly strategic 'career-linked' objectives for many individuals (Waters and Brooks, 2010a). These findings do not correspond to conventional wisdom, which states that international students are highly strategic and focussed primarily on subsequent careers, and where their choice of institutions and subjects reflects explicit attempts to maximize their accumulation of 'cultural capital' (Bourdieu, 1984). Nor do they obviously connect with assumptions underpinning much work on the sociology of education, where the concept of middle-class 'strategies' around education (and the need to gain 'positional advantage') is liberally invoked. Instead, Waters and Brooks (2010a) found that for many of their interviewees, international education seemed to represent an active shunning of 'life-planning' and the responsibilities associated with employment (Brooks and Everett, 2008). Going overseas offered opportunities for 'excitement', 'glamour' and 'fun' and a way of deferring the inevitable encroachment of a career. Waters and Brooks (2010a) conceptualized their findings in terms of the 'accidental achievement' of UK students who, despite their claims of disinterestedness, nevertheless appear to be generally 'successful'. The theoretical ideas of Pierre Bourdieu (1984, 1996) are particularly illuminating: he argues that for the most privileged members of society, amongst whom many of these students would count, strategies of reproduction are not necessarily conscious or deliberate, but are subsumed within a more general 'aesthetic disposition', wherein 'ordinary urgencies' and material concerns are put to one side and in their place can be found the tendency to pursue pleasure and experience for experience's sake. Importantly, however, Waters and Brooks (2010a) also argue that the choices which these individuals make with regards to their education may nevertheless result in the reproduction of their privilege. This becomes clear when we examine the destinations of UK students. As has been already noted, they are focussed on 'world class' institutions abroad, and particularly Ivy League universities in the United States. The opportunities to study at these institutions presented themselves not at all by 'accident', but most usually in association with particular experiences of (private) schooling and parental involvement in education.

## Experiences and outcomes from overseas study

Research on different international student groups indicates the many and significant advantages that can accrue from acquiring 'overseas' (particularly 'Western') credentials (Ong, 1999; Waters, 2008; Williams, 2009). As we have argued in Chapter 3, labour market advantages, in the case of Chinese students, would seem to be particularly pronounced. These occur when graduates of a Western university return home to search for work, armed with their international qualifications. In certain occupations (such as banking and accountancy), a degree from a recognized British or North American university represents valuable cultural capital. Overseas educated graduates find that they are able to net the 'top jobs' as a direct consequence of their international credentials. The findings of research on the employment outcomes of British graduates educated overseas are far more ambiguous when it comes to deciphering the (dis)advantages of holding an international degree.

To begin, however, with the research on 'credit mobility', a comparison of mobile and non-mobile students yields few differences when it comes to career and employment outcomes (Findlay et al.,

2006). There is, Findlay et al. (2006) note, a lamentable absence of employer surveys, which would indicate if and how mobility is valued in the labour market. A small study of University of Sussex Year-Abroad students did suggest some significant advantages to overseas mobility: mobile students were more likely to be found in professional or managerial jobs and to be earning high salaries that their non-mobile counterparts (King and Ruiz-Gelices, 2003). HEFCE [Higher Education Funding Council for England] data suggest, however, that outcomes for Erasmus and non-Erasmus students do appear to be similar (Findlay et al., 2006). The results, therefore, are inconclusive in relation to credit-mobility.

Research by Brooks and Waters sought explicitly to examine the significance of employment-related concerns for students' choices around international higher education. Contrary to their expectations, they found very little evidence that study abroad was seen by students as a means of securing a labour market advantage (Brooks and Waters, 2009a; Brooks et al., 2012). While a considerable number of postgraduate respondents had been motivated to pursue higher-level study in order to distinguish themselves from peers with only an undergraduate degree, the overseas nature of the education *per se* was not deemed important. In their research, they asked respondents who had completed an undergraduate or postgraduate degree abroad to reflect upon their subsequent labour market advantages, and it became clear that in some cases their overseas qualifications had been a discernible *disadvantage*. Often, this related to the longer duration of their qualification (four years for an undergraduate degree, two years for a Masters degree or five or more years for a PhD), compared to its shorter equivalent in the UK. Others contended that many British employers knew little about overseas universities and, as such, were unsure about the value of a degree from an institution outside the UK (Brooks and Waters, 2009b).

However, while an overseas education was not considered to offer any automatic advantage within the UK labour market, it was believed to be important in opening up work opportunities abroad (especially in the country of study) (Brooks et al., 2012). For a minority of UK students, the possibility of an 'international' career has been one of the most important reasons for pursuing education overseas (Findlay and King, 2010; Brooks et al., 2012). This was inextricably linked to the desire to live and, in some cases, gain permanent residency, abroad. It is to this point that we now turn.

In their survey, King and Ruiz-Gelices (2003) found that three times as many 'Year-Abroad' as 'non-Year-Abroad' students were living overseas following graduation. Indeed, there is a growing body of evidence

to suggest that studying overseas can be linked to permanent relocation abroad, although the exact causal relationship is not always clear.
In some cases, individuals had always intended to return to the UK
after graduating, but a romantic relationship had forced them to
change their plans. Waters and Brooks (2010b) observed several examples of where individuals had married or established a life with long-
term partners whom they had met when studying overseas. There are
indications of what Scott and Cartledge (2009) have described in their
study of UK citizens working in France as 'going native'. They stressed the
significance of 'mixed nationality relationship migrants'; in other words,
'migrants who have committed to a life outside their home country
because of the presence of a foreign partner' (Scott and Cartledge, 2009,
p.60). Whilst it is likely that the majority of overseas students do not
develop relationships in this way, a small number clearly do.

There is also some evidence in the literature to suggest that UK students
use studying overseas as a way of securing permanent residency abroad
(such strategies have been frequently reported for other national student
groups – see Baas, 2006). This would seem to be more common amongst
those studying in Australia (Findlay and King, 2010) (see Chapter 7);
although Waters and Brooks (2010b) have found that this was also true
for many sixth formers looking to study in the US, who stressed the
significance of life-style considerations in their decision-making. For
those with an eye on future employment opportunities abroad, gaining
qualifications from their chosen country was seen as an important step
in this process, believing that employers there would look much more
favourably on those with a degree from a 'domestic' university, than
on one gained in the UK (Brooks et al., 2012). Implicit in these
discussions is the assumption that higher education qualifications are
less 'mobile' than we might assume, or be led to believe. We should not
dismiss the possibility that acquiring overseas credentials may, for UK
students, be inextricably linked to other longer-term mobility objectives.

A final point that we wish to make with regards to students' experiences overseas concerns the nature of their social and cultural encounters. We might expect that international students would report rich
inter-cultural experiences. However, research by Waters and Brooks
(2010b) has clearly shown the *limits* placed upon UK students' interactions when overseas, and the fact that these restrictions were often not
obviously of their choosing (see also King and Ruiz-Gelices, 2003).
Many students talked of an insular and tightly bound 'international
student community', from which it was difficult to 'escape' (Fincher
and Shaw, 2009). The enforced separation of international students by

host institutions is clearly good, in one respect, for the development of strong friendships and enduring social capital. On the whole, however, students lamented the fact that they had little contact with others beyond a narrow social circle, one interviewee invoking the notion of a 'bubble', shut off from the 'real world' outside. This, we argue, resonates strongly with the findings of research on British expatriate enclaves overseas (e.g. Beaverstock, 1996; Yeoh and Willis, 2005). Inadvertently, an international student community may serve an important function, in the creation of a segregated and separated educated 'elite'.

## Conclusion

This chapter has examined a hitherto neglected group of international students – those from the UK. Whilst anecdotal evidence would suggest that British students have for many years gone abroad in search of a different, more exciting or more valuable educational experience, until recently very little was known about this group – how many there are, where they go and, perhaps more intriguingly, *why* they go. We are drawn, in particular, to the question of 'why' not least because the UK retains a global reputation for academic excellence at university level, housing some of the oldest and most prestigious institutions in the world. Consequently, the UK is a significant net *importer* of international students, second only to the United States as the biggest importer, globally. We understand, now, a great deal about why many international students choose to study abroad – often related to the allure of the English language or world-class institutions. We have sought therefore to throw some light on British students in particular as a notably *under*-researched group.

During the last five or so years, a picture of UK international students has begun to emerge, as a result of several in-depth empirical studies of their experiences and motivations. In this chapter, we were able to draw out the following points with respect to UK students overseas. First, we noted the changing policy context that has, over the last decade, begun (albeit modestly) to facilitate *outward* mobility from the UK. In terms of the characteristics of internationally mobile UK students, we found, perhaps unsurprisingly, that they were often privileged on various measures, such as having parents with professional or managerial occupations and attending private schools. These students have a rich pot of familial capital (social, cultural and economic) from which they can draw. And contra to the usual depictions of elite transnational migrants as individualistic and footloose, these findings emphasized the embedded social networks that, in various ways, facilitated students' mobility. We also stressed the salience of the notion of habitus, within which the sense of travel is embedded.

As noted in Chapter 3, there has been very little said on the issue of gender in relation to UK international students, and even less on ethnicity. In terms of the geography of student mobility, however, we have shown that the United States is overwhelmingly dominant in terms of students' intentions and perhaps slightly less dominant when it comes to actual destinations of study. On the whole, the research shows that the US, Canada and Australia are favoured by UK international students. Attempts to explain this fall back partly on the importance of (English) language: UK students generally have poor second-language skills, and partly on the powerful influence of the media (particularly Hollywood films and television shows depicting images of glamour and excitement). In relation to the motivations of students, we emphasized two in particular: the need to attend a 'world class' educational institution; and the desire to seek adventure abroad. In our own study (e.g. Brooks and Waters, 2009a), we found that international education can offer students a 'second chance' at accessing the most prestigious institutions, usually following their failure to secure a place at Oxford or Cambridge, although these claims have been contested by others (Findlay and King, 2010). All of the studies reviewed in this chapter have also stressed the importance of more 'experiential' goals and objectives, centring on notions of enjoyment, adventure and self-actualization.

# 6
# Geographies of Student Mobility

## Introduction

There is a need, we argue here, for an overtly *geographical* perspective on international student mobility. At its most simple, such a perspective enables us to map contemporary patterns and flows of students from one region or country to another, highlighting, in the process, similarities and differences over space. In foregrounding the spatially differentiated nature of such flows, however, a geographical perspective can also indicate the social, political and economic implications of this spatial differentiation – internationalization is a notoriously uneven process, representing a plural landscape of opportunity for some (individuals, institutions and countries), and disadvantage for others. The importance of a geographical perspective has been implicit throughout the book: this chapter, however, represents an explicit attempt to bring the geographies of student mobility to the forefront of discussion. It does so in three, interconnected ways.

First, we highlight the spatially uneven and differentiated patterns of higher education internationalization, and the variegated flows of students that result. This is, in the words of Cresswell (2006), 'mobility as a brutal fact' – an empirical, measurable reality. Cognizance of these hard facts is a necessary first step towards exposing the 'power-geometries' (Massey, 1993; Robertson, 2005) hidden beneath a prevalent 'universalising' internationalization discourse. Second, we discuss the importance of 'contemporaneous plurality' (Massey, 2005) within international geographies of student mobilities. Internationalization is a multi-dimensional process – whilst some countries and institutions are thriving in this environment, others quite simply are not. The chapter considers the 'winners' and 'losers' from international HE and the mobility of students. This brings us to a third section in our discussion, which posits the need to take seriously, first, the concept of 'mobilities' and the political connotations with which it is imbued and, related to this, the importance of 'transnationalism' – a theme that has emerged throughout the chapters so far. Here we discuss the purported emergence of a 'new mobilities' paradigm within the social sciences (Sheller and Urry, 2006). As Cresswell (2006) argues, 'movement is the general fact of displacement before the type, strategies and social implications of that movement are considered' (p.3). Mobility, in contrast, is full of social, cultural and political *meaning*. Throughout this book, we have attempted to uncover the contemporary meanings (material and symbolic) of international student 'mobility' (as opposed to simply describing their movements). Whilst the mobilities paradigm has quite a wide remit, we consider the implications of this perspective specifically for understanding international students. Similarly, we draw on theories of transnational mobility to make explicit the light that such perspectives can throw on understanding student mobilities.

We begin, however, with a detailed examination of extant spatial patterns associated with the contemporary mobilities of international students. In Chapter 4, a number of useful distinctions were made, that it is helpful to reiterate here. First is the distinction between 'diploma' mobility (i.e. mobility to study for the *whole* of a degree) and 'credit' mobility (i.e. international movement as *part* of a degree course). Studies have also distinguished between 'spontaneous' and 'organized' forms of mobility. In what follows, the discussion refers to the most common of these types – 'diploma' and 'spontaneous' mobility. Most educational migration occurs outside of organized mobility programmes (such as Erasmus), and is dependent upon the motivation and initiative of individual students and their families.

## Spatial patterns of student mobility

As we have asserted, far from being a uniform process, international student mobility (equating to 3.3 million individuals worldwide – OECD, 2009) is spatially differentiated and highly uneven in nature. From global flows to highly localized individual and familial preferences, geographies of student mobility also manifest simultaneously at several different scales. At the coarsest scale, students generally move from East to West and from non-English-speaking to English-speaking countries: whilst the US, the UK, Canada, Australia and New Zealand receive almost half of all international students, 58 per cent originate from China, India, Malaysia,

Hong Kong and Singapore – a figure predicted (in 2004) to increase to 75 per cent by 2020 (British Council, 2004).[1] At the same time, students are increasingly attracted to a relatively small number of 'elite' institutions (e.g. Ivy League universities in the US and Oxbridge universities in the UK) – from the perspective of students and their families there exists a distinctive global, regional and national *hierarchy* of higher education institutions (Marginson and van de Wende, 2007), the implications of which are felt at the institutional as well as at the national level.

These broad patterns are, however, complicated by smaller movements that appear to contradict the trends – UK students leaving to study overseas, for example, and the development of educational migration *within* and *between* institutions in traditional 'student-sending' regions such as East Asia. Despite being the largest student exporter, China is also increasingly competing *for* international students (THE, 2010). In addition, students now have the opportunity to obtain an 'international' education without ever leaving home. Here, we are referring to the burgeoning number of degree programmes involving partnerships between local and foreign HEIs. So, for example, a partnership between Queen's University of Belfast and Shenzhen University means that 'local' Chinese students can receive a degree from Queen's University whilst attending a HEI in China. Such partnerships with foreign educational providers are springing up in places as diverse as Japan, India, Hong Kong and Qatar.

It is also pertinent to stress that the *relative significance* of international student mobility for national economies and individual institutions can vary substantially, depending upon the measures used to assess their impact. So, for example, the US received by far the greatest number of international students in 2003 – 586 000 compared to 273 000 for the UK (ranked 2nd in terms of international student numbers). However, if we take a different measure, and consider numbers of international students as a percentage of total numbers enrolled in tertiary education, then the US is ranked only 13th, behind Finland (12th), Ireland (7th) and New Zealand (2nd) (OECD, 2007). Using this measure, international students are most significant for Australia, where over 17 per cent of total tertiary enrolments are classified as 'international'. We should also note that different countries often use different ways of counting their international students. The UK recently 'discovered' that it had over a hundred thousand more international students than had been originally thought. This follows an analysis by the British Council, which calculated international students for the first time based on their nationality (rather than the previous measure of 'domicile', which discounted students already in the UK on foundation or language courses or at private schools) (International Focus, 2009b). Consequently, the 389 330 international students in 2008 based on the old measure rose to 513 570 (International Focus, 2009b).

These global, regional and national patterns have significant political, social and economic implications. With the marketization of higher education, institutions within countries are increasingly competing directly with each other to attract international students and the money that they bring with them. As we outlined in Chapter 2, with relative cuts in government spending on HE, individual institutions in many countries are more reliant than ever on the fees of international students for maintaining programmes and growing their institutions in the immediate and longer terms. National differences when it comes to interest in international student recruitment have, until recently, been quite stark. Whilst Australia, it is widely recognized, has the most organized and aggressive recruitment and marketing strategy for its HEIs in the world (coordinated by IDP [International Development Project] Education Australia), and the UK has coordinated international activities through the highly successful British Council, until recently the United States and Canada have had little of note when it comes to an internationalization strategy. A recent commentary by the President of the Association of American Geographers (Pandit, 2009) suggests that the US is and should be increasingly concerned with the internationalization of HE. Pandit (2009) notes that in 2006 the US Departments of State and Education convened a summit on International Education at the White House to highlight the potential 'national' importance of international education. Despite this, it is still widely assumed that international students remain largely insignificant for US HEIs and for the US economy more generally. In the next part of the chapter, we outline some global trends in international student mobility.

### Global flows of international students

Trends in international student mobility can be conceptualized at different scales, from the global 'region' to the level of the HEI and even patterns of enrolment within educational establishments. Figure 6.1 indicates the regional demand for international student places in 2003 (British Council, 2004).

As can be seen quite clearly from the figure, as a region, Asia dominates global demand for international student places. At the crudest scale of analysis, then, a quite distinctive geography of international student mobility is emerging, involving students coming from Asia to HEIs in Europe, North America and Oceania.

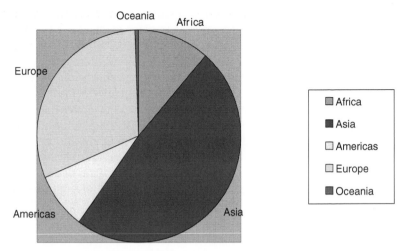

*Figure 6.1*   Regional share of international student demand, 2003 (Source of data – British Council 2004)

If we break these numbers down further, a clearer picture of the geography of international student demand emerges. Almost two-thirds of international students from 'Asia' in fact come from *East* Asia (over 500 000 individuals in 2003), and a large proportion of these originate from the People's Republic of China. Other major sources of international students from East Asia are Hong Kong, Taiwan, Japan and South Korea. As discussed in Chapter 3 of this book, these students are seeking the prestige of an English-medium education from a Western university. In their home countries, such credentials are often highly valued within particular desired occupations (such as in the financial services industry). There is also, however, another reason for the tendency of wealthy families from East Asian countries to seek an 'overseas education' for their children – as a strategy to avoid highly competitive, 'life-or-death' national examinations (such as the Hong Kong Certificate of Education Examination in Hong Kong and the National College Entrance Examination in China) (Waters, 2008).

If we look at where students are going, the national scale gives us a more useful picture than does a regional portrait. A recent report from the OECD observes that the US, UK, France and Germany are the top four ranked countries by international student numbers – together they receive more than 50 per cent of all foreign students worldwide (OECD, 2007). As noted by Bone (2010), Germany, especially, is increasingly offer-ing courses to students *in English*, in an attempt to meet demand from students in Asia but also from students elsewhere in Europe. The importance of English-speaking destination countries is highlighted by the British Council, which coined the phrase 'Main English-Speaking Destination Countries' (MESDCs) to indicate what it perceives to be the UK's biggest competitors when it comes to attracting international students. The MESDCs are Australia, US, Canada, New Zealand and the UK.

The implications of these global patterns will be discussed in more detail later on in the chapter. Here, it will suffice to say that global flows of international students generally represent the entrenching of existing patterns of power and influence in higher education. These patterns are a legacy of colonialism and imperialism; international HE would seem to do little to redress historical patterns of dependency and uneven development.

### An example: the UK

The UK provides an interesting and significant example of an international student-receiving country. A result of its history as a colonial power, the age and historical profile of its institutions, and the work of the British Council, the UK is second only to the US for total number and global share of international students; 51 603 were accepted by UK institutions in 2008 (UCAS, 2009). However (and unlike the US), international students *also* represent a significant share of the total tertiary intake of students in the UK (14 per cent in 2007) (OECD, 2007). As much as 20 per cent of all degrees conferred by UK institutions are awarded to international students (International Focus, 2009b). Many postgraduate courses in the UK now rely on international students for their existence – an analysis of HESA data by the British Council showed that they make up more than 70 per cent of total postgraduate students within social and biological science departments and more than 80 per cent of those on business and administrative postgraduate courses (International Focus, 2009b). The British Council report, published in 2004 in partnership with Universities UK and IDP Education Australia forecast demand for international student places in the UK. In summary, this report noted that:

- Countries in Asia (especially China, Malaysia, Hong Kong and India) will become increasingly important whilst the relative significance of Europe will decrease;
- China will be the largest 'source country' for students in the UK in 2020, with an 11.4 per cent growth in numbers (from 2003) – from 20 000 to 131 000;

- Demand from India will grow considerably by 2020, from 7 000 students (in 2003) to 30 000 students;
- By 2020 there will be *less diversity* in student-sending countries – the top ten countries will account for 61 per cent of the total number of international students compared to 55 per cent in 2003.

Other countries that will experience a significant growth in numbers of students coming to the UK by 2020 are Malaysia (7 per cent annually) and Pakistan (10 per cent annually). By 2020, 79 per cent of the total global demand for student places in the UK is forecast to come from *Asia* – this is compared to only 13 per cent from Europe (British Council, 2004). Although Bone's (2010) recent comments may throw some doubt upon the exact accuracy of these forecasts, there is a widespread consensus that the *general* trends they report will continue. As such, the composition of the international student body in the UK will become increasingly Asian in region of origin.

Whilst the UK is generally thought of as a receiver of international students, however, we should mention also its growing presence overseas. First, this is a result of UK HEIs engaging in and helping to develop more and more partnerships with HEIs abroad, delivering a 'British' education to students *in situ*. More will be said of this shortly. Second, the UK has a role as a student-*sending* country. Until recently, very little was known about UK students who chose to go overseas study. Indeed, the assumption of policy makers and universities has always been that students in the UK will want to stay in the UK. There has been a slight shift in thinking around this recently – the second 'Prime Minister's Initiative' (as noted in Chapter 5) included the objective of sending more British students abroad. The motivations and experiences of UK students overseas have already been detailed in Chapter 5 of this book.

### Contra-flows of international students

Going against these large-scale emergent trends are some examples of 'non-traditional' countries marketing to, and attracting, international students, such as Malaysia, the United Arab Emirates and Hong Kong. As observed in an article accompanying the *Times World University Rankings* for 2009, 'The US domination of the top ranks of global higher education is not as strong as it has been in previous years... institutions in Asian countries such as Hong Kong and Japan are growing in stature' (Baty, 2009a, p.iii). The US still, clearly, dominates these rankings, with 54 institutions ranked in the top 200 in the world.

However, Malaysia, South Korea, Hong Kong and Japan have moved up to become 'significant players' on the world stage of higher education. The reasons given for this include recent, heavy investment in HE and, significantly, an attempt to raise their global profile and 'visibility' by 'internationalizing' their staff and student bodies (Baty, 2009a). Japan and Hong Kong feature most strongly in the *Times World University Rankings*. Hong Kong has three universities in the top 50, whilst Japan has 11 in the top 200. The significantly improved placing of countries in Asia in rankings such as these will undoubtedly have an impact on international student recruitment in the next few years. 'Official' rankings are consulted by students seeking an international education. The success of universities outside the 'core' (even if it is success according to a very Western measure) may go some way to redress the power imbalances inherent within the internationalization of HE to date.

Although Malaysia has arguably failed to meet even domestic demand for HE in the public sector, private institutions, often established in partnership with UK, US or Australian HEIs, are beginning to 'export' their English-medium education to students in China, India and the Middle-East (Yonezawa, 2007). Like other countries in the region (e.g. Singapore, Hong Kong) the Malaysian government is attempting to brand Malaysia as an education 'hub' (Yonezawa, 2007). China is perhaps the best example of the development of international HE outside the 'West'. In terms of servicing home demand, China has around 23 million students in HE (there are over 1700 institutions) (Baty, 2009b). In the last ten years, numbers of international students hosted by institutions in China have increased from 50 000 to 240 000 in 2010 (THE, 2010). The *Times Higher Education* noted recently that universities in Beijing alone were hosting 80 000 foreign students in 2010, which was an increase of 10 000 on figures for 2009 (THE, 2010). There has also been a corresponding increase in the number of scholarships available to international students (ibid.). The national government has experimented in an extreme concentration of funding – investing the equivalent of 2.9 billion pounds in just 36 institutions. This has led, it is argued, 'to large disparities in quality and opportunities for students' (Baty, 2009b, p.5). There are also other potentially problematic issues arising with the speed at which HE in China has developed – whilst money has provided the infrastructure, problems with human capital remain. Only 9 per cent of university staff in China have PhDs (Baty, 2009c). International interest in China as a destination country for international students appears, however, to be strong, with current figures at 165 000 (Baty, 2009c). Growth in these numbers will depend, at least in part, on how China is able to place itself within international league tables for higher education.

## Transnational education and immobility

Whilst the mobility of students represents one of the most *conspicuous* indicators of internationalization in HE, very recently a number of less obvious yet highly significant developments have occurred, involving the increasing *overseas presence* of 'Western' HEIs in East Asia, where market demand for international HE is especially high. In contrast to the 'traditional' pattern of international HE, where students spend the duration of their studies abroad, in these new programmes 'international' education is largely delivered *locally,* potentially negating the need for student mobility. Several writers have suggested that overseas travel is an essential part of creating a highly desirable (from the perspective of employers) 'cosmopolitan sensibility' amongst international students (Ong, 1999; Waters, 2006). This raises a number of questions concerning the necessity of physical mobility in the 'international student experience'. To what extent can these 'international' programmes, delivered locally and without the need for travel, develop in students the desired social and cultural capital (Bourdieu, 1986), consequently enhancing 'employability' in a global knowledge based economy?

Historically, the UK has exerted a strong influence on educational structures in Hong Kong, and this relationship continues to manifest itself. UK HEIs have initiated a series of partnerships between UK and 11 local Hong Kong HEIs. According to the Hong Kong Education Bureau, in January 2008 there were over 400 such courses run by 36 different UK HEIs in Hong Kong. More than 40 per cent of joint initiatives were begun after 2003 (Tang and Nollent, 2007). In comparison to other 'non-local [i.e. international] providers', the significance of the UK in Hong Kong HE is notable. Of the total number of collaborative (so-called 'exempted') courses, UK provides 63 per cent of supply, compared to 22 per cent from Australia, 5 per cent from the USA and 1 per cent from Canada. These links were bolstered by the 'Memorandum of Understanding on Education Cooperation' signed on 11th May 2006 by Arthur Li (Secretary for Education and Manpower in Hong Kong) and Bill Rammell (Minister of State for Higher Education and Lifelong Learning in the UK). The memorandum aims, amongst other things, to strengthen partnerships and strategic collaboration between the UK and Hong Kong. UK HEIs' involvement in delivering HE in China is ostensibly less well developed. However, in 2006 UK HEIs provided the QAA [Quality Assurance Agency for Higher Education in the UK] with information on 352 individual links with 232 Chinese HE institutions or organizations (QAA, 2007). Some recent significant developments with respect to international 'partnerships' with Chinese institutions include Xi'an Jiaotong Liverpool University, located in Suzhou in China, which opened its doors in September 2006 to approximately 160 students, with 900 students in 2008. Other examples of UK-China international partnerships include: Leeds Metropolitan University and Zhejiang University of Technology; Queen Mary, University of London and Beijing University of Posts and Telecommunications; The Queen's University of Belfast and Shenzhen University; and the University of Bedfordshire and the China Agricultural University.

In 2006, the QAA conducted audits of ten selected partnerships between UK and Chinese HEIs in order to establish how UK institutions were maintaining academic standards and the quality of education within these partnerships (QAA, 2007). A similar exercise was carried out in 2007 on partnerships between six UK HEIs and Hong Kong HEIs. Despite this interest, very little is known about the *students* undertaking these degree courses – their backgrounds, motivations or experiences. In addition, students' subsequent labour market outcomes remain unclear, as do employers' (crucial) perceptions regarding the quality of such degree programmes.

This book is predicated on the importance of mobility in the international student experience. The physical mobility of the individual, involving immersion in a new country and culture for a period of time, reflects the honing of language skills and the accumulation of other forms of embodied 'cultural and social capital' (Murphy-Lejeune, 2002; Waters, 2006, 2007). And yet, intriguingly, these new overseas programmes rarely involve this element of mobility. Models incorporating *some* element of mobility are increasingly being developed (e.g. the development of '2+2' and '3+1' programmes where students spend two years or one year at the overseas institution respectively) as a way of ensuring a steady stream of international students into UK HEIs. However, many of these programmes can be studied for entirely 'at home'. This raises a number of important issues concerning how the 'value' of an overseas degree is generated – whether its value rests partly or largely in the experience of overseas mobility and residence, or whether an 'international' degree undertaken 'at home' is just as worthwhile (from the perspective of students and employers).

So far in this chapter we have described and discussed the variegated global and regional patterns of international student mobility in relation to the process of internationalization. The next two sections introduce some specifically geographical ways of conceptualizing these patterns: firstly, in terms of recent thinking around 'space' and relationality and, secondly, with reference to an emergent 'mobilities paradigm' within the social sciences and the dominance of a transnational perspective. We begin with a discussion of the concept of 'contemporaneous plurality' (Massey, 2005).

## Plural landscapes of student mobility

As we have stressed throughout the book, the internationalization of HE is far from uniform – it is an uneven and 'messy' process, where not every country and institution is moving smoothly towards internationalizing its curricula and student body. Thus, whilst some countries and institutions thrive in an environment of internationalization, others do not. It helps, therefore, to think of the internationalization of HE in terms of 'contemporaneous plurality' (Massey, 2005). This has two key aspects: first, recognition that there exists extreme *spatial diversity* within international HE. Second, the notion emphasizes the fact that different places are nevertheless deeply connected and implicated in each others' fortunes and outcomes (i.e. a relational understanding of space). This latter point suggests the need (for countries, institutions and individuals) to act responsibly and to take responsibility for their actions with respect to international education. Governments, HEIs and individual students should be aware of how their decisions about higher education directly affect others elsewhere. In this section, we discuss the 'spatiality' of international student mobility with reference to three theoretical ideas: an 'engaged pedagogy', a 'relational' HE market place, and geographies of cultural capital.

Clare Madge, Parvati Raghuram and Patricia Noxolo (2009) have recently addressed the tendency, in contemporary debates, 'to present the internationalization of UK HE as a "neutral experience" within normalizing conceptions of internationalization' (p.35). Instead, their paper offers 'a more "layered" understanding that highlights the connections between the geographical, historical, political, economic and cultural spheres in order for a more "engaged pedagogy" to emerge' (p.35). Although this point has much wider resonance, their argument focuses in particular upon the history and geographies of colonialism, and the implications this has for understanding contemporary international student experiences. HEIs in the UK, they argue, are increasingly embedded within a global neo-liberal agenda, which itself is built upon 'previous repertoires of global inequality' (p.42). Academics are struggling with the contradictions of lecturing about neo-imperialism and global inequalities whilst at the same time being themselves directly involved in the recruitment of international students. These, Madge et al. (2009) argue, are the 'structures of academic imperialism' (p.42), and need to be responded to by an 'engaged pedagogy' (p.43). Engaged pedagogy can be summarized as: a) actively attempting to contest 'the centre'; b) engaging in genuine dialogue (with international students); and c) practising care and responsibility beyond the classroom. It also demands awareness that there is no 'one size fits all' – engaged pedagogy is necessarily contextual and place-specific. In practice, this might mean:

> refusing to take (yet another) international postgraduate student in order to 'bolster' recruitment targets...[or] refusing to collude with line managers, marketing committees and the like, who actively recruit students without taking the pedagogic responsibilities entailed by taking recruitment seriously...[or] It may involve recognising and critiquing the role of UK HEIs in creating the underdevelopment of individuals and families in poorer countries who are making horrendous financial sacrifices... (p.44)

The issues raised in Madge et al.'s (2009) paper are important ones, and indicate a geographical understanding of international student mobility.

Discussions in geography around 'space' and its 'relational' nature provide a different and useful perspective on the internationalization of higher education and student mobility. As Simon Marginson (2008, p.303) has argued, 'worldwide higher education is [itself] a relational environment'. Consequently, there will be winners and losers – on the whole it represents a zero-sum game. The 'marketplace' in international education exemplifies this point: countries, localities and institutions increasingly compete aggressively against each other to attract full fee-paying students. This competition is aided and abetted by league tables and rankings, which serve to create a myth around various national education systems and individual educational institutions, perpetuating the geographical unevenness of international education. We will touch upon some of the most important implications of these relational geographies here.

First, despite the growth in the internationalization of 'domestic' education worldwide, it remains the case that very few national economies benefit substantially from international student mobility. This is suggested in the discussion, above, in relation to *where* students are going to (and coming from) for higher education. A very small number of countries (four) receive over half of all international students worldwide (OECD, 2007). Most of these countries (with the exception of the United States) have invested monetarily in developing a strong brand image for their 'national' education system. And international students *do* bring significant financial benefits to countries and HEIs. In the UK, the turnover of the British Council for 2009–2010 was reportedly £705 million (British Council, 2010). Australia is perhaps the single county with the greatest reliance on trade in international education services, as noted in a recent government-commissioned report (Bradley et al., 2008). Education is Australia's *largest* service-sector export and its third largest overall export (ibid.). Very few countries can make such claims regarding the financial benefits of global patterns of international student mobility. However, as noted in Chapter 2, for some countries encouraging *outward* mobility is actually more cost effective that creating additional new university places to meet domestic demand.

Secondly, a relatively small number of HEIs benefit significantly from their positioning on an imagined global map of distinction and cultural capital (Marginson and van der Wende, 2007; Marginson, 2008). Much of the impetus for student mobility comes from a perception of the 'value' attached to attaining credentials from particular universities – thus, the Ivy League institutions in the US and Oxbridge (and to a lesser extent the Russell Group) in the UK attract applications from the greatest numbers of international students, even if many of those students are unsuccessful in their attempts to gain a place. Indeed, as was mentioned earlier, much of the geography of international student mobility has been shaped by global rankings (such as the *Times Higher Education* QS World University Rankings and Shanghai Jiao Tong University rankings) in higher education. The impact of influential global ranking systems in HE has been examined by Simon Marginson and Marijk van der Wende (2007). They describe an international HE environment in which 'international comparisons are constantly made' (2007, p.307). However, as noted in the introduction to this chapter, 'the rise of global referencing does not signify that higher education has simply become a single worldwide network of HEIs' (p.307). They continue:

> In global markets, studies of international student choice making indicate that, on the whole and with the partial exception of the

small group of HEIs, the Harvards and Oxfords that are household names all over the world, the national identity of HEIs continues to be more important in the eyes of the world than the institutional identity of the individual HEIs. (p.307)

Thus, despite the marketing strategies of individual HEIs, and the availability of more information on individual institutions and courses (accessible to most on-line), crude *international* geographies still do matter.

At the same time as we acknowledge the apparent 'stranglehold' that the richest and most successful Western universities have over global ranking systems, it is nevertheless worth remembering that many 'newer' universities, especially in the UK, are heavily engaged in attempts to attract international students, and are very proficient at this. Roughly half of all collaborations between universities in Hong Kong and the UK involve institutions that were previously (prior to 1992) polytechnics (Tang and Nollent, 2007). Some have developed 'special relationships' with particular countries that stretch back several years – an excellent example of which is the relationship between the University of Greenwich in the UK and India. With a relationship stretching back to the 1950s, it has more students from India than any other UK university (International Focus, 2009a). The university has recently opened a Centre for Indian Business in Delhi, as part of its 'international strategy' (International Focus, 2009a). Some of these universities, where teaching is prioritized over research activity, rely on international student fees to replace shortfalls in funding from research. This dependency on international students is not a particularly healthy one and, arguably, actually exacerbates inequalities in education by solidifying the division between 'research-intensive' and 'teaching-led' institutions.

The issue of 'spatial diversity' and 'relationality' in international HE can be thought of in another way, with respect to how different credentials are appraised and evaluated in different places. Put simply, the value of credentials varies spatially. This assertion flies in the face of 'human capital' theory, where investment in one's education can be made, and the resultant qualifications exchanged unproblematically for employment, anywhere in the world. This point has several dimensions to it. First (and perhaps obviously), some qualifications (from certain institutions) are more valuable than others, and the HEIs producing the most sought after credentials tend to be concentrated in particular (Western) countries. Thus, degrees from an Ivy League institution in the United States, or from Oxbridge or the University of London in the UK are the most desired in the world. This fact speaks directly to Madge et al.'s (2009) concerns around the ongoing salience of academic imperialism in contemporary international HE. A second, related point concerns the dominance of the English-language and English-medium education. It is not surprising that more and more (non-English-speaking) countries are offering higher education degree courses through the medium of English (see Chapter 4, which discusses English-medium instruction in Europe). This, quite simply, reflects international student demand. Again, this can only be understood in relation to the history of colonialism and its links to contemporary academic imperialism. A third aspect of the geography of credential value is perhaps less obvious: the same degree may be valued differently between one labour market and another. In their study of British international students, for example, Brooks et al. (2012) found that a 'foreign' degree was often less valued in the UK than it was in the country within which it was obtained. Conversely, Waters (2008), in her study of migrant students from Hong Kong, found that a 'Canadian' university degree was more valuable when taken 'back to Hong Kong' than it was for individuals choosing to stay and look for work in Canada. The reason for this was two-fold – in Hong Kong a 'Canadian' degree had, amongst other things, 'rarity value' (Waters, 2006). At the same time, Hong Kong immigrants to Canada reported experiencing (racial) discrimination in the Canadian labour market. Thus, a geographical perspective on international HE (including the way in which credentials are evaluated and exchanged for employment) is crucial, underlining the fact that the meanings attached to education are, ultimately, context-specific. In the section that follows, we discuss another aspect to the geographies of international students, by focussing specifically on their mobility and the ways in which 'mobility', as a concept, might be critically examined.

## Theorizing the 'mobility' of international students

In this next section, we turn to consider how mobility might be conceptualized 'geographically', drawing upon theoretical ideas emanating from within and beyond the discipline of geography. It begins by examining what has been called a 'mobilities paradigm' (Sheller and Urry, 2006), which alludes to spatial theory but also draws heavily from contemporary sociological work. We then examine the concept of 'transnationalism', which emerged during the early to mid-1990s and has grown into a dominant means of theorizing migration (Basch et al., 1994).

## A mobilities paradigm

A 'new mobilities' paradigm is said to have emerged, recently, within the social sciences (Sheller and Urry, 2006). This paradigm interrogates the social, cultural and political *meanings* of 'mobility' – meanings created in response to differential power relations, at multiple scales (Cresswell, 2006). Concern with mobility has arisen, at the most basic level, in response to the recent apparent increase in international population flows, of different kinds. These can include the longer-term and temporary migration of asylum seekers, students, journalists, business executives, tourists, and so on (Sheller and Urry, 2006). The mobility of human populations is generally on the increase. And yet, as Sheller and Urry (2006) observe, social scientists have largely neglected studying people's movements, focusing instead upon pre- and post-migration experiences. This is partly a result of the widespread implementation of so-called 'methodological nationalism', wherein the nation-state becomes the *de facto* unit of analysis. Recent inter-disciplinary research on *trans*nationalism has gone some way towards addressing this shortcoming (Basch et al., 1994). However, even within this body of work, the tendency has been to examine migrants' experiences 'at home' and 'overseas', rather than focussing on the actual process of and meanings attached to mobility itself. Instead, we need to examine the power inherent in the ability to move from A to B – the resources that enable and disable mobility. This leads us to an equally important and related point – the mobility of some individuals is inevitably accompanied by the immobility of others. As Doreen Massey (1993) has indicated, there is a 'power-geometry' inherent within (transnational) mobility. She writes:

> ...different social groups and different individuals are placed in very distinct ways in relation to these flows and interconnections. Different social groups have distinct relationships to this anyway-differentiated mobility: some are more in charge of it than others; some initiate flows and movement, others don't; some are more on the receiving end of it than others; some are effectively imprisoned by it. (1993, p.61)

Alongside the 'jet-setters' and those who have access to e-mail and fax-machines, are juxtaposed the experiences of refugees and undocumented migrant workers. It is imperative, Massey argues, that we draw a distinction between those who control mobility and those who are *controlled by* it. Linked to this, research has shown that transnational communities of various kinds are sustained by individuals who are

decidedly *immobile* and rooted in place. The transnational practices of the hyper-mobile businessman, for example, are often supported fundamentally by his 'static' wife (Waters, 2002). Sheller and Urry (2006) have observed the 'highly embedded and immobile infrastructures' that enable mobility (p.210). Fixed platforms (such as airports, petrol stations, roads and stations) function to facilitate mobility. Thus, any examination of increased mobility must also take into account the simultaneous rise in forms of immobility. This, of course, has implications for studies of the mobility of international students. It forces us to perceive the various and mushrooming embedded, material resources that allow their mobility – their use of planes and mobile technologies; visa processing offices; the growth of accommodation blocks, teaching facilities and restaurants catering specifically to international students, and so on.

Applying such a perspective to understanding international student mobility has several outcomes. First, we are consequently cognizant of the fact that student mobility is never a neutral act – something that 'just happens'. Rather, it is filled with social, cultural and political meaning. The mobility of international students, therefore, is a worthy subject of study – how they come to travel, how they travel, how often, and to what effect. In studying students' mobility, we are inevitably opening up to scrutiny the power relations that underpin that mobility. Here, power is manifest at a number of different levels, from the differential power of nation states to control and direct internationalization and international student flows, to the power of individual educational institutions to attract and retain large numbers of international students, to the power of individual students and their families to draw upon the sometimes vast resources necessary to make educational mobility happen. As noted in Chapter 4, although the available evidence is competing, on balance research has shown that international students emanate from relatively wealthy and privileged backgrounds (Cammelli et al., 2008; Findlay et al., 2006; Kenway and Fahey, 2007; Krzaklewska, 2008; Olero and McCoshan, 2006).

Whilst often considered powerful actors in their own right, therefore, we should not overlook that fact that international students are themselves increasingly subject to technologies of power and surveillance, inextricably linked to the fact that their mobility is corporeal and embodied (Cresswell, 2006; Gogia, 2006). International students are gendered, raced and classed in various ways. Their bodies are subject to increasing scrutiny as they travel, through an expanding use of biometrics and biosecurity measures. The recently implemented 'points system' in the UK requires international students to carry bio-metric identity cards. A literature is emerging on the 'racialization' of international student bodies – of stereotyping and 'othering' (Collins, 2004, 2006). More generally, in many ways the voices of international students have been silenced within contemporary debates and their opinions rarely sought (Madge et al., 2009). This is, potentially, one con-sequence of the tendency to perceive international students as 'cash cows' – the quality of their social and pedagogical experiences comes second to and far below the need to attract international students within some educational institutions. The growth of 'bogus colleges' in the UK and Canada, offering 'fake' diplomas, is one example of how international students may be exploited. Baas (2007) discusses how some tertiary institutions in Australia are willing to recruit inter-national students with very limited ability to speak English (and very little prospect of achieving on their chosen course). For these institu-tions, students' money was the driving concern.

We also need to interrogate prevalent discourses around mobility and the valorization of student mobility in particular. Holdsworth (2009) has discussed this in relation to the mobility of domestic students, moving within the UK. She writes:

in celebrating students' mobility we are valorising a particular model of the transition to adulthood which focuses on separation, self-reliance, and responsibility for the self, rather than one based on inter-dependencies, mutual support, and responsibility for others. (p.1861)

Her work was produced in the context of the expansion of a local higher education sector in the UK (linked to ideas around widening parti-cipation) and fears that this may lead to a 'two-tier' system, between those who can and cannot 'afford' to leave home to attend university. Holdsworth critiques the assumptions underpinning these ideas – parti-cularly that the 'ideal' university experience necessarily involves move-ment from home. Similarly, we must be equally critical of discourses of mobility embedded in the international student experience. Why should, we ask, mobility *per se* be valued? What cultural and particularly class-based beliefs undergird the valorization of international travel?

With the empowerment of some countries, institutions and individuals comes, however, a related and simultaneous disempowerment of other places and people, evoking Massey's (2005) notion of 'contemporaneous pluralities' and their underlying 'power-geometries' (Massey, 1993). Waters (2008), for example, has considered how international HE may be related to processes of 'social exclusion' in the home country. This occurs when international credentials become valorized to the detriment of locally-acquired qualifications. In her work on higher education and employment in Hong Kong, Waters has shown how fear of 'failure' in a highly competitive local higher education system led some middle-class families to migrate to Canada, where access to higher education was assumed to be 'easier'. Paradoxically, however, when these same individuals decided to return to Hong Kong armed with their Canadian university degrees, they found themselves successfully competing for the best and most desirable jobs, often excluding (working-class) individuals with 'local' HE credentials. Throughout East and Southeast Asia, 'Western' educational credentials are imbued with symbolic value, often irrespective of their 'real' pedagogic value. We need, therefore, to think about the wider social implications of internationalization, and the role of higher education in society. What are the connections between the mobility of some international students and the immobility of other young people? As discussed in Chapter 5, other studies (Brooks and Waters, 2009a; Wiers-Jenssen, 2008) have shown how international education enables high-aspiring middle-class students to have a 'second-chance' at success overseas, when they have failed to get onto their first-choice course at home.

When we discuss the mobility of international students, then, we need to take a *critical* perspective. It is not enough to describe their patterns of movement. Rather, we need to be cognizant of and strive to uncover the social, cultural and political meanings of their mobility.

## Transnationalism

Since the mid-1990s, the concept of 'transnationalism' has been prominent within discussions of population mobility, spanning both social science and humanities disciplines. It is used, most commonly, to denote the various ties (political, social, economic, emotional) that contemporary migrants can be seen to maintain to more than one country simultaneously (Basch et al., 1994). As Collins (2009) observes, in many ways interest in 'transnationalism' as a topic of study emerged out of debates – prolific at the time – about globalization and its effects. It reflected a dominant view that the nation-state was no longer (if it ever was) a sovereign and sacrosanct entity, and this applied to the movement of people as well as to goods and money. Older, established conceptions of immigration as a more or less permanent and discrete move from one country to another, were being challenged 'from the grass-roots', by migrants themselves (Vertovec, 1999).

Aihwa Ong's (1999) now iconic book, *Flexible Citizenship*, was extremely timely in its publication, emerging out of and alongside a surge of academic interest in transnationalism. In short, Ong provided a theoretical framework for understanding contemporary transnationalism amongst *more privileged* migrant groups; up until this point, research on transnational migration had focussed largely on relatively impoverished migrants, where migration enabled access to better jobs, more money and a better standard of living for family residing back in the country of origin (e.g. Basch et al., 1994; Glick Schiller and Fouron, 1999). These migrants were seen as victims of a harsh and unforgiving global capitalist system and oppressive local political regimes, and transnational practices offered a limited degree of 'empowerment'. In contrast, Ong (1999) described wealthy and powerful migrants with 'an élan for thriving in conditions of political insecurity, as well as in the turbulence of global trade' (p.1). They have been seen as an integral part of the modern capitalist system – what Sklair (2001) has since called the 'transnational capitalist class'. Through transnationalism, citizenship was transformed: a new generation of 'hyper-mobile' super-migrants perceived citizenship as something *to be collected* (the so-called 'multiple passport holder'). Citizenships facilitated travel (and particularly travel with a business or professional purpose). Consequently, in relation to contemporary transnationalism, citizenship would appear to have lost much of its original meaning, at least amongst elites. This is clearly most relevant when it comes to the so-called *affective* aspects of citizenship – the feelings of belonging, pride and responsibility that it is supposed to evoke amongst newly naturalized immigrants (Kymlicka and Norman, 1994). Debates in sociology, social anthropology and cultural studies have proffered notions of 'deterritorialised' and 'cosmopolitan' forms of identity associated with transnationalism and the transgressing of boundaries (Hannerz, 1996; Kearney, 1991; Mitchell, 1997; Rouse, 1995).

Work integrating ideas around transnationalism and student mobilities is an even more recent undertaking. Research in this vein only really began to appear in print in the early to mid-2000s, although the volume of work linking transnationalism and student migration continues to grow apace (Baláž and Williams, 2004; Collins, 2004, 2006; Gargano, 2009; Ghosh and Wang, 2003). It touches on a number of diverse themes, including the transnational accumulation of (human, social and cultural) capital, students' cosmopolitan identities, and transnational consumption practices. Most of this work focuses on students' *embodied mobility* and particularly how they negotiate multiple identities as they move through space and between places (see Ghosh and Wang, 2003, for a personal account of the embodied transnationalism of international students). Our discussions in this volume have been informed by these debates. We view contemporary student mobility not as a singular move between one country and another (usually followed by return), but as a complex array of transnational networks and connections, linking students' 'home' and 'host' societies. These linkages do not end when a student graduates, but will in most cases persist over time, into their working lives and beyond. As emphasized in Chapter 3, international students are not the only kind of mobile students and we need to be cognizant of the important role that young immigrants play in this process. Consequently, a 'life-course' perspective on transnational family migration may prove particularly useful – many studies have shown the importance of children's education in influencing mobility at key moments in people's lives (Ley and Kobayashi, 2005; Kobayashi and Preston, 2007).

Students are also, often, part of transnational families, as discussed in detail in Chapter 3. East Asian student mobility in particular sometimes involves the international relocation of *entire families* (Kobayashi and Preston, 2007; Ley, 2010; Waters, 2005), in contrast to a prevalent view of international students as footloose and independent. However, just as common is the transnational splitting of families for educational ends – 'wild geese' or *kirogi* families, originating principally from South Korea, epitomize this trend. 'Astronaut' families and 'parachute' or 'satellite' kids found in North America and originating from Hong Kong, Taiwan or mainland China during the 1990s are similarly exemplary of transnational migration (Bohr and Tse, 2009; Ho, 2002; Kobayashi and Preston, 2007; Lam et al., 2002; Man, 1995; Orellana et al., 2001; Teo, 2007; Waters, 2002, 2003, 2008; Zhou, 1998). The important point to stress here is that these families live out transnationalism on a daily basis – it is fundamental to their lives. Furthermore, it is profoundly geographical, involving the negotiation of physical and emotional separation and distance and yet technological nearness.

## Conclusion

Worldwide, every year, more students are participating in some form of international education. Prevalent discourses around internationalization might suggest that higher education institutions around the globe are following the same 'internationalizing' path (to be found at different stages along this path). The view from within HEIs, as well as the opining of governments, would imply that internationalization is, ultimately, a highly positive process, wherein 'everyone wins'. To date, we have generally lacked a critical geographical perspective on the internationalization of higher education and the mobility of students. In this chapter we have endeavoured to provide such a perspective. By thinking geographically about international higher education, we are forced to acknowledge the 'contemporaneous plurality' that exists, the 'relational' nature of the international HE market place, and the social, cultural and political implications of students' mobilities (Massey, 2005).

A geographical perspective on international student mobility highlights the spatial inequalities inherent in the process. These inequalities can be conceptualized at different scales and are most clearly apparent between individuals, on the one hand, and geographical regions on the other. In relation to regions, far from representing the universal 'rolling out' of internationalization policies around the world, what has emerged is a highly uneven map, with distinctive 'winners' and 'losers'. As noted, at the crudest level, international education continues to favour the 'West' over non-Western countries – the US, UK and Australia are dominant when it comes to attracting internationally mobile students. At the same time, however, we have also noted some subtle changes and developments – involving, for example, the growth of international HE *within* East and Southeast Asia. The initiatives detailed in Singapore (around the 'global schoolhouse') exemplify what would appear to be a growing subversive trend, wherein Asian countries are becoming active players in *competing for* international students. This may begin, also, to challenge neo-colonial discourses and practices around international HE (Madge et al., 2009). When it comes to individuals, adopting a critical perspective on mobilities highlights the social inequalities often inherent within international student mobility, and the need to be cognizant of these. Physical mobility in relation to education is almost always a privileged undertaking, and accessible to only a minority of individuals. At the same time, work on transnational mobility and education has pointed to some rather different issues, highlighting the sacrifices made and significant difficulties faced by families (and especially women within families) in pursuit of international education.

# 7
# Student Mobility and the Changing Nature of Education

## Introduction

There is an important historical legacy to student migration: the 'Junior Year Abroad' has long been part of the American higher education experience, while a qualification obtained from the 'mother country' carried high levels of prestige in certain countries under conditions of colonialism (Madge et al., 2009). Moreover, Rivza and Teichler (2007) have emphasized the medieval precedents of much contemporary migration, suggesting that about a tenth of the student population in medieval universities came from outside countries. Nevertheless, as we have intimated in earlier chapters, the scale of international student migration is considerably larger than previously witnessed and, in contrast to the past, is now associated with significant and explicit policy formulation – at national, regional and international levels (see Chapter 2 for further details). As we have noted in preceding chapters, countries that have traditionally been seen primarily as 'destination' countries are now actively encouraging more *outward* migration of domestic students. In the US, for example: the Abraham Lincoln Study Abroad Fellowship Program has called for the number of Americans studying overseas to be increased to one million by 2016; Harvard University has announced that study abroad will become a requirement for the majority of its degrees; and the University of Minnesota has set a goal for 50 per cent of its students to spend part of their degree programme studying overseas within ten years (Fielden, 2007). Within Australia similar trends have emerged: both the federal government and individual universities have provided scholarships for home students to study in Asia. Conversely, areas of the world from which most international students have tended to *originate* are now taking energetic steps to enter the market for overseas students themselves. This has been particularly marked within East and South-East Asia (Sidhu, 2009). As noted in the previous chapter, the number of international students at Chinese universities increased by 190 000 between 2000 and 2010 (THE, 2010), while in Taiwan, numbers increased from 6380 in 2001 to 21 005 in 2007 (Roberts et al., 2010).

However, despite what might appear to be a growing global convergence in relation to student migration, as Chapters 3, 4 and 5 have indicated, regional disparities remain significant; both nations and regions have an important role in mediating 'global social policy' as well as global trends more generally (see Chapter 2).

While changes in HE are strongly linked to the wider policy context, they are also explained by other aspects of societal change which are explored in this chapter. Firstly, we consider the increasing importance of travel within young people's lives, the links between travel and HE, and the resources offered by overseas experiences for 'identity construction' within late modern society (Conradson and Latham, 2005). Secondly, we extend this analysis by considering the relationship between international HE and other types of migration, focussing specifically on the acquisition of citizenship and/or permanent residency of another country. We then go on to explore the ways in which international HE may be affected by the changing nature of the graduate labour market and, as a result of the emergence of 'mass' HE systems in many parts of the world, the increased competition for professional and managerial jobs. Finally, we focus on some of the pedagogical and social issues that are brought into sharp relief by significant increases in student migration. We consider the impact on knowledge creation and transfer, and on the intercultural experiences of both mobile and immobile students.

To some extent, the changes discussed in this chapter can be seen as broadly positive. The increase in student mobility is associated with: the introduction of a more international curriculum in many subject areas in universities across the world; greater diversity of student bodies in many HEIs; new cross-national friendships; and a more cosmopolitan outlook amongst those who choose to study overseas (and, perhaps, amongst those with whom they come into contact). It is also the case that, for some students, increased opportunities for mobility have allowed them to secure better financial support and/or pay lower fees abroad than if they had remained within their own country. However, this chapter will also point to the ways in which increasing student mobility may be serving to exacerbate educational inequalities and the consequences of such trends for the way in which education is understood and experienced by both international students and others in society.

## The role of travel in young people's lives

As we suggested above, contemporary trends in international HE can, in part, be related to wider social changes. One such change, which has had a considerable impact on the inclination and ability of some young people to take up opportunities for overseas study is the increasing importance of travel, generally, in young people's lives. Conradson and Latham (2005) contend that for 'an increasingly diverse mix of people, a period spent abroad – whether to study, develop a career, as part of travelling, or as an experimentation with the possibility of emigrating permanently – is becoming a normal and almost taken-for-granted part of the life cycle' (p.288). Others have pointed to the increasing importance of travel for the young, in particular – as fares become cheaper and, as a result, long-haul destinations become increasingly accessible to those on lower incomes and/or without full-time jobs. Technological developments, such as mobile phones, cheap long-distance phonecalls, social networking pages and Skype have also made it easier for young people to stay in touch with friends and family at home, and thus made travel (and overseas study) seem easier (see, for example, Vertovec, 2004).

In theorizing these developments, some writers have suggested that travel can be understood as constituting an important part of the 'biographical construction' of the young (Beck, 1992; Giddens, 1991). Conradson and Latham (2005) suggest that while travel could be seen as a strategic attempt to assemble cultural capital to be deployed on the return home, their research with young adults from Australia and New Zealand who had settled in London leads them to the conclusion that it should be understood, instead, as part of a broader culture of self-exploration and self-development. Indeed, they contend that it is part of wider societal individualization, in which huge emphasis is placed on 'the culture and nurture of the individual self' (p.292). A similar argument is developed by Desforges (2000), who maintains that travel is used by young people to re-imagine themselves, particularly at periods in their lives when their self-identity is open to question. He suggests that, for his respondents, 'travel played a relatively powerful role in helping them feel as though they were moving towards a rewarding self in the future' (p.935) by providing them with a range of new experiences to draw upon to re-narrate and re-present their identity.

Some scholars have framed educational mobility, more specifically, in a similar way. King and Ruiz-Gelices (2003), for example, suggest that young people who travel abroad as a result of a decision to study overseas, 'are taking a significant step in setting in motion their own individualized life projects' (p.245). Moreover, recent work that has focussed on UK students who have chosen to study overseas has pointed to the ways in which such experiences are valued for the opportunities they offer for 'being "different"' (Findlay and King, 2010), even if the nature of that difference is rather circumscribed (Waters and Brooks, 2010b). However, scholars have also pointed to the ways in which such markers of 'difference' should perhaps not be understood *solely* as part of projects of self-development; they can also have a more strategic purpose – achieving 'distinction' and differentiating oneself from others through the pursuit of more unusual and exotic experiences (Findlay and King, 2010). Indeed, the 'mobility capital' developed by students, through studying overseas, has been argued to be an important resource which can be 'deployed over the subsequent life-course for personal, social or career enhancement' (Findlay et al., 2006, p.293; see also Brooks and Waters, 2010).

The links between travel and higher education are reciprocal in nature. On the one hand, there is some evidence to suggest that an increasing propensity to travel for leisure purposes, on the part of the young, has increased interest in studying overseas – or at least travelling further afield to pursue such opportunities. Students who had lived or travelled abroad prior to higher education, for example during a gap year, have been found to be more likely that their peers to engage in formal mobility schemes (such as Erasmus exchanges) during their time at university (Sussex Centre for Migration Research, 2004). Similarly, the increasing number of British students who are choosing to pursue a degree at Asian and Australasian universities is held to be an effect of the popularity of these destinations for gap year travel (Findlay et al., 2006). On the other hand, higher education itself can be seen as an important means through which travel can be facilitated, through the 'integration' of periods abroad within degree courses in a student's home country (such as the American 'Junior Year Abroad' and the European Erasmus scheme), and also through the opportunities it offers for sampling life abroad in a relatively 'safe' way. Indeed, as we noted in Chapter 4, Murphy-Lejeune (2002) suggests that mobile students can travel 'more lightly' than other migrants:

> Their experience is less dramatic since their in-between position is only temporary. Their attachment or detachment from the home culture is merely loosened rather than seriously tested....If they

experience an identity crisis, it may remain superficial rather than profound. (pp.232–233)

Here, student travel is seen as qualitatively different from that undertaken in other contexts and as a useful way of first encountering other cultures.

## Higher education and migration

As we have discussed in earlier chapters, the pursuit of an international higher education can also be framed within wider debates about migration in order to secure citizenship of a particular state. A growing body of work has demonstrated the ways in which education is deployed, by those keen to move abroad, as a means of gaining entry to another country (Baas, 2006; Findlay and King, 2010; Jackling, 2007; Shanthi Robertson, 2009) or as a 'trial run' for living abroad (Favell, 2008; King and Ruiz-Gelices, 2003). There are differences, however, within this literature in the extent to which the acquisition of citizenship (or permanent residency) is seen as an end in itself or, conversely, as a step towards attaining economic advantage. In Ong's (1999) analysis, for example, the pursuit of a Western education by students from Hong Kong has commonly been driven by a desire to secure citizenship of another country as part of a broader strategy to accumulate economic capital. On the basis of her empirical work, she argues that citizenship is often understood by such migrants as 'flexible' in nature, and a means of furthering one's own (or one's family's) economic position:

> Although citizenship is commonly thought of as based on political rights and participation within a sovereign state, globalization has made economic calculation a major element in diasporan subjects' choice of citizenship…seeking to both circumvent and benefit from different nation-state regimes by selecting different sites for investments, work and family relocations. (p.63)

Similar themes pervade other studies. For example, Baas (2006) has shown how many Indian students are drawn to study in Australia because of the economic advantages they assume will follow from gaining permanent residency there. He argues that the families of the young people he interviewed 'are upwardly mobile but often seem to think that their mobility is too limited within India itself….Having a family member abroad will not only generate more money, but will also increase the family's reputation' (p.23). Within the US, those international students who choose to remain in the country on completion of their degrees also seem to be motivated, primarily, by economic factors. On the basis of their research at the University of Minnesota, Hazen and Alberts (2006) suggest that 'economic and professional factors typically dominate among incentives to stay in the US, while personal and societal factors tend to draw the students back to their home countries' (p.213). In contrast, however, Brooks et al. (2012) have argued that in their sample of UK students, the acquisition of citizenship was often seen as an end in itself, rather than a means of furthering one's economic position. They argue that amongst their group of respondents who had a strong desire to live abroad on completion of their studies, it was commonly believed that, in order to gain citizenship of their chosen country, it would first be necessary to find employment in that country, and that gaining an overseas qualification would facilitate this process. Indeed, many asserted that employers in their desired country of residence would look much more favourably on those with a degree from a 'domestic' university, rather than one gained from the UK.

There are, however, important geographical disparities in these motivations, which relate to both the students' countries of origin as well as of destination. As Baláž and Williams (2004) note, 'there are sharp national and spatial differences in staying-on versus returning home practices' (p.218). The research conducted in the US by Alberts and Hazen (2005) is instructive here. They contend that while the vast majority of the international students involved in their study said that they felt torn between remaining in the US and returning to their home country, responses were differentiated along national lines. Greek students, for example, tended to think that they would be better off both professionally and economically if they stayed in the US but, because of the significant weighting they placed on personal and societal factors, typically favoured a return home. Similarly, students from Tanzania also emphasized the importance of family ties and their preference for their home culture, and expressed a desire to return home promptly. In contrast, for the Chinese students in the sample, 'constraints on a wider level, such as the insecure political situation in China and the economic and environmental problems in the country, seemed to override personal and societal pressures to return to some degree' (ibid., p. 149). On the basis of this evidence, Alberts and Hazen conclude that discussion of return migration decisions must be sensitive not only to the personal preferences of the individuals concerned, but to the wider political and economic characteristics of both country of origin and country of destination, which help to structure decision-making (see also Lee and Kim, 2010).

In explaining differences by country of destination, it is also helpful to consider the ways in which host governments have sought to market their tertiary education to overseas students, and to examine the impact this has had on student flows. For example, there is little evidence from the US to suggest that a large majority of incoming students are motivated primarily by a strong desire to gain permanent residency (Hazen and Alberts, 2006; Szelényi, 2006). In contrast, extant research suggests that international students who choose to pursue their HE in Australia are more likely than international students elsewhere to be motivated by a desire to seek citizenship or permanent residency in the host country (Findlay and King, 2010; Jackling, 2007; Shanthi Robertson, 2009). In part, such students have been encouraged by the immigration policies of the Australian government (Baas, 2006; Ziguras and Law, 2006). Since 1998, various policies have been introduced which have favoured international students as political migrants (Shanthi Robertson, 2009). These have included the award of extra 'migration points' for holding Australian educational qualifications and the establishment of a new visa category that allows students to switch to migrant status by applying for permanent residency during their time as students in Australia (ibid.). Shanthi Robertson (2009) suggests that 38 per cent of Chinese students and 66 per cent of Indian students who graduated from Australian universities in 2002 obtained permanent residency in this way. She thus concludes that, in Australia, 'international education and skilled migration have become inextricably linked, creating new and distinct migration pathways' (no pagination). Baas (2007) goes further, arguing that the migration industry has, in effect, 'hijacked' the education industry – pointing to the growth in the number of 'smaller colleges at the bottom-end of a very price-competitive market' (p.58), which do not always offer international students a high quality education.

This explicit attempt by the Australian government to hold on to well-qualified young adults has been replicated, to varying degrees, by other governments around the world and can be seen as evidence of what Brown and Tannock (2009) have termed the global 'war for talent'. This war, they argue, is predicated on the assumption that the expansion of HE in many parts of the world has done nothing to alleviate the scarcity of 'top talent' and it is thus necessary to look beyond the borders of the nation-state to find the best brains and the most talented employees. They go on to suggest that although such discourses originated within management consultancy companies, they have since been taken up by governments around the world:

> Because of these alleged labour shortages, because talent has never been more globally mobile or sought after, and because previous cycles of liberalisation of global capitalism and trade have created global supply chains and production systems which require internationally mobile professional and managerial workforces in order to operate effectively, political elites around the world argue that they have no choice but to enter the war for talent. (Brown and Tannock, 2009, p.381)

Although such mobility is often discussed in terms of 'brain drain' (the losses suffered by nations who send considerable numbers of students abroad) or 'brain gain' (the associated advantages to receiving nations), research with those students who have been internationally mobile suggests that they subscribe more to the concept of 'brain circulation' (Jöns, 2009; Lowell and Findlay, 2001) – seeing no necessary contradiction between taking up employment in the country in which they have studied and being supportive of their home nation. Indeed, Szeléyni's (2006) interviews with international graduate students in the US revealed that while most felt some sense of social responsibility towards their home country, a considerable number were not concerned about returning home as they 'defined their contributions as situated in a regional or global sphere' (p.205), and saw foreign residence as not incompatible with a strong focus on their country of origin.

## Graduate employment

Such debates about the economic drivers of student mobility are underpinned, to some extent, by the shift witnessed in many parts of the world over the past few decades from an elite system of higher education to a mass system. As a result of this change, it is argued, graduate labour markets have become increasingly congested and the upper middle classes who have, historically, dominated HE for much of the 20th century, have had to find new ways of both ensuring their social reproduction and distinguishing themselves from other graduates of a mass system. Brown and Hesketh (2004) argue that this has led to the emergence of an 'economy of experience' whereby students and graduates aim to supplement their degree with a range of other qualifications, skills and attributes, which will give them the 'edge' in applications for competitive graduate positions. For example, they highlight the importance, to many graduate recruiters, of a range of 'soft skills' such as leadership, drive and determination – gained through participation in particular extracurricular activities. Other writers have suggested that this differentiation from fellow graduates is sought through aiming to gain entry to only the most prestigious universities (Reay et al., 2005) and engaging in postgraduate-level education and training (Brooks and Everett, 2009). Moreover, Heath (2007) argues that some aspects of youth travel can be seen as part of this growing economy, with young people using their 'gap years', in particular, to gain overseas experience which may help to differentiate them from other graduates in possession of 'only' a degree. This competition is exacerbated, it is argued, by the increasingly global nature of labour markets. No longer is it played out solely within national arenas; the market for some jobs, at least, is now international and immigrants constitute an increasing proportion of the upper levels of the labour market. It appears that the expansion of HE worldwide has done nothing to alleviate employer views about the scarcity of 'top talent'; indeed, many organizations have only relatively recently started to look further afield for their graduate employees (Brown and Tannock, 2009).

As we have suggested in previous chapters, within this changing labour market, there is some evidence to suggest that an international education can be an effective means of securing 'distinction' from other graduates. Indeed, Brown and Tannock argue that middle-class parents have responded to the increasingly global nature of the labour market by seeking 'to position their children in the most desirable and prestigious schools and programmes, to become one of the select members of the internationally sought after, high skill elite' (p.384). Similar arguments have been made in relation to HE, specifically, with a period abroad being seen as a means of differentiating oneself from other graduates of a mass higher education system within one's own nation state (Findlay et al., 2006; Murphy-Lejeune, 2002). An overseas education can also be viewed as an effective means of gaining some of the 'soft skills' or 'personal capital' required by many employers, generally, as well as the more specific inter-cultural skills and international exposure desired by global recruiters (Crossman and Clarke, 2010; King and Ruiz-Gelices, 2003; Murphy-Lejeune, 2002). On the basis of their research with Slovakian students who had studied in the UK, Baláž and Williams (2004) argue that the informal learning (such as developing self-confidence, an openness to learning and greater flexibility) undertaken during a period abroad was valued much more highly by their respondents than the formal learning that had taken place. In particular, they contend that the establishment of social networks is a very important outcome of international student migration, and helps to open up a wide variety of economic opportunities – through providing: information and knowledge; the basis for constructing business partnerships; and a means of accessing particular markets and/or resources. The development of this social and personal capital can have quite a significant impact in 'distinguishing' those who have studied overseas from their less mobile peers.

However, as we have discussed in earlier chapters, the way in which this 'distinction' is configured differs considerably between national contexts. Chapter 3 demonstrated how, for Asian students, it is often an overseas (English-medium) qualification *per se* that is desired (preferably from an Anglophone country). In contrast, for many UK students (discussed in Chapter 5), much greater emphasis is placed on the status of the university attended. In part, this difference can be explained by differences in the value ascribed to overseas qualifications within national labour markets. The evidence suggests that a degree awarded by a 'Western', Anglophone country often has considerably higher status within the labour markets of many 'Eastern' countries than an equivalent domestic qualification (Ong, 1999; Rizvi, 2000; Singh et al., 2007; Waters, 2007); this then provides strong motivation to seek such advantage through overseas study. In contrast, in those countries such as the UK from where prestigious degrees often emanate, calculations are different; indeed, an overseas qualification may be seen by employers as of *less value* than one secured from a British university (Brooks et al., 2012). The hierarchical positioning of universities internationally (Marginson, 2008) and the privileging of western, Anglophone forms of knowledge (particularly in the disciplines of management, commerce and economics) (Kenway and Fahey, 2007; Mazlish and Morss, 2005) may encourage assumptions amongst graduate recruiters about the 'superior' quality of a UK qualification. Indeed, Findlay and King (2010) conclude their report on international education, written for the UK's Department for Business, Innovation and Skills, by suggesting that considerably more thought needs to be given by government and employers 'as to how best to tap the human, social and cultural capital of UK students after their graduation from foreign universities' (p.43).

Although the extant literature in this area is small, there is some, albeit limited, evidence that similar patterns to the UK may be found in other European countries. Wiers-Jenssen (2008), for example, has argued that

Norwegian graduates who have an overseas qualification often face greater difficulties in entering the national labour market than their peers in possession of a degree from a domestic institution. On the basis of his sample, he argues that both unemployment and 'over-education' were more prevalent amongst those who had studied overseas. Moreover, analysis of migration within Europe more generally has pointed to the relatively 'risky' nature of this endeavour. As discussed in Chapter 4, Favell et al. (2008) maintain that mobile Europeans take 'much more marginalised, risky career decisions compared to those in nationalised careers from welfare states with stable pay-offs at home' (p.9). They go on to suggest that, because of this level of risk, mobility is more likely to be pursued by so-called 'social spiralists' than their peers from more privileged backgrounds. They contend that:

> the so-called 'elites', who have opted to be move internationally under present conditions of globalization, are often not from elite backgrounds but provincial, career-frustrated 'spiralists' who have gambled with dramatic spatial mobility in their education and careers abroad to improve social mobility opportunities that are otherwise blocked at home. (p.9)

There is also some evidence to suggest that despite the widespread encouragement of highly skilled migration, migrants often face difficulties in accessing the most well-paid and prestigious jobs. Brown and Tannock (2009) suggest that many such people 'are actually slotted into second-tier jobs, filling positions that the native-born who are trained in their occupational specialties won't touch' (p.385) (such as teaching in particularly demanding schools and covering the night shifts as a doctor) – denied access to the first tier on the basis of their citizenship and/or national status. Nevertheless, as we have demonstrated in Chapters 3, 4 and 5, while the immediate labour market rewards which accrue to the holders of an overseas qualification may differ by national context, other evidence points to the enduring social advantages that are common to many mobile students across the globe.

The tendency for young people and their families to seek out overseas education as a means of responding to labour market pressures has much in common with what Mitchell (2003) describes as the shift from the 'multicultural self'– those who value diversity and are able to work with difference within the nation-state – to the 'strategic cosmopolitan' – individuals who are focussed, primarily, on the need to act strategically to maximize personal advantage within a highly competitive global arena (discussed in Chapter 1). Indeed, pursuing a similar argument, Singh et al. (2007) maintain that the role of the state in many countries has changed significantly. No longer is it concerned to provide a public education that instils character and virtue, with the aim of promoting both the socio-economic security of individuals and the cohesion of the nation-state. Instead, it appears to be intent on producing a different kind of subject (akin to Mitchell's strategic cosmopolitan) through the expectation that students will take advantage of the opportunities offered by the global expansion of higher education 'while graduates are expected to have the capacity to see, imagine and experience labour market possibilities beyond the nation-state' (p.195). Thus, strategic competitiveness seems to be encouraged, implicitly, by the workings of graduate labour markets and, explicitly, through the expectations of national governments.

## Pedagogical issues

One of ways countries have responded to the growth in student mobility and the increasingly intense pressure of the international market for such students is by taking steps towards 'internationalizing' the HE curriculum. The new curriculum to be introduced in Hong Kong is a good example of this: a new four-year degree structure will be offered in all of the Special Administrative Region's eight universities from 2012 as a means of inculcating 'global citizenship' among their students and strengthening the region's appeal to the overseas market (Morgan, 2010). All students will be expected to: engage in experiential learning; study or work overseas for a period of time; and take a number of common core modules in addition to the specialist ones required for their degree specialism (Fearn, 2010). The University of Hong Kong's website states explicitly:

> To prepare students for global citizenship, it is essential that an international perspective pervades the curriculum across the University. Explicit attention must be paid to the global relevance of our programmes if they are to be attractive to a diverse student population. (University of Kong Kong, 2010)

Although such far-reaching reforms are, to date, relatively unusual, smaller-scale initiatives can be seen elsewhere. In the UK, for example, Leeds Metropolitan University has required every module offered within the institution to be redesigned to meet 'international' requirements

(Jones and Brown, 2007), while the University of Southampton runs a number of 'Global Graduate' activities, for which students can earn points to add to their 'Graduate Passport'. These include: attending intercultural workshops, completing a language class, attending an international event or conference and studying, working or volunteering abroad. Furthermore, the Higher Education Funding Council for England funded a 'Global People' project, to develop a range of competencies to drive the internationalization of the curriculum (www. globalpeople.org.uk).

Such initiatives can be seen, to a significant extent, as means of recruiting international students (along with home students who wish to develop a more 'international' outlook). However, student mobility has also been used by policymakers and the higher education community as a means of knowledge transfer and capacity building, rather than as an end in itself. The attempt to establish a 'European Research Area' is an example of this, in which mobility is seen largely as an instrument for the transfer of scientific knowledge (CEC, 2000). In policy texts about such developments (as well as about the institutional innovations outlined previously), there is nevertheless, as Kenway and Fahey (2007) note, 'a relative dearth of discussion about the kinds of knowledge that readily travels, the knowledge that most and least benefits from travel, how knowledge travels or why it travels in the manner that it does' (p.171). Most importantly, the power relationships that often structure knowledge transmission are rarely mentioned.

Despite this silence within official documents, scholars have pointed to the asymmetries in knowledge transmission which affect the nature of regional initiatives such as the European Research Area, as well as pedagogy within individual classrooms (Clifford, 2009; Doherty and Singh, 2005). As we discussed in Chapter 4, the various European programmes to encourage the mobility of researchers across the region have been seen by some as a means of institutionalizing the flow of knowledge from central points of power within the European university system to more marginal locations – in effect a transfer from 'old' to 'new' Europe (Kenway and Fahey, 2007, p.172). Moreover, Choi (2010) claims that the reforms in Hong Kong – particularly proposals that the Chinese University of Hong Kong increase the number of courses taught in English (justified on the grounds of the need to 'internationalize') – are manifestations of both English hegemony and neo-colonialism. Similarly, Rizvi (2000) describes how the majority of Malaysian students who move to Australia to pursue degrees in management, commerce or economics are taught a 'seemingly universal' organizational ideology, which is welcomed by Malaysian businesses on their return home. It is not, however, the ideology that is taught by domestic institutions, and has the effect of privileging Western modes of thought and modes of knowledge.

Robinson-Pant's (2009) research with international doctoral students in the UK has shown how some came to see themselves as pedagogical 'change agents' on return home – through encouraging greater emphasis to be placed within their home institutions on both 'being critical' and considering the ethical implications of research. She outlines in some detail the strategies the students intended to use to effect this change, for example: questioning the dominant hierarchy of language used in academia, experimenting with writing styles and introducing new research approaches. However, the extent to which they could also act as change agents within UK universities was seen as much more limited, with several respondents commenting that in the host country they felt that they had much less space available to them to challenge the dominant culture. Taking a more specific, disciplinary perspective, Madge et al. (2009) point to the ways in which geography curricula have been influenced by student migration – with that offered in Korea, for example, strongly shaped by American approaches as a result of the large number of Korean academics who gained their doctoral degrees in the US, while Williams and Baláž (2008) outline similar asymmetries in their research on the nature of knowledge transfer by doctors who train abroad.

Sidhu's (2006) analysis of marketing materials emanating from various popular international student destinations also highlights particular assumptions about the direction of knowledge transfer. As discussed in Chapter 2, she argues that British materials – from universities themselves as well as from the British Council, which has overall responsibility for promoting the 'national brand' of higher education – present a clear 'Othering discourse', constructing overseas students as both passive and in need of instruction from Western nations. Moreover, she asserts that the recourse to various icons of Empire within marketing materials helps to reinforce perceptions about the continuity of the Western canon, while the pedagogical practices evident in UK institutions and other Western universities offer few discursive spaces for developing more 'transformative scholarship' or 'for building non-territorial solidarities that liberate humane and democratic expressions of cosmopolitanism and foster authentic international collaborations' (p.313).

While accepting the broad thrust of some of these arguments, other researchers have suggested that knowledge flows are more complex than some of the accounts above suggest, and rarely only one-way.

Madge et al. (2009), for example, point to the legacy of colonial education and its important role in shaping many of the anti-colonial movements of the first half of the 20<sup>th</sup> century. They argue that similar contestations are apparent today, and that international students should not be seen as passive recipients of an overseas education but as active agents in knowledge-making in the country of destination as well as of origin. There are also notable differences by country in the extent to which international students are able to effect 'knowledge transfer' on their return home: their influence in Chinese HEIs, which typically have a highly centralized, government-prescribed curriculum, is likely to be considerably less than in Singapore, for example, which is much more open to global influence (ibid.).

Alongside this literature on the asymmetries of knowledge flows, is another body of work which has focussed on the problems faced by international students within the classroom – pointing to, for example, teachers' negative attitudes to some overseas students (Singh and Doherty, 2008) and the exclusionary tactics used by some groups of 'home' students (Madge et al., 2009). It is important, however, to note the geographical specificity of this work. Such 'problems' have been noted largely within Western universities and, even within this group, there are significant disparities: recent research suggests that universities in Australia, South Africa, the US and the Netherlands are considerably better at integrating international students than their UK counterparts (Madge et al., 2009). Within the UK, there has been a discernible shift in emphasis within this literature over recent years (Morrison et al., 2005). Early work often problematized the international student, drawing on a deficit model in which difficulties with language, study skills and adapting to cultural norms were attributed to the individual and used to explain poor academic performance. More recently, emphasis has come to be placed, instead, on the host institution and its responsibility for adapting to the needs of a diverse student body, recognizing that overseas students cannot be treated as a homogenous block. Moreover, diversity is now commonly presented as a benefit for both incoming students and home students (Jones and Brown, 2007), and as an effective means, for both groups, of developing the inter-cultural skills and other attributes increasingly demanded by employers. The nature of these inter-cultural experiences is explored in more detail below.

## Inter-cultural experiences

As noted above, overseas education is often promoted, to students and employers alike, on the basis that it helps to develop a range of inter-cultural skills that will have value in later life, particularly within the workplace. For example, in 2007, Bill Rammell, the then Minister of State for Higher Education in the UK, claimed that:

> For students, a period of study or work abroad brings positive benefits both personally and professionally. It enhances their understanding of other languages and cultures, and increases their confidence and self-reliance. In a global economy, these skills and competencies are increasingly sought by employers, and students with this experience will find that their employability is higher than without it. (Fielden, 2007, p.1)

As discussed in previous chapters, the important emphasis placed on the inculcation of inter-cultural skills is evident in many different regions of the world, from south-east Asia (see Chapter 3) to mainland Europe and the UK (Chapters 4 and 5). Such skills are, for example, seen as central to the effective functioning of the European Union, at both a political and economic level, and to the development of a European identity, critical to the wider project of European integration (King, 2003). There are certainly some very positive accounts of the ways in which international education can indeed facilitate such skill development. In his historical overview of the internationalization of HE, Teichler (2004b) suggests overseas study can be both an effective, as well as relatively safe, means of challenging attitudes and engrained perspectives 'because of an all-embracing confrontation to a culture different from that at home' (p.11). A similar argument is pursued by Murphy-Lejeune (2002) who documents the increasingly questioning stance of the students in her study who were educationally mobile, in relation to both the concept of national borders and the meaning of 'home'. Other studies have also highlighted the way in which young people, themselves, believe their perspectives had changed through a period studying overseas (King and Ruiz-Gelices, 2003). As mentioned earlier in this chapter, Slovak students who had spent a period of time at a UK university, for example, tended to value informal learning, and particularly the opportunity to study and work in a different cultural environment, much more highly than the formal education they received (Baláž and Williams, 2004). Similarly, overseas students enrolled at Taiwanese universities described one of the most rewarding aspects of their time abroad as experiencing life outside their home country and becoming 'better citizens' because of their increased understanding of another part of the world (Roberts et al., 2010), while Chinese students studying in Australia were deemed to have become more culturally flexible and reflexive as a result of their overseas education (Singh et al., 2007). More generally, studies have indicated that students often understand the term 'being international' as referring, primarily, to attitudes of mind and inter-cultural competencies (Hayden et al., 2000). Some scholars have suggested that the greater mobility of students can also have a positive impact on those who remain at a home institution but, during their studies, interact with international students. Brown and Jones (2007) present a very positive account of the way in which overseas students are seen in the UK, arguing that there has been a shift away from focussing on the problems of a culturally diverse classroom to recognizing the learning opportunities that such environments offer. They argue that international students are increasingly seen as 'a source of cultural capital and intentional diversity, enriching the learning experience both for home students and for one another, expanding staff horizons, building a more powerful learning community and thus developing the higher education experience' (p.2).

There is, however, a body of literature that paints a rather different, and less positive, picture of the inter-cultural learning undertaken by international students. Firstly, some scholars have argued that the opportunities for learning about different cultures within the class-room are limited, within Western countries at least, by the dominance of Western bodies of knowledge. As noted above, it remains relatively difficult for those from non-Western countries to share their own approaches to particular subject areas within Western universities (Kenway and Fahey, 2007; Robinson-Pant, 2009).

Secondly, informal learning outside the classroom is often limited by the social segregation of international students – seemingly evident in many parts of the world (Fincher and Shaw, 2009; Montgomery and McDowell, 2009). Studies of Erasmus students have shown how they often mix with other international students rather than the host community (Caudery et al., 2009; Tsoukalas, 2008). Indeed, Tsoukalas claims:

> The Erasmus students saw themselves as members of an exclusive community...with strong internal cohesion and solidarity and with a common purpose. In comparison to this, the class of local students contributes an inclusive social category, is made up mostly of imagined others, has a weak sense of social cohesion and solidarity and includes no common goals. (p.142)

He goes on to argue that the Erasmus students in his study not only failed to establish contact with the local community but also engaged in relatively little inter-cultural learning within the group of international students. There are, he argues, various explanations for this: the difficulty of young exchange students standing as 'fully fledged representatives of their country' (p.144); the difficulty of teaching any foreigner one's own particular 'ways' outside of the relevant cultural context; the problems caused by communicating in a second or third language; and the ways in which an experience of living abroad tends to strip away many traits of one's home country. While the relatively short duration of the Erasmus exchange may be seen as an additional explanation of the lack of social integration and inter-cultural learning, similar trends have also been identified amongst students who have gone abroad for the whole of a degree. Overseas students in Taiwan, for example, have been shown to be reluctant to engage in extra-curricular activities and not fully immersed in the local culture (Roberts et al., 2010), while Waters and Brooks' (2010b) work with mobile UK students has highlighted both the difficulties of integrating with local communities, experienced by some, but also the perceived 'safety' of remaining within predominantly international student groups. In many ways, this reflects some of the more general literature on cosmopolitanism. For example, Savage et al.'s (2005) research amongst different communities in the north-west of England has shown how those who claim a 'cosmopolitan' identity are 'attracted to the idea of appreciating global cultures yet their actual cultural reference points show very little engagement with cultures outside the English speaking metropolises' (p.206).

Thirdly, inter-cultural learning is impeded when international students face racism and/or discrimination in the host country. Collins (2010) argues that South Korean students in Auckland, New Zealand face many challenges as they settle into their new lives as international students, one of which is the racism they sometimes encounter from the local population. Similarly, drawing on evidence from the UK, Madge et al. (2009) discuss the 'passive xenophobia' experienced by some overseas students within university classrooms. They also make the point that the diverse nature of many UK classrooms is frequently downplayed in marketing material. Indeed, they argue that 'although the authority of colonialism and post-colonialism is continuously drawn upon to recruit students, it is precisely through the erasure of their presence [within marketing campaigns] that this authority is garnered' (p.41).

Finally, there is some ambivalence in the literature about the degree of cultural difference that is most conducive to inter-cultural learning.

Rivza and Teichler (2007) distinguish between two forms of educational mobility: 'vertical' mobility, which refers to the movement of students who aim to benefit from higher education of a higher quality or in an area of specialism not available in their home country, and 'horizontal' mobility, understood as movement to neighbouring countries with similar HE systems. Teichler (2004b) argues that while the former may be a more efficient means of ensuring rapid knowledge transfer, the latter 'offers a better framework for border-crossing communication and discourse' (p.14). He suggests that this is because destructive culture shocks are less likely during horizontal mobility and, as a result, insight into the host culture will be achieved more quickly. The available empirical evidence certainly suggests that the culture shocks associated with 'vertical' mobility can be significant. Indeed, Singh et al. (2007) contend that Chinese students who move to Australia to pursue a degree often have considerable difficulties when they return home, finding it hard to settle back into the local and national spaces they once occupied. However, in contrast to Teichler's position, Singh et al. maintain that such difficulties can ultimately be productive. They assert that their respondents, while unable simply to slot back into the communities from which they came, responded in a positive manner, forming new 'cosmopolitan spaces' of their own. They argue that, as a direct result of their experiences, they became more culturally flexible and reflexive, developed a capacity to deal with the contradictions in their situation, and adopted a much broader global outlook. Moreover, 'against the familiarity of multiple cultural spaces, and with the confidence of their own skills of cultural negotiation, they now seek new orientations to their world and new forms of cosmopolitan bridging' (p.208). Similar arguments are made by Rizvi (2000) on the basis of his research with Malaysian students in Australia:

> With formative international experiences, they [the Malaysian students] are able to look at the world as dynamic and multicultural. This is so because they operate within a hybridised space and are equally comfortable in more than one cultural site. Their identity is intercultural with multiple cultural defining points. They typify a new global generation. (p.223)

There is, therefore, considerable ambivalence about the role of international education in promoting intercultural learning. While there is some evidence that educational mobility promotes a more questioning stance to one's 'home' culture and a greater openness to the cultures of others, this is not experienced by all. Research has also pointed to the frequent social segregation of international students, the discrimination they sometimes face, and the dominance of Western bodies of knowledge.

## Exacerbating inequalities

Political rhetoric is replete with claims about the benefits that educational mobility offers to both the student who takes up such opportunities and society more generally. This quotation from the 2009 European Commission green paper on learning mobility is typical in emphasizing the advantages that accrue to the students, employers and the European Union as a whole:

> Studies confirm that learning mobility adds to human capital, as students access new knowledge and develop new linguistic skills and intercultural competences. Furthermore, employers recognise and value these benefits....It can also strengthen Europe's competitiveness by helping to build a knowledge-intensive society, thereby contributing to the achievement of the objectives set out in the Lisbon strategy for growth and jobs. (CEC, 2009, p.2)

Such mobility is often argued to have helped stimulate the development of a more global curriculum in many subject areas, and to have brought about more diverse learning environments in universities worldwide. Indeed, we have outlined above a number of important advantages associated with student mobility, including the inculcation of more tolerant, questioning and culturally reflexive attitudes on the part of students who move abroad for some or all of their higher education. However, we have also cited strong evidence that international HE, in its current form, has had a less positive impact in a number of ways and, in some contexts, is clearly implicated in the exacerbation of educational and social inequalities. Such inequalities are played out at two levels: between individuals and between nations and/or geographical regions.

As we have suggested above, the pursuit of international education can be seen as part of a wider strategy to achieve distinction – from other graduates of a mass HE system and within an increasingly congested graduate labour market. 'Mobility capital' can be accumulated through studying overseas (as well as other forms of youth travel) and can be drawn upon on graduation as well as later in life to differentiate oneself from others and secure positional advantage within some (but not all) labour markets. For some students (particularly those from East Asian countries), this distinction is generally related to the acquisition of an overseas qualification *per se*; for others (particularly those from Western countries), it is related to the status of the university at which one studied. For both groups, the 'soft skills' and social networks developed as a result of a period overseas bestow considerable labour market advantage. Theorists have suggested that this instrumental pursuit of overseas education should be seen as part of a broader shift towards what Mitchell (2003) has called 'strategic cosmopolitans', people with a strongly competitive global outlook, who are motivated 'not by ideals of national unity in diversity, but by understandings of global competitiveness and the necessity to strategically adapt as an individual to rapidly changing personal and national contexts' (p.388).

Some scholars have argued that the increase in the number of students pursuing higher education abroad is indicative of a democratization of mobility (Roberts et al., 2010). Indeed, we have suggested above and in Chapters 4 and 5 that there may be some evidence to suggest that, amongst European students, a failure to excel within the domestic system may be one reason for taking up a place at an overseas university. However, in general, educational mobility still seems to be much more prevalent amongst groups with high levels of economic, cultural and/or social capital and correlated strongly with social privilege (Brooks and Waters, 2009a; Findlay et al., 2006; Singh et al., 2007). Thus, it appears that different socio-economic groups – across the world – have very different abilities to overcome the 'friction of distance' (Harvey, 1989, p.211). The inequalities that follow from these differential abilities to travel are exacerbated, some researchers maintain, by the way in which policymakers treat international and domestic students. On the basis of her analysis of higher education reform in Singapore, Sidhu (2009) suggests that, by the energetic pursuit of outstanding overseas students, the Singapore government has set up an unhelpful binary between '"ordinary" locals and exceptional global talent' (p.251). This argument is developed by Brown and Tannock (2009) who contend that, as the number of international students in any one country increases, so it becomes harder for students and the electorate more generally to expect or require universities to pursue social justice:

> With international students, there are no strong equity demands to accept students from disadvantaged social backgrounds, provide free

or heavily subsidised student tuition, emphasise social science or humanities education relevant to students' personal identities or support the needs and interests of local communities surrounding college campuses as there are for higher education students domestically. (p.384)

It is also the case, however, that mobile students, themselves, sometimes suffer within university classrooms. Indeed, earlier parts of this chapter have pointed to various ways in which racism, discrimination and social segregation can all have a significant and negative impact upon a period abroad.

Student mobility can also help to perpetuate inequalities between nations or regions. There is evidence to suggest that Western modes of thought and approaches to knowledge creation are often used, by mobile students from 'Eastern' countries, to critique domestic practices when they return home. Due to the significantly greater numbers moving from East to West than from West to East, it is perhaps unsurprising that Western bodies of knowledge have not been subjected to the same kind of critique. Such trends may well be reinforced by the frequent use of Western partners to drive higher education expansion within Asian countries (Olds, 2007b; Sidhu, 2009) and the high value accorded to Western qualifications within Asian labour markets (Waters, 2009). Some scholars have suggested that inequalities are also apparent within regions. As we have discussed above (and in Chapter 4), Kenway and Fahey (2007) argue that, within Europe, for example, mobility policies aid 'knowledge transfer' from richer Western European countries to poorer, less powerful nations on the continent.

The emergence of a clearer and more competitive 'market' for international students over the last two decades has, it is argued, helped to entrench differences between national higher education systems. League tables of world universities, produced on an annual basis (and discussed in more detail in Chapter 2), have helped to construct a clear global hierarchy of institutions. Indeed, Marginson (2008) has argued that the global field of higher education is structured by 'an opposition between the elite sub-field of restricted production, and the sub-field of large scale mass production' (p.305). The elite sub-field, he suggests, is comprised of institutions such as the top American universities and the universities of Oxford and Cambridge in the UK, whose global power 'rests on the sub-ordination of other institutions and nations' (ibid.). US hegemony, in particular, he contends, is underpinned by: the global use of English; research concentration and knowledge flows; and its success as a 'people attractor', through offering superior salaries for staff and scholarships for students. Thus, he claims that the dominance of the US within the field of higher education is akin to its global hegemony in other areas such as media, finance and technology. Although there are some signs of change, with recent growth in Asian markets for overseas students and an improvement in the league table positions of Asian HEIs, clear inequalities remain.

## Conclusion

The significant growth in the number of mobile students witnessed worldwide over recent years is, in part, inextricably linked to the policy developments at international, regional, national and local level discussed in Chapter 2. However, it is also bound up with other aspects of social change, which have been explored in this chapter. We have shown how travel has assumed an important place in the lives of many young people and how overseas experiences often provide useful resources for 'identity construction' within contemporary society. Educational mobility can, therefore, be seen as part of this wider shift in the lives of young men and women. The pursuit of an international higher education can also be framed within wider debates about migration to secure citizenship of another country. This chapter has argued that there is now considerable evidence to indicate that education is often used as either a means of gaining entry to another country or as a 'trial run' for living abroad. In some countries (notably Australia), measures have been taken by national governments to ease the route from international student to permanent resident. Student migration is also, we have suggested, a response to the increasingly congested nature of the graduate labour market in many parts of the world – a means of 'distinguishing' oneself from other graduates of a mass HE system, and developing the soft skills and social networks valued by employers. However, we have highlighted geographical disparities in the way in which this 'distinction' is configured: in Asian countries an overseas qualification *per se* is often desired, whereas in the UK overseas education is often valued primarily because of the greater opportunities it offers for accessing elite institutions.

This chapter has also explored the impact of student migration on the nature of higher education itself. We have argued that one way in which universities in various parts of the world have responded to the increasing number of mobile students is by 'internationalizing' the curriculum; this is also frequently part of a wider institutional strategy to increase the number of such students. While we have acknowledged the emancipatory potential of some of this work – for example, encouraging students to question traditional bodies of knowledge and to enhance their understanding of those from other cultures – we have also suggested that, to date, this potential has often not been realized. Indeed, the chapter has provided evidence of the way in which knowledge transmission is often rather one-way, and the continuing dominance of 'Western' traditions of thought. Developing this argument, we have drawn on material from Chapters 3, 4 and 5 to suggest that there is now convincing evidence that international HE, in its current guise, is clearly implicated in exacerbating educational and social inequalities – between individuals and also between nations and/or geographical regions. The consequences of this for policy and practice are addressed in Chapter 8.

# 8
# Conclusion

Over the last two decades, the meaning of 'internationalization' for higher education has undergone a fundamental and decisive shift. From being a topic of vague, peripheral interest to colleges and universities, it now represents an issue that is highly prioritized in strategic plans and policy agendas. The recruitment of large numbers of international students to HEIs is no longer simply a welcome although largely incidental addition to domestic enrolments, but instead is seen as *critical* to the survival of many academic programmes and even some institutions. Australia's universities are perhaps symbolic of this growing and deepening relationship of dependency between domestic and international higher education. A recent government-commissioned report, *Review of Australian Higher Education*, describes the impact of internationalization on domestic educational institutions (Bradley et al., 2008). International student numbers have grown on average by 14 per cent annually since 1982, and education is now Australia's largest service-sector export and third largest export overall (ibid.). Several universities rely on international students for over 25 per cent of their total income (the figure is as much as 44 per cent for Central Queensland University) (ibid.). In relation to these figures, the report makes the following observations:

> It appears that many [Australian higher education] institutions use international student revenue to support services to domestic students and bolster research infrastructure [...] There appears to be a systematic pattern across institutions of cross-subsidisation to supplement other institutional activities. This suggests that funds available for teaching of domestic students and for research activities may be insufficient and that services for international students

would improve if more funds were made available to institutions. (Bradley et al., 2008, p.93)

Australia's reliance on international students is clearly one major concern voiced within this review, hinting at the fact that fees from international students are no longer supplementing income from public sources, but have been *replacing* it. In the UK, recent media reports have similarly suggested that, as a consequence of trenchant funding cuts by the national government, and an ongoing cap on the number of domestic students that institutions can admit in any one year, the future of many universities may hinge on their ability to be competitive in an international educational market. Attracting students from overseas is clearly a pivotal part of such internationalization strategies (Curtis, 2009). As described in Chapters 6 and 7 of this book, educational institutions (particularly in the Western economies) are increasingly aware of the importance of developing and maintaining a 'brand image', and are cognizant of their 'global positioning'. Countries, too, are subject to scrutiny by prospective students seeking a national education 'brand'. And yet, despite their unequivocal importance to Western universities and economies more broadly, international students are not universally welcomed. Media coverage has focussed on very recent attempts by several Western governments to limit immigration (including the UK and Australia), with direct implications for international student numbers as well as for how students perceive their reception within these countries. The issue of student migration is therefore often highly politicized. A number of violent attacks on Indian international students in Australian cities and Korean students in Canada over the last few years have also highlighted the vulnerability of international students and, correspondingly, the potential vulnerability of the international student market (e.g. Park, 2010). The global reputations of countries (as desirable study destinations) are not immutable, but are intertwined with wider political-economic and social circumstances.

Available statistics are illustrative of the contemporary importance of international students, with more than three million individuals now studying for a tertiary-level qualification outside of their home country (OECD, 2009). In fact, as we have observed, this figure greatly under-represents the true number of students acquiring an 'international education': Chapter 3 shows that many families now partake in 'educational immigration' (Butcher, 2004), involving the relocation of entire households (parents and children) overseas (Waters, 2005). In addition, hundreds of thousands of students are studying for a foreign qualification 'at home', as more universities 'off-shore' their degree programmes, whether through 'franchising' educational materials, utilizing flying faculty, or opening branch campuses and whole new universities abroad. The notion of 'student mobility' has therefore evolved beyond the typical characterization of the 'foreign student', to encompass a wider range of practices and mobilities.

The clear qualitative and numerical importance of the internationally mobile student, however, has not been matched by academic interest in the topic, which has until recently been surprisingly muted. It is clear that over the last twenty years, research has failed to keep up with the pace of developments in the internationalization of education, and although a surge of work in this area has gone some way to rectify the shortfall, significant gaps in our knowledge remain. Academic understanding of the internationalization of education is usually piecemeal and often anecdotal. Nevertheless, as we have shown, there *is* a substantial body of richly empirical work on the mobility of different student groups, emerging out of diverse disciplinary fields. Until now, this work has not been brought together in any substantive or systematic way. *Student Mobilities, Migration and the Internationalization of Higher Education* reflects our sense of the considerable importance of international education for countries, societies, communities and institutions, as well as for individuals and their families and the pressing need, therefore, to engage critically with the extant academic literature. In this book, we have drawn upon this rich empirical work to proffer new and constructive ways of conceptualizing international student mobility, which will help us begin to see the larger picture, detailing the transformation of education and society, of which student mobility is clearly just a part. In what follows, we draw out the main themes from our case studies on which these new conceptualizations (discussed in detail in Chapters 6 and 7) rest.

In *Student Mobilities, Migration and the Internationalization of Higher Education*, we have drawn upon specific empirical case studies (Chapter 3 on East Asian students, Chapter 4 on students within Europe and Chapter 5 on the international mobility of UK students) as a vehicle for extracting wider themes, with a view to developing existing theorizations of international student mobility and the internationalization of higher education. In this conclusion, we frame these themes in terms of the *geographies* of student mobility – the need for a geographical perspective on international education is an assertion running both implicitly and explicitly throughout the book. We consider first the different *scales* at which these issues can be approached – from the personal to the national and the transnational. We then examine some conceptual concerns that cross-cut these different scales of analysis, discussed in terms of the *uneven* geographies of student mobilities. The next section of the conclusion offers up some policy implications emerging from our findings, which is an attempt to bring together, in a far more systematic way, academic work on the internationalization of education and practitioner debates that are, in many cases, largely divorced from scholarship. Finally, we draw to a close with some brief reflections on the internationalization of higher education.

## Deciphering the meaning and significance of student mobility

Unlike many discussions around the internationalization of education – particularly those initiated by practitioners of international education – we have been cognizant of the need for a people-centred perspective on student mobility. To this end, we have deliberately attempted to look beyond crude economic and political assessments of student motivations, towards understanding the often highly personal and always social reasons why individuals migrate for education. The decision to relocate overseas, however temporarily, is not taken lightly, and involves complex deliberations and doubts, as well as a sense of excitement, anticipation and adventure. The fact that every year more students are travelling abroad in search of education mirrors to a large degree the picture for international migration as a whole. This has resulted, at least in part, from the conjoining of technological developments (telecommunications, media and transportation) and an expanded *imagination*. Cultural theorist Arjun Appadurai (1996, p.4) captures well this powerful relationship, which is said to drive mobility:

> Electronic mediation and mass migration mark the world of the present not as technically new forces but as ones that seem to impel (and sometimes compel) the work of the imagination. Together, they create specific irregularities because both viewers and images are in simultaneous circulation. Neither images nor viewers fit into circuits or audiences that are easily bound within local, national, or regional spaces. Of course, many viewers may not themselves migrate. But few important films, news broadcasts, or television spectacles are entirely unaffected by other media events that come from further afield. And few persons in the world today do not have a friend, relative, or co-worker who is not on the road to somewhere else or already coming back home, bearing stories and possibilities. [...] This mobile

and unforeseeable relationship between mass-mediated events and migratory audiences defines the core of the link between globalization and the modern.

Young people, like other potential migrants, are therefore increasingly exposed to images from overseas and consequently to the *idea* of mobility. Rizvi (2009) attributes an increase in international student mobility specifically to the 'social imaginaries' of individuals. As we have shown in several chapters, travel as a child has an important part to play in this: many international students had significant prior experiences of overseas travel with parents, friends or independently (Findlay and King, 2010; Teichler, 2004a). Many also have family members living abroad (Brooks and Waters, 2010; Findlay and King, 2010). All of this further instils in young people the possibility of mobility and what it can offer.

From the literature, two particular perspectives on student motivations for international mobility have emerged, which we will briefly review here. The first emphasizes student 'strategies' linked to employability concerns, and the second discusses a more experiential side to the decision to embark on study abroad. Beginning with the notion of 'strategies': as we have shown, much of the literature suggests that international students are often acutely concerned with 'investing qualitatively' in their futures (Murphy-Lejeune, 2002, p.100). Murphy-Lejeune (2002) discusses the accumulation of what she calls 'mobility capital' by international students – a period spent overseas is believed to equip students with the skills, attributes and bodily comportment prized in an international labour market (Ong, 1999). Several other writers have mooted similar ideas with reference to 'cultural capital', drawing on Pierre Bourdieu's (1986) concept and its relationship to social reproduction. Cultural capital is said to exist in three states: 'institutionalized' by the academic qualification, 'embodied' in the attributes and characteristics of the person, and 'objectified' in material artefacts (Bourdieu, 1986). The first and second of these have been directly discussed in relation to the strategies of international students (Waters, 2006): it is argued that the cultural capital inherent in an international degree certificate is valuable and in some contexts highly prized; at the same time, international students also 'embody' various traits that employers seek, not least the ability to converse fluently in a second language (usually English). This links to wider debates emanating from research on the sociology of education, which have discussed 'employability' and the related tactics deployed by middle-class families concerned with 'positional advantage' in a saturated graduate labour market (Ball, 2003; Brown et al., 1997; Brown et al., 2003). Obtaining international qualifications is increasingly seen as a potentially useful way of securing a positional advantage. As we have shown throughout the chapters in *Student Mobilities, Migration and the Internationalization of Higher Education*, some notion of 'positional advantage', ensuing directly from the possession of international qualifications, is commonly expressed by internationally mobile students.

At the same time, empirical research on international student mobility also lays stress on what Krzaklewska (2006) terms an 'experimental dimension', wherein personal motivations for study overseas are less overtly strategic. Instead they reflect vaguer notions of fun, excitement, exploration and self-actualization (Waters and Brooks, 2010b). Chapter 7, in particular, discussed the role of overseas mobility in young people's lives and how, increasingly, travel abroad is being seen as 'a normal and almost taken-for-granted part of the life-cycle' (Conradson and Latham, 2005, p.288). This has been theorized as encompassing young people's 'biographical constructions' (Beck, 1992; Giddens, 1991), what King and Ruiz-Gelices (2003) describe as the initiating of students personal 'life projects' (p.245). At the same time, however, we have also shown how in some contexts (particularly in relation to students from East Asia, as discussed in Chapter 3) migration for education is anything but 'individualized' and, in fact, enlists in some way several other family members, not least when 'international education' involves the relocation overseas of entire households. This is especially the case where students move overseas at a young age, *prior* to their application for university entrance (Lee and Koo, 2006; Waters, 2008).

We now move from an examination of the 'personal' and 'familial' to consider the salience of a more commonly invoked scale of analysis – the *national*. The chapters in this book point to the enduring significance of the nation-state as a key player in policy-making, and a key driver of international student mobility. As indicated above, and as described in Chapter 2, one of the major ways in which nation-states interact with student mobility is through national immigration policy. In fact, it is hard to over-estimate the importance of policies related to immigration for facilitating and/or limiting flows of international students. Most usually, internationally mobile students enter countries on a student visa or study permit. However, we have also shown how other types of immigration (such as 'business' or 'skilled' migration) can also involve educationally-motivated family relocation (see, for example, Chapter 3). Furthermore, states control, to a certain extent, what happens to students at the end of their studies – in Chapter 7 we discussed how some countries, such as Australia, have actively encouraged foreign students to become permanent residents following their studies. In contrast, the US and UK have enacted policies that force students to leave the country following the completion of their course. Other examples of the relationship between national-level policy and the internationalization of higher education include the development of a 'Global Education Hub' in Singapore (Olds, 2007a), the ultimate aim of which has been to attract large numbers of international students into the city-state and then to retain them, boosting the skill base of the national economy.

Shifting scale once again – the research on international student mobility discussed throughout *Student Mobilities, Migration and the Internationalization of Higher Education* has emphatically demonstrated the value of a *transnational* perspective. As suggested above, whilst we have argued (particularly in Chapter 2) that the nation-state remains pivotal in directing international student mobility – not least through the creation of various policy contexts – it is nevertheless impossible to understand fully its meaning and significance without due attention to 'the transnational'. Commonly defined as the ways in which contemporary migrants maintain significant ties (social, economic, political and emotional) with two or more countries simultaneously (Basch et al., 1994), the concept of 'transnationalism' has provided a fruitful way of conceptualizing the frequent physical movement and emotional connections of contemporary migrants. This would seem to be particularly germane to the practices of international students, who by their nature are expected to move repeatedly (and unproblematically) between home and host societies.

However, it is perhaps also worth stating that the existence of '*transnationalism*' is fundamentally dependent upon the enduring power of the nation-state, without which the term would lose any meaning. Furthermore, the geographical differences that exist between (national) societies would seem still to matter to transnational migrants – the movement of many international students is far removed from the depictions of the seamless mobility of cosmopolitan elites (e.g. Ong, 1999). On the contrary, as we have shown, international students can experience significant problems associated with being 'out of place' in their host country and yet are expected to re-adjust without difficulty to returning home during and after study (e.g. Ghosh and Wang, 2003). We have also shown (as summarized in Chapter 7) the problematic nature of students' 'intercultural experiences' when studying abroad. It is widely assumed by educational practitioners and policymakers that a period spent in education overseas will bring 'positive benefits' such as enhancing 'understanding of other languages and cultures' whilst increasing 'confidence and self reliance' (Fielden, 2007, p.1). Such benefits will enable employability down the line as 'these skills and competencies are increasingly sought by employers' (ibid.). And there is some evidence of these positive outcomes, as observed in several studies (King and Ruiz-Gelices, 2003; Murphy-Lejeune, 2002; Teichler, 2004b). However, this view has to be balanced against a more substantial body of work that has painted a quite different picture, showing the socially limited experiences of international students – both inside and outside of the formal learning environment (e.g. Fincher and Shaw, 2009).

As Vertovec (1999) has clearly indicated, transnationalism can occur both 'from above' and 'from below'. If we turn, then, to consider the 'top-down' nature of transnationalism, its relevance to understanding regional initiatives in relation to educational mobility – most notably found within the European Union – and the role played by supra-national organizations such as the World Bank, UNESCO and the OECD, is clear. In Chapter 4, we highlighted Susan Robertson's (2009) discussion of the evolution of higher education in Europe, which emphasizes the significance of the Bologna Process, the Erasmus scheme and the development of a European Higher Education Area. Although the intention of these initiatives has been to create a seamless, unbounded educational space, in reality these are *transnational* initiatives, entailing all the stickiness of enduring national difference. We have also discussed the increasingly prominent role of the OECD, UNESCO and the World Bank in helping to shape international education from 'above'. The OECD, for example, implements regular educational 'benchmarking' exercises, provides easy access to international comparisons based on various indicators, and produces policy reviews and recommendations. UNESCO, too, has been involved in measuring and drawing comparisons between national education systems, with the goal of developing international standards in education at all levels. We have shown, throughout this book, the value of approaching international student mobility from different angles with an awareness of the various (albeit socially constructed) scales at which it can be understood. In the next section of the conclusion, we consider some of the major themes to have emerged from within this book – themes which generally apply at all scales of analysis.

## Uneven geographies: class, power and neo-colonialism

Whilst the social and cultural 'diversity' argument, in favour of the internationalization of higher education, is frequently and widely espoused by educational practitioners and policymakers, the academic literature is generally less celebratory and far more cautionary in its approach. The view that international education represents the 'democratization' of mobility and the expansion of access to quality education on a global scale is a minority one (e.g. Roberts et al., 2010). In contrast, the academic research that we have reviewed here overwhelmingly suggests that internationally mobile students are privileged individuals in possession of far higher levels of capital (economic, social and cultural) than their non-mobile peers and, furthermore, pursuing higher education overseas serves to reproduce that capital and, consequently, their privileged position in society (Bourdieu, 1984). Whilst this capital accumulation may not always be overtly strategic, as discussed above (see Waters and Brooks, 2010a), even less calculating motives for overseas study (such as the search for self-actualization or adventure) will often nevertheless produce the same advantageous result (Findlay and King, 2010). We are not suggesting that 'international' credentials are *always* favoured in the market place, as this is clearly not the case (see Brooks et al., 2012). However, the privileged social position of mobile students is rarely challenged through their international experiences and there is a need, we suggest, to understand better the uneven geographies of international credentials from students', graduates' and employers' perspectives at multiple geographic scales.

Geographies of international education also point to the uneven, larger-scale power dynamics inherent in this multi-billion pound industry. Discussed in Chapter 6, very few national economies benefit substantially from international student mobility, as the figures on flows of students globally attest. In fact, the majority of international students are found in a very small number of countries, and these countries are located in the West. Put crudely, rich countries benefit most from the economic advantages that accrue from international student mobility, and their present-day uneven (power) relationship with student 'sending' countries is often built on a recent exploitative colonial past (Madge et al., 2009).

The application of ideas in geography around 'space' and its 'relational' nature can throw these unequal power relations into sharper relief. As Marginson (2008, p.303) has argued, 'worldwide higher education is a relational environment', and therefore represents a zero-sum game. Countries and institutions compete against each other to attract full fee-paying students, aided and abetted by published league tables. Every year, the same national education systems and institutions top these tables, perpetuating the geographical unevenness of international education. Presently, however, a subtle change is occurring, wherein 'non-traditional' regions (such as Hong Kong and the People's Republic of China) are beginning to figure more prominently within global rankings. The implications of this change in terms of a re-dressing of existent power relations around international student mobility are yet to be seen.

The influence of neo-colonialism through international education can be seen in other, more conspicuous ways, too. Perhaps the most obvious of these is the enduring allure of the English-language in continuing to attract students to English-speaking Western countries and institutions. This is often couched in discourses pertaining to 'the global language', but nevertheless serves to perpetuate the kinds of pre-existing uneven power relations discussed above. As observed in Chapter 3, the attraction of English is often a key driver underpinning educational migration. This, as we have discussed, is what Chew (2010) has termed 'linguistic migration' and Park and Bae (2009) describe in terms of 'language ideologies': 'the belief that good English skills are an indispensable requirement for success in the global economy, that early exposure to an English-speaking environment is necessary for successful acquisition of English, and [...] the belief that competence in English conducive to social mobility can only be obtained at specific geographical locations, namely the English speaking countries of the West' (p.368). Linguistic migration, Park and Bae argue, is driven by 'globally dominant ideologies of English that constitute highly specific views of language, place and social space' (ibid.). The accusation of 'neo-colonialism', enacted through mobility and language acquisition, is implicit in this discussion. We also discussed, in Chapter 7, the pervasive influence of Western bodies of knowledge in educational instruction and the limited opportunities available, to international students, for learning about different cultures within the classroom or lecture hall setting. Other (non-Western) approaches to learning or knowledge are often not valued or simply ignored within Western universities (Kenway and Fahey, 2007; Robinson-Pant, 2009). This latter point is clearly something that can, and should be addressed, and reflects Madge et al.'s (2009) call for the implementation of an 'engaged pedagogy' in and through international education.

## Bringing it all together: policy implications

As we have shown in several earlier chapters, neo-liberalism drives much student mobility. This is evidenced both by the expensive marketing strategies deployed by universities throughout the world to increase overseas revenue, and by the decision-making processes of potentially mobile young people, conscious of the need to distinguish themselves from other graduates in an increasingly competitive labour market. It seems naïve to assume that much can be done to change this wider context. Nevertheless, we suggest that there are a number of policies that can be enacted at a variety of scales, which may help to redress some of the inequalities highlighted throughout this book.

We have emphasized the ways in which educational mobility is often taken up by only the most privileged groups in society, and thus helps to perpetuate social advantage. There are various steps national governments, regional bodies and individual universities could take to open up such opportunities to a wider cross-section of young people. More could be done to instil in young people, during their time in compulsory education, a greater awareness of other education systems and the advantages (as well as the disadvantages) of gaining a qualification abroad. As young people move closer to the age at which they are required to make decisions about higher education, publicity about overseas opportunities could be targeted more specifically at lower income groups. Harvard University has, for example, recently employed an outreach officer to work with state schools in the UK, partly in response to concern that the majority of its incoming students from the UK had studied at private schools (Smith, 2006). In many cases, the financial barriers to studying abroad are not insuperable. Indeed, the variation in tuition fee level between countries and the wide array of scholarships on offer can sometimes make studying abroad a cheaper option than remaining at home. Ensuring that such financial information is widely disseminated may help to stimulate interest in mobility among young people with few economic resources of their own to draw upon. While such measures may help to address some of the social inequalities that are often exacerbated by student migration, they may also ensure that the inter-cultural skills and capacity to work across national borders, which have been called for by employers (Fielden, 2007), are developed by a wider cross-section of the labour force.

We have drawn attention to the significant variations in student migration between countries and, in particular, the dominance of rich, Anglophone nations in the international marketplace. While it is difficult to imagine countries with net inflows of students being prepared to adopt policies which compromise their position, regional mobility schemes such as the Erasmus programme perhaps offer more potential for 'managing' student flows, and encouraging students to study in less well-off and non-English-speaking nations. Currently, all Erasmus students receive a 'mobility grant'; the level of this grant could be varied by country of destination so as to incentivize study in those parts of the continent which are currently less attractive to mobile students. Such policies may also help to address the inequities in the flow of *knowledge*, which we have discussed above and in previous chapters. By providing incentives for students to study in less popular areas of Europe, the dominance of what Kenway and Fahey (2007) identify as the 'central points of power in the European university system' (p.172) may be eroded. At a more local level, in universities throughout the world, introducing a more critical and 'engaged pedagogy' (along the lines suggested by Madge et al., 2009) may help students to be more sensitive to the power relations implicit in processes of knowledge transfer and thus to develop their own critique of assumptions that underpin teaching and learning in different parts of the world.

Finally, the recent cases of violence against international students in Australia and Canada testify to the urgent need for policymakers, particularly at the national and institutional levels, to do more to protect the well-being of such young people. In part, this may be achieved by taking greater steps to ensure that they are integrated fully with domestic students. Research, cited in a number of chapters of this book, has indicated that international students are often housed separately from other students and, as a result, find it difficult to engage fully with local communities. Integrated student accommodation, the pairing of overseas students with 'link' families in the local area and more attention to the ways *all* students can be brought together through particular pedagogies within university classrooms may go some way to increasing both the safety of mobile young people and the depth of their inter-cultural encounters.

## Final remarks on the internationalization of education

There can be little doubt that the future of higher education, globally, will be inexorably bound to the process of internationalization. Yet, just as globalization has now been exposed as a politically laden discourse – depicting an inevitable and unstoppable juggernaut – so too must the political and economic imperatives, underpinning many internationalization strategies, be exposed. The neo-liberal vision of 'international education' (invariably driven largely by mercenary concerns) is not inevitable, and alternative futures for HE, involving *different versions* of internationalization, must be imagined, deliberated and discussed. Our review of the current state of internationalization in higher education (albeit one focussing on student mobilities) suggests some very mixed outcomes. On the one hand, there is a great deal to be lauded – many students benefit from international mobility, as do some national economies and educational institutions. There are clear 'winners' when it comes to international student mobility. At the same time, as we have endeavoured to show, the geographies of internationalization are highly uneven and an overwhelming focus on the 'inevitability' of international higher education fails to acknowledge the countries, economies, societies and individuals for which there are no gains to be had from this process. In fact, domestic education within many countries may be consistently undermined by large numbers of internationally mobile students. We must also look at international student mobility alongside other forms of internationalization that have grown and developed over the last ten years – the most conspicuous of these being the expansion of 'off-shore' campuses and 'non-local' degree courses offered by foreign providers. At first glance, this might appear to suggest that the physical mobility of students may become a less important aspect of internationalization in the future. However, we might also be seeing the emergence of a differentiated international education, where 'mobile' (i.e. generally more privileged) students continue to be advantaged in international labour markets *vis-à-vis* their 'non-mobile' peers. Despite this, all official statistics would suggest that international student mobility is far from in demise. Further research is therefore needed, we would argue, which attempts to understand how mobile students fit into the larger picture of the contemporary transformation in the spaces of higher education and how, also, the advantage that accrues from international mobility can be made more accessible to all students, and not just the most privileged sections of society.

# Notes

## Chapter 2  Policy Context

1  The 'Tuning' project was originally conceived as a means of linking the political objectives of the Bologna Process to the higher educational sector within Europe. However, since 2003, it has been 'rolled out' to Latin America, with the aim of creating a more unified Latin American higher education area.

2  The 'Asia Link' project was established by the EU in 2002 to promote networking and partnerships between universities in Europe and developing countries in Asia.

## Chapter 3  Mobility of East Asian Students

1  Although there has been quite a lot of work on 'Asian American' students and their academic performance relative to other immigrant groups in the United States (e.g. Louie (2004)), research on East Asians as 'mobile' or transnational students is a much more recent undertaking. This chapter focuses on this latter body of work.

2  Some parents will move their children back into the home education system before tertiary education, with the hope that their experiences of living abroad will put them at an advantage when attempting to get into one of the highly competitive local universities.

3  In addition to the 'children's education', the main reasons given by families from Hong Kong and Taiwan for immigration are 'political uncertainty' and the security offered by obtaining a 'second passport', and environmental/ lifestyle factors (Kobayashi and Preston, 2007). Unlike most 'economic' migrants, it would seem that these families never migrate to pursue 'economic opportunities' abroad (Ley, 2010).

## Chapter 5  International Mobility of UK Students

1  The research informing this chapter includes: 1) Three questionnaire surveys of University of Sussex students in 2000–2001 (King and Ruiz-Gelices, 2003). The main survey was of (261) graduates who had spent a year abroad in Europe as part of their degree. 2) A report by the Sussex Centre for Migration Research, University of Sussex, and the Centre for Applied Population Research, University of Dundee (2004). This reported on a study that included institutional questionnaires from 80 UK HEIs, interviews with 46 academics and 'mobility managers', 1200 questionnaires from students and 180 interviews with students. 3) A British Academy-funded study (2007–2008) into the mobility of UK students. This study included in-depth interviews with 85 individuals – 40 seriously thinking about going overseas for a degree, and 45 having completed a

degree abroad. 4) A study funded by the UK Department for Business, Innovation and Skills (BIS), which included a metadata analysis of sources providing statistics on international student mobility; a survey of the application intentions of 1400 final-year pupils from schools in two regions of England, and a survey of 560 UK students currently enrolled for study at universities in the USA, Ireland, Australia, the Czech Republic, France and Germany (Finlay and King, 2010).

2 SATs are 'Scholastic Aptitude Tests', used for admission to universities in the United States.

3 Bourdieu (1984) uses 'habitus' in his work to describe the formative relationship between individuals and their socio-cultural environment. A group (usually class) 'identity' is inculcated through habit and everyday experiences in a way that is largely unconscious.

## Chapter 6    Geographies of Student Mobility

1 Although it should be noted that Bone (2010), in a recent report to the Department for Business, Innovation and Skills questions the reliability of these 'demographic' projections based, as they were, on 'the last 13 years or so [which] have seen an extraordinary expansion of global trade in general, and an extremely benign financial environment relatively speaking, neither of which can be relied upon in the future' (p.1).

# References

Ackers, L. (2010) 'The "Forceps" question: Understanding the dynamics of knowledge transfer and translation processes in North-South health care partnerships'. Presentation to the Spatial Mobility of Knowledge Symposium, 15–18 September, Heidelberg, Germany.

Alberts, H. and Hazen, H. (2005) '"There are always two voices...": International students' intentions to stay in the United States or return to their home countries', *International Migration*, 43, 3, 131–154.

Altbach, P. and Knight, J. (2007) 'The internationalization of higher education: Motivations and realities', *Journal of Studies in International Education*, 11, 3–4, 290–305.

Appadurai, A. (1996) *Modernity at Large: Cultural Dimensions of Globalisation*. Minneapolis: University of Minnesota Press.

Araujo, E. (2007) 'Why Portuguese students go abroad to do their PhDs', *Higher Education in Europe*, 32, 4, 387–397.

Archer, L. (2008) 'The new neoliberal subjects? Younger academics' constructions of academic identity', *Journal of Education Policy*, 23, 3, 265–285.

Arthur, M.B. and Rousseau, D.M. (1996) 'Introduction: The boundaryless career as a new employment principle', in Arthur, M.B. and Rousseau, D.M. (eds) *The Boundaryless Career: A New Employment Principle for a New Organizational Era*. New York: Oxford University Press, pp.3–20.

Baas, M. (2006) 'Students of migration: Indian overseas students and the question of permanent residency', *People and Place*, 14, 1, 9–24.

Baas, M. (2007) 'The language of migration: The education industry versus the migration industry', *People and Place*, 15, 2, 49–60.

Baláž, V. and Williams, A. (2004) '"Been there, done that": International student migration and human capital transfers from the UK to Slovakia', *Population, Space and Place*, 10, 217–237.

Ball, S. (2003) *Class Strategies and the Education Market: The Middle-Classes and Social Advantage*. London: Routledge Falmer.

Ball, S. (2007) 'Big policies/small world: An introduction to international perspectives in education policy', in Lingard, B. and Ozga, J. (eds) *The Routledge-Falmer Reader in Education Policy and Politics*. London: Routledge, pp.36–47.

Ball, S.J., Bowe, R. and Gewirtz, S. (1995) 'Circuits of schooling: A sociological exploration of parental choice of school in social-class contexts', *Sociological Review*, 43, 52–78.

Basch, L., Glick Schiller, N. and Szanton Blanc, C. (1994) *Nations Unbound: Transnational Projects, Postcolonial Predicaments, and Deterritorialized Nation-States*. Amsterdam: Gordon and Breach.

Baty, P. (2009a) 'Asia advances', *Times Higher Education*, 8 October 2009, iii–iv.

Baty, P. (2009b) 'China is set to demand respect', *Times Higher Education*, 29 October 2009, 5.

Baty, P. (2009c) 'The long march', *Times Higher Education*, 29 October 2009, 31–35.

Baty, P. (2009d) 'Mobility slows but EU wants many more to join Erasmus', *Times Higher Education*, 29 October 2009, 16–17.

BBC News (2009) 'More overseas students found', *BBC News Online*, http://news.bbc.co.uk/go/pr/fr/-/1/hi/education/8060219.stm (Accessed 21 May 2009).

Beaverstock, J.V. (1996) 'Migration, knowledge and social interaction: Expatriate labour within investment banks', *Area*, 28, 4, 459–470.

Beck, U. (1992) *Risk Society*. London: Sage.

Beck, U. (2002) 'The cosmopolitan society and its enemies', *Theory, Culture and Society*, 19, 1–2, 17–44.

Beck, U. and Beck-Gernsheim, E. (1995) *The Normal Chaos of Love*. Cambridge: Polity Press.

Birtwistle, T. (2007) 'European and European Union dimensions to mobility', in Jones, E. and Brown, S. (eds) *Internationalising Higher Education*. London: Routledge, pp.181–192.

Bodycott, P. (2009) 'Choosing a higher education study abroad destination. What mainland Chinese parents and students rate as important', *Journal of Research in International Education*, 8, 3, 349–373.

Bohr, Y. and Tse, C. (2009) 'Satellite babies in transnational families: A study of parents' decision to separate from their infants', *Infant Mental Health Journal*, 30, 3, 265–286.

Bondi, L. and Matthews, M.H. (1988) (eds) *Education and Society: Studies in the Politics, Sociology and Geography of Education*. London: Routledge.

Bone, D. (2010) *Internationalisation of HE: A Ten Year View*. Available online at: http://webarchive.nationalarchives.gov.uk/tna/+/http://www.bis.gov.uk/wp-content/uploads/2009/10/HE-Internationalisation-Bone.pdf/ (Accessed 13 September 2010).

Bourdieu, P. (1984) *Distinction: A Social Critique of the Judgement of Taste*. Cambridge, Massachusetts: Harvard University Press.

Bourdieu, P. (1986) 'The forms of capital', in Richardson, J.G. (ed.) *Handbook of Theory and Research for the Sociology of Education*. New York: Greenwood Press, pp.241–258.

Bourdieu, P. (1998) *Acts of Resistance*. Cambridge: Polity Press.

Bracht, O., Engel, C., Janson, K., Over, A., Schomburg, H. and Teichler, U. (2006) *The Professional Value of Erasmus Mobility*. Final report presented to the European Commission, Directorate-General Education and Culture.

Bradley, D., Noonan, P., Nugent, H. and Scales, B. (2008) *Review of Australian Higher Education: Final Report*. Commonwealth of Australia.

British Council (2004) *Vision 2020: Forecasting International Student Mobility*. Design Department.

British Council (2010) *British Council Annual Report, 2007–08*. Available online at: http://www.britishcouncil.org/annual-report/index.htm (Accessed 15 July 2010).

Brooks, R. (2005) *Friendship and Educational Choice. Peer Influence and Planning for the Future*. Basingstoke: Palgrave.

Brooks, R. (2007a) 'Government rhetoric and student understandings. Discursive framings of higher education "choice"', in Epstein, D., Boden, R., Deem, R., Rizvi, F. and Wright, S. (eds) *Geographies of Knowledge, Geometries of Power: Higher Education in the 21st Century* (World Year Book of Education 2008). New York: Routledge, pp.232–247.

Brooks, R. (2007b) 'Young people's extra-curricular activities: Critical social engagement – or "something for the CV"?', *Journal of Social Policy*, 36, 3, 417–434.

Brooks, R. and Everett, G. (2008) 'The prevalence of "life planning": Evidence from UK graduates', *British Journal of Sociology of Education*, 29, 3, 325–337.

Brooks, R. and Everett, G. (2009) 'Post-graduation reflections on the value of a degree', *British Educational Research Journal*, 35, 3, 333–349.

Brooks, R. and Waters, J. (2009a) 'A second chance at "success": UK students and global circuits of higher education', *Sociology*, 43, 6, 1085–1102.

Brooks, R. and Waters, J. (2009b) 'International higher education and the mobility of UK students', *Journal of Research in International Education*, 8, 2, 191–209.

Brooks, R. and Waters, J. (2010) 'Social networks and educational mobility: The experiences of UK students', *Globalisation, Societies and Education*, 8, 1, 143–157.

Brooks, R., Waters, J. and Pimlott-Wilson, H. (2012) 'International education and the employability of UK students', *British Educational Research Journal*, 38, 2, 281–298.

Brown, P. (1990) 'The "third wave": Education and the ideology of parentocracy', *British Journal of Sociology of Education*, 11, 1, 65–85.

Brown, P., Halsey, A.H., Lauder H. and Wells, A.S. (1997) 'The transformation of education: An introduction', pp. 1–44, in Halsey, A.H., Lauder, H., Brown, P. and Wells, A.S. (eds) *Education, Culture, Economy, Society*. Oxford: Oxford University Press.

Brown, P. and Hesketh, A. (2004) *The Mismanagement of Talent: Employability and Jobs in the Knowledge Economy*. Oxford: Oxford University Press.

Brown, P., Hesketh, A. and Williams, S. (2003) 'Employability in a knowledge-driven economy', *Journal of Education and Work*, 16, 107–126.

Brown, P. and Lauder, H. (2006) 'Globalisation, knowledge and the myth of the magnet economy', *Globalisation, Societies and Education*, 4, 1, 25–57.

Brown, P. and Lauder, H. (2009) 'Globalization, international education and the formation of a transnational class', in Popkewitz, T. and Rizvi, F. (eds) *Globalization and the Study of Education* (108th Yearbook of the National Society for the Study of Education). Malden, Massachusetts: Wiley-Blackwell, pp.130–147.

Brown, P. and Tannock, S. (2009) 'Education, meritocracy and the global war for talent', *Journal of Education Policy*, 24, 4, 377–392.

Brown, S. and Jones, E. (2007) 'Introduction: Values, valuing and value in an internationalised higher education context', in Jones, E. and Brown, S. (eds) *Internationalising Higher Education*. London: Routledge, pp.1–6.

Butcher, A. (2004) 'Educate, consolidate, immigrate: Educational immigration in Auckland, New Zealand', *Asia Pacific Viewpoint*, 45, 2, 255–278.

Butler, T. (2003) 'Living in the bubble: Gentrification and its "others" in North London', *Urban Studies*, 40, 12, 2469–2486.

Cammelli, A., Ghiselli, S. and Mignoli, G. (2008) 'Study experience abroad: Italian graduate characteristics and employment outcomes', in Byram, M. and Dervin, F. (eds) *Students, Staff and Academic Mobility in Higher Education*. Newcastle: Cambridge Scholars Publishing, pp.217–236.

Cantwell, B. and Maldonado-Maldonado, A. (2009) 'Four stories: Confronting contemporary ideas about globalisation and internationalisation in higher education', *Globalisation, Societies and Education*, 7, 3, 289–306.

Castells, M. (1996) *The Rise of the Network Society*. Oxford: Blackwell.

Castles, S. and Miller, M.J. (1993) *The Age of Migration: International Population Movements in the Modern World*. Basingstoke: Palgrave.

Castles, S. and Miller, M. (2009) *The Age of Migration: International Population Movements in the Modern World* (fourth edition). Basingstoke: Palgrave.

Caudery, T., Petersen, M. and Shaw, P. (2008) 'The motivation of exchange students at Scandinavian universities', in Byram, M. and Dervin, F. (eds) *Students, Staff and Academic Mobility in Higher Education*. Newcastle: Cambridge Scholars Publishing, pp.114–130.

Chew, P.G. (2010) 'Linguistic capital, study mothers and the transnational family in Singapore', in Vaish, V. (ed.) *Globalization of Language and Culture in Asia*. London: Continuum, pp.82–105.

Choi, P.K. (2010) '"Weep for the Chinese university": A case study of English hegemony and academic capitalism in higher education in Hong Kong', *Journal of Education Policy*, 25, 2, 233–252.

Chubb, J. and Moe, T. (1997) 'Politics, markets and the organisation of schools', in Halsey, A., Lauder, H., Brown, P. and Wells, A. (eds) *Education. Culture, Economy, Society*. Oxford: Oxford University Press, pp.363–381.

Clark, B. (1998) *Creating Entrepreneurial Universities: Organizational Pathways of Transformation*. Oxford: Pergamon Press.

Clark, T. (2006) 'A free lunch in Uppsala', *The Guardian*, 24 October 2006, 31.

Clayton, J., Crozier, G. and Reay, D. (2009) 'Home and away: Risk, familiarity and the multiple geographies of higher education experience', *International Studies in the Sociology of Education*, 19, 3–4, 157–174.

Clifford, V. (2009) 'Engaging the disciplines in internationalising the curriculum', *International Journal of Academic Development*, 14, 2, 133–143.

Coleman, J. (1988) 'Social capital in the creation of human capital', *American Journal of Sociology*, 94, S95–S120.

Collins, F. (2009) 'Transnationalism unbound: Detailing new subjects, registers and spatialities of cross-border lives', *Geography Compass*, 3, 1, 434–458.

Collins, F.L. (2004) '(Trans)national bodies, (trans)national languages, and the transformation of local urban space', *New Zealand Geographer*, 60, 52–59.

Collins, F.L. (2006) 'Making Asian students, making students Asian: The racialisation of export education in Auckland', New Zealand, *Asia Pacific Viewpoint*, 47, 2, 217–234.

Collins, F.L. (2008) 'Of *kimchi* and coffee: Globalisation, transnationalism and familiarity in culinary consumption', *Social and Cultural Geography*, 9, 2, 151–169.

Collins, F.L. (2010) 'Negotiating un/familiar embodiments: Investigating the corporeal dimensions of South Korean international student mobilities in Auckland, New Zealand', *Population, Space and Place*, 16, 1, 51–62.

Commission of the European Communities (CEC) (1989) *ERASMUS Programme. Annual Report 1988* (Brussels, COM (89) 192 final).

Commission of the European Communities (CEC) (1995) *Towards the Learning Society (White Paper)* COM (95) 590 Final. Brussels, Commission of the European Communities.

Commission of the European Communities (CEC) (2000) *Towards a European Research Area* COM (2000) 6 Final. Brussels, Commission of the European Communities.

Commission of the European Communities (CEC) (2002) *Commission's Action Plan for Skills and Mobility* COM (2002) 72 Final. Brussels, Commission of the European Communities.

Commission of the European Communities (CEC) (2009) *Promoting the Learning Mobility of Young People* COM (2009) 329 Final. Brussels, Commission of the European Communities.

Conradson, D. and Latham, A. (2005) 'Friendship, networks and transnationality in a world city: Antipodean transmigrants in London', *Journal of Ethnic and Migration Studies*, 31, 2, 287–305.

Cresswell, T. (2006) *On the Move*. London: Routledge.

Crossman, J. and Clarke, M. (2010) 'International experience and graduate employability: Stakeholder perceptions on the connection', *Higher Education*, 59, 5, 599–613.

Curtis, P. (2009) 'Universities facing new cash crisis and job cuts', *The Guardian*, 21 November 2009, 13.

Deem, R. (2001) 'Globalisation, new managerialism, academic capitalism and entrpreneurialism in universities', *Comparative Education*, 37, 1, 7–20.

Department for Education and Skills (DfES) (2006) *Prime Minister Launches Strategy to Make UK Leader in International Education*. Press Notice 2006/0058, 18 April 2006.

Desforges, L. (2000) 'Travelling the world. Identity and travel biography', *Annals of Tourism Research*, 27, 4, 926–945.

Deumert, A., Marginson, S., Nyland, C., Ramia, G. and Sawir, E. (2005) 'Global migration and social protection rights. The social and economic security of cross-border students in Australia', *Global Social Policy*, 5, 3, 329–352.

Dicken, P. (2003) *Global Shift: Reshaping the Global Economic Map in the 21st Century* (fourth edition). London: Sage.

Dillabough, J., Kennelly, J. and Wang, E. (2007) 'Warehousing young people in urban Canadian schools: Gender, peer rivalry, and spatial containment', in Gulson, K. and Symes, C. (eds) *Spatial Theories of Education: Policy and Geography Matters*. New York: Routledge, pp.131–154.

Doherty, C. and Singh, P. (2005) 'How the West is done: Simulating Western pedagogy in a curriculum for Asian international students', in Ninnes, P. and Hellsten, M. (eds) *Internationalising Higher Education. Critical Explorations of Pedagogy and Policy*. Hong Kong: Springer.

Dolby, N. and Rizvi, F. (2008) 'Introduction. Youth, mobility and identity', in Dolby, N. and Rizvi, F. (eds) *Youth Moves*. New York: Routledge, pp.1–14.

Education Bureau (2007) *Other Education and Training*, http://www.edb.gov.hk (Accessed 5 February 2008).

Edwards, R. and Usher, R. (2008) *Globalisation and Pedagogy: Space, Place and Identity* (second edition). Oxford: Routledge.

Ehrenreich, S. (2008) '"Teaching for residence abroad": Blending synchronic and diachronic perspectives on the assistant year abroad', in Byram, M. and Dervin, F. (eds) *Students, Staff and Academic Mobility in Higher Education*. Newcastle: Cambridge Scholars Publishing, pp.65–81.

Elliott, A. and Urry, J. (2010) *Mobile Lives*. London: Routledge.

Ertl, H. (2006) 'European Union policies in education and training: The Lisbon agenda as turning point?', *Comparative Education*, 42, 1, 5–27.

Faggian, A., McCann, P. and Sheppard, S. (2007) 'Some evidence that women are more mobile than men: Gender differences in UK graduate migration behaviour', *Journal of Regional Science*, 47, 3, 517–539.

Favell, A. (2006) 'London as Eurocity: French free movers in the economic capital of Europe', in Smith, M. and Favell, A. (eds) *The Human Face of Global Mobility*. New Brunswick: Transaction Publishers, pp.247–274.

Favell, A. (2008) *Eurostars and Eurocities. Free Movement and Mobility in an Integrating Europe*. Oxford: Blackwell Publishing.

Favell, A., Feldblum, M. and Smith, M. (2008) 'The human face of global mobility: A research agenda', in Smith, M. and Favell, A. (eds) *The Human Face of Global Mobility*. New Brunswick: Transaction Publishers, pp.1–25.

Fearn, H. (2010) 'Extreme make-over', *Times Higher Education*, 4 February 2010, 38–41.

Fielden, J. (2007) *Global Horizons for UK Students: A Guide for Universities*. London: The Council for Industry and Higher Education. Available online at: http://www.cihe.co.uk/category/knowledge/publications/ (Accessed 13 September 2010).

Fincher, R. and Costello, L. (2003) 'Housing ethnicity: Multicultural negotiation and housing the transnational student', in Yeoh, B., Cherney, M. and Kiong, T. (eds) *Approaching Transnationalisms: Studies on Transnational Societies, Multicultural Contacts and Imaginings of Home*. Boston, MA: Kluwer, pp.161–186.

Fincher, R. and Shaw, K. (2009) 'The unintended segregation of transnational students in central Melbourne', *Environment and Planning A*, 41, 8, 1884–1902.

Findlay, A. and King, R. (2010) *Motivations and Experiences of UK Students Studying Abroad*. BIS Research Paper No. 8. London: Department for Business, Innovation and Skills.

Findlay, A., King, R., Stam, A. and Ruiz-Gelices, E. (2006) 'Ever reluctant Europeans: The changing geographies of UK students studying and working abroad', *European Urban and Regional Studies*, 13, 4, 291–318.

Fine, R. (2007) *Cosmopolitanism*. London: Routledge.

Fitzpatrick, T. (2001) *Welfare Theory: An Introduction*. Basingstoke: Palgrave.

Fukuyama, F. (1992) *The End of History and the Last Man*. New York: Free Press.

Gargano, T. (2009) '(Re)conceptualizing international student mobility: The potential of transnational social fields', *Journal of Studies in International Education* 13, 3, 331–346.

Ghosh, S. and Wang, L. (2003) 'Transnationalism and identity: A tale of two faces and multiple lives', *Canadian Geographer/Le Géographe Canadien*, 47, 3, 269–282.

Gibson, A. and Asthana, S. (1998a) 'School performance, school effectiveness and the 1997 White Paper', *Oxford Review of Education*, 24, 2, 195–211.

Gibson, A. and Asthana, S. (1998b) 'School pupils and examination results: Contextualising school "performance"', *British Educational Research Journal*, 24, 3, 269–283.

Gibson, A. and Asthana, S. (2000) 'Local markets and the polarization of public-sector schools in England and Wales', *Transactions of the Institute of British Geographers*, 25, 303–319.

Giddens, A. (1991) *Modernity and Self-identity: Self and Society in the Late Modern Age*. Cambridge: Polity Press.

Giddens, A. (1999) *Runaway World*. London: Profile Books.

Glick Schiller, N. and Fouron, G. (1999) 'Terrains of blood and nation: Haitian transnational social fields', *Ethnic and Racial Studies*, 22, 340–361.

Gogia, N. (2006) 'Unpacking corporeal mobilities: The global voyages of labour and leisure', *Environment and Planning A*, 38, 359–375.

Green, A. (2003) 'Education, globalisation and the role of comparative research', *London Review of Education*, 1, 2, 83–97.

Green, A. (2006) 'Education, globalization and the nation-state', in Lauder, H., Brown, P., Dillabough, J. and Halsey, A. (eds) *Education, Globalization and Social Change*. Oxford: Oxford University Press, pp.192–197.

Gribble, C. (2008) 'Policy options for managing international student migration: The sending country's perspective', *Journal of Higher Education Policy and Management*, 30, 1, 25–39.

Gulson, K. and Symes, C. (eds) (2007) *Spatial Theories of Education: Policy and Geography Matters*. New York: Routledge.

Gurría, A. (2009) *The New Dynamics of Higher Education and Research for Societal Change and Development*. Speech to the UNESCO World Conference on Higher Education, UNESCO, Paris, 5 July 2009.

Guth, J. and Gill, B. (2008) 'Motivations in East-West doctoral mobility: Revisiting the question of brain drain', *Journal of Ethnic and Migration Studies*, 34, 5, 825–841.

Habu, T. (2000) 'The irony of globalization: The experience of Japanese women in British higher education', *Higher Education*, 39, 1, 43–66.

Hannerz, U. (1996) *Transnational Connections: Culture, People, Places*. New York: Routledge.

Hanson Thiem, C. (2008) 'Thinking through education: The geographies of contemporary educational restructuring', *Progress in Human Geography*, 33, 154–173.

Harvey, D. (1989) *The Condition of Postmodernity*. Oxford: Blackwell.

Hayden, M., Rancic, B.A. and Thompson, J.J. (2000) 'Being international: Student and teacher perceptions from international schools', *Oxford Review of Education*, 26, 1, 107–123.

Hazelkorn, E. (2009) 'Rankings and the battle for world class excellence: Institutional strategies and policy choice', *Higher Education Management and Policy*, 21, 1, 1–22.

Hazen, H. and Alberts, H. (2006) 'Visitors or immigrants? International students in the United States', *Population, Space and Place*, 12, 201–216.

Heath, S. (2007) 'Widening the gap: Pre-university gap years and the "economy of experience"', *British Journal of Sociology of Education*, 28, 1, 89–103.

Held, D. and McGrew, A. (eds) (2005) *The Global Transformation Reader: An Introduction to the Globalisation Debate* (3rd edition). Cambridge: Polity Press.

Henry, M., Lingard, B., Rizvi, F. and Taylor, S. (2001) *The OECD, Globalization and Education Policy*. Oxford: Pergamon.

Herbert, D.T. (2000) 'School choice in the local environment', *School Leadership and Management*, 20, 79–97.

Hirst, P. and Thompson, G. (1996) *Globalisation in Question*. Cambridge: Polity.

Ho, E. (2002) 'Multi-local residence, transnational networks: Chinese "astronaut" families in New Zealand', *Asian and Pacific Migration Journal*, 11, 1, 145–164.

Holdsworth, C. (2009) '"Going away to uni": Mobility, modernity, and independence of English higher education students', *Environment and Planning A*, 41, 20, 1849–1864.

Holloway, S., Hubbard, P., Jöns, H. and Pimlott-Wilson, H. (2010) 'Geographies of education and the significance of children, youth and families', *Progress in Human Geography*. Online Advance Publication.

House of Commons Home Affairs Select Committee (2009) *Bogus Colleges. Eleventh Report of Session 2008–09*. Available online at: www.publications. parliament.uk/pa/cm200809/cmslect/cmhaff/595/595.pdf (Accessed 5 August 2010).

Huang, S. and Yeoh, B. (2005) 'Transnational families and their children's education: China's "study mothers" in Singapore', *Global Networks*, 5, 4, 379–400.

Hunt-Grabbe, C. (2010) 'Why British students are flocking to America', *The Sunday Times*, 31 January 2010.

International Focus (2009a) *International Focus: 04/02/09*. London, UK HE International Unit. Available online at: http://www.international.ac.uk/resources/ International%20Focus%20issue%2032.04.02.09.pdf (Accessed 7 February 2009).

International Focus (2009b) *International Focus: 03/06/09*. London, UK HE International Unit. Available online at: http://www.international.ac.uk/resources/ International%20Focus%20issue%2039.03.06.09.pdf (Accessed 5 June 2009).

Jackling, B. (2007) 'The lure of permanent residence and the aspirations and expectations of international students studying accounting in Australia', *People and Place*, 15, 3, 31–41.

Jarvis, P. (2000) 'Globalisation, the learning society and comparative education', *Comparative Education*, 36, 3, 343–355.

Jones, E. and Brown, S. (eds) (2007) *Internationalising Higher Education*. London: Routledge.

Jöns, H. (2009) '"Brain circulation" and transnational knowledge networks: Studying long-term effects of academic mobility to Germany', 1954–2000, *Global Networks*, 9, 315–338.

Kearney, M. (1991) 'Borders and boundaries of state and self at the end of empire', *Journal of Historical Sociology*, 4, 539–561.

Keating, A. (2009) 'Educating Europe's citizens: Moving from national to post-national models of educating for European citizenship', *Citizenship Studies*, 13, 2, 135–151.

Kelly, A. (2009) 'Globalisation and education: A review of conflicting perspectives and their effect on policy and practice in the UK', *Globalisation, Societies and Education*, 7, 1, 51–68.

Kelo, M., Teichler, U. and Wachter, B. (eds) (2006) *Eurodata – Student Mobility in European Higher Education*. Bonn: Lemmens Verlags.

Kenway, J. (1992) *Marketing Education in the Post-Modern Age*, Paper to the AARE Conference, San Francisco.

Kenway, J. and Bullen, E. (2008) 'The global corporate curriculum and the young cyberflâneur as global citizen', in Dolby, N. and Rizvi, F. (eds) *Youth Moves*. New York: Routledge, pp.17–32.

Kenway, J. and Fahey, J. (2007) 'Policy incitements to mobility: Some speculations and provocations', in Epstein, D., Boden, R., Deem, R., Rizvi, F. and Wright, S. (eds) *Geographies of Knowledge, Geometries of Power: Higher Education in the 21st Century (World Year Book of Education 2008)*. New York: Routledge, pp.161–179.

Kim, J. (2010) '"Downed" and stuck in Singapore: Lower/middle class South Korean wild geese (*kirogi*) children in Singapore', *Research in Sociology of Education*, 17, 271–311.

King, R. (2003) 'International student migration in Europe and the institutionalisation of identity as "Young Europeans"', in Doomernik, J. and Knippenberg, H. (eds) *Migration and Immigrants: Between Policy and Reality*. Amsterdam: Askant, pp.155–179.

King, R. and Ruiz-Gelices, E. (2003) 'International student migration and the European "year-abroad": Effects on European identity and subsequent migration behaviour', *International Journal of Population Geography*, 9, 3, 229–252.

Knight, J. (2004) 'Internationalization remodeled: Definition, approaches, rationales', *Journal of Studies in International Education*, 8, 1, 5–31.

Kobayashi, A. and Preston, V. (2007) 'Transnationalism through the life course: Hong Kong immigrants in Canada', *Asia Pacific Viewpoint*, 48, 2, 151–167.

Kraftl, P. (2006) 'Ecological architecture as performed art: Nant-y-Cwn Steiner School, Pembrokeshire', *Social and Cultural Geography*, 7, 927–948.

Krzaklewska, E. (2008) 'Why study abroad? An analysis of Erasmus students' motivations', in Byram, M. and Dervin, F. (eds) *Students, Staff and Academic Mobility in Higher Education*. Newcastle: Cambridge Scholars Publishing, pp.82–98.

Kymlicka, W. and Norman, W. (1994) 'Return of the citizen: A survey of recent work on citizenship theory', *Ethics*, 104, 2, 352–381.

Lam, T., Yeoh, B. and Law, L. (2002) 'Sustaining families transnationally: Chinese-Malaysians in Singapore', *Asian and Pacific Migration Journal*, 11, 1, 117–144.

Lanzendorf, U. (2006) 'Inwards and outwards European students', in Kelo, M., Teichler, U. and Wachter, B. (eds) *Eurodata – Student Mobility in European Higher Education*. Bonn: Lemmens Verlags, pp.54–77.

Lauder, H. and Hughes, D. (1999) *Trading in Futures: Why Markets in Education Don't Work*. Buckingham: Open University Press.

Leathwood, C. and Read, B. (2009) *Gender and the Changing Face of Higher Education. A Feminised Future?* Buckingham: SRHE and Open University Press.

Lee, J. and Kim, D. (2010) 'Brain gain or brain circulation? US doctoral recipients returning to South Korea', *Higher Education*, 59, 627–643.

Lee, Y. and Koo, H. (2006) '"Wild geese fathers" and a globalised family strategy for education in Korea', *IDPR*, 28, 4, 533–553.

Lewis, N. (2005) 'Code of practice for the pastoral care of international students: Making a globalising industry in New Zealand', *Globalisation, Societies and Education*, 3, 5–47.

Ley, D. (2010) *Millionaire Migrants: Trans-Pacific Lifelines*. RGS-IBG Book Series. Oxford: Wiley-Blackwell.

Ley, D. and Kobayashi, A. (2005) 'Back to Hong Kong: Return migration or transnational sojourn?', *Global Networks*, 5, 2, 111–127.

Li, L., Findlay, A., Jowett, A. and Skeldon, R. (1996) 'Migrating to learn and learning to migrate', *International Journal of Population Geography*, 2, 51–67.

Louie, V. (2004) *Compelled to Excel: Immigration, Education and Opportunity among Chinese Americans*. Stanford: Stanford University Press.

Lowell, B.L. and Findlay, A. (2001) *Migration of Highly Skilled Persons from Developing Countries: Impact and Policy Responses* (International Migration Papers 44). Geneva: International Labour Office.

Madge, C., Raghuram, P. and Noxolo, P. (2009) 'Engaged pedagogy and responsibility: A postcolonial analysis of international students', *Geoforum*, 40, 34–45.

Maiworm, F. (2001) 'ERASMUS: Continuity and change in the 1990s', *European Journal of Education*, 36, 4, 459–472.

Man, G. (1995) 'The experience of women in Chinese immigrant families: An inquiry into institutional and organizational processes', *Asian and Pacific Migration Journal*, 4, 2–3, 303–327.

Marginson, S. (2007) 'Have global academic flows created a global labour market?', in Epstein, D., Boden, R., Deem, R., Rizvi, F. and Wright, S. (eds) *Geographies of Knowledge, Geometries of Power: Higher Education in the 21st Century (World Year Book of Education 2008)*. New York: Routledge, pp.305–318.

Marginson, S. (2008) 'Global field and global imagining: Bourdieu and worldwide higher education', *British Journal of Sociology of Education*, 29, 3, 303–315.

Marginson, S. and Rhoades, G. (2002) 'Beyond national states, markets and systems of higher education: A glonacal agency heuristic', *Higher Education*, 43, 281–309.

Marginson, S. and van der Wende, M. (2007) 'To rank or to be ranked: The impact of global rankings in higher education', *Journal of Studies in International Education*, 11, 3–4, 306–329.

Massey, D. (1993) 'Power-geometry and a progressive sense of place', in Bird, J., Curtis, B., Putnam, T., Robertson, G. and Tickner, L. (eds) *Mapping the Futures: Local Cultures, Global Change*. London: Routledge, pp.59–69.

Massey, D. (2005) *For Space*. London: Sage.

Matsuura, K. (2009) *The New Dynamics of Higher Education and Research for Societal Change and Development*. Address to the opening ceremony of the 2009 World Conference on Higher Education, 5 July 2009.

Matthews, J. and Sidhu, R. (2005) 'Desperately seeking the global subject: International education, citizenship and cosmopolitanism', *Globalisation, Societies and Education*, 3, 1, 49–66.

Mazlish, B. and Morss, E. (2005) 'A global elite?', in Chandler, A. and Mazlish, B. (eds) *Leviathans. Multinational Corporations and the New Global History*. Cambridge: Cambridge University Press, pp.167–186.

McBurnie, G. and Ziguras, C. (2001) 'The regulation of transnational education in South East Asia', *Higher Education*, 42, 85–105.

Mitchell, K. (1997) 'Transnational subjects: Constituting the cultural citizen in the era of Pacific Rim capital', in Ong, A. and Nonini, D. (eds) *Ungrounded Empires: The Cultural Politics of Modern Chinese Transnationalism*. New York: Routledge, pp.228–256.

Mitchell, K. (2003) 'Educating the national citizen in neo-liberal times: From the multicultural self to the strategic cosmopolitan', *Transactions of the Institute of British Geographers*, 28, 387–403.

Montgomery, C. and McDowell, L. (2009) 'Social networks and the international student experience: An international community of practice?', *Journal of Studies in International Education*, 13, 4, 455–466.

Montsios, S. (2009) 'International organisations and transnational education policy', *Compare*, 39, 4, 469–481.

Morano-Foadi, S. (2005) 'Scientific mobility, career progression, and excellence in the European research area', *International Migration*, 43, 5, 133–160.

Morgan, J. (2010) 'Hong Kong academy set to take a great leap forward', *Times Higher Education*, 8 April 2010, 19–20.

Morrison, J., Merrick, B., Higgs, S. and Le Metais, J. (2005) 'Researching the performance of international students in the UK', *Studies in Higher Education*, 30, 3, 327–337.

Murphy-Lejeune, E. (2002) *Student Mobility and Narrative in Europe. The New Strangers*. London: Routledge.

Murphy-Lejeune, E. (2008) 'The student experience of mobility, a contrasting score', in Byram, M. and Dervin, F. (eds) *Students, Staff and Academic Mobility in Higher Education*. Newcastle: Cambridge Scholars Publishing, pp.12–30.

Musselin, C. (2004) 'Towards a European labour market? Some lessons drawn from empirical studies on academic mobility', *Higher Education*, 48, 55–78.

Naidoo, V. (2006) 'International education. A tertiary-level industry update', *Journal of Research in International Education*, 5, 3, 323–345.

Ning, Q. (2002) *Chinese Students Encounter America*. Aberdeen: Hong Kong University Press.

Nordheimer, J. and Frantz, D. (1997) 'Testing giant exceeds roots, drawing business rivals' ire', *New York Times*, 30 September 1997.

Norman, P. (2010) 'Sham wedding and bogus college crackdown', *Sky News Online*, 23 July 2010. Available online at: http://news.sky.com/skynews/Home/Politics/ Immigration-Minister-Confirms-Crackdown-On-Sham-Marriages-And-Bogus-Colleges/Article/201007415669445 (Accessed 5 August 2010).

Oakman, D. (2005) *Facing Asia: A History of the Colombo Plan*. Canberra: Australian National University Press.

OECD (2007) *Education at a Glance*. Paris: OECD Publications.

OECD (2009) *Education at a Glance*. Paris: OECD Publications.

Olds, K. (2007a) 'Global assemblage: Singapore, foreign universities and the creation of a "global education hub"', *World Development*, 35, 6, 959–975.

Olds, K. (2007b) *The Ripple Effects of the Bologna Process in the Asia-Pacific*. Available online at: http://globalhighered.wordpress.com/2007/09/29/the-ripple-effects-of-the-bologna-process-in-the-asia-pacific (Accessed 5 August 2010).

Olero, M. and McCoshan, A. (2006) *Survey of the Socio-Economic Background of Erasmus Students*. DG EAC 01/05, European Commission.

Olssen, M. (2006) 'Neoliberalism, globalization, democracy: Challenges for education', in Lauder, H., Brown, P., Dillabough, J. and Halsey, A. (eds) *Education, Globalization and Social Change*. Oxford: Oxford University Press, pp.261–287.

Ong, A. (1999) *Flexible Citizenship: The Cultural Logics of Transnationality*. Durham: Duke University Press.

Ong, A. and Nonini, D. (eds) (1997) *Ungrounded Empires: The Cultural Politics of Modern Chinese Transnationalism*. New York: Routledge.

Ono, H. and Piper, N. (2004) 'Japanese women studying abroad, the case of the United States', *Women's Studies International Forum*, 27, 101–118.

Orellana, M., Thorne, B., Chee, A. and Lam, W. (2001) 'Transnational childhoods: The participation of children in processes of family migration', *Social Problems*, 48, 4, 572–591.

Ozga, J. and Lingard, B. (2007) 'Globalisation, education policy and politics', in Lingard, B. and Ozga, J. (eds) *The RoutledgeFalmer Reader in Education Policy and Politics*. London: Routledge, pp.65–82.

Page, R. and Silburn, R. (1999) *British Social Welfare in the Twentieth Century.* Basingstoke: Palgrave.

Pandit, K. (2009) 'Leading internationalization', *Annals of the Association of American Geographers*, 99, 4, 645–656.

Papatsiba, V. (2005) 'Political and individual rationales of student mobility: A case-study of ERASMUS and a French regional scheme for studies abroad', *European Journal of Education*, 40, 2, 173–188.

Papatsiba, V. (2006) 'Making higher education more European through student mobility? Revisiting EU initiatives in the context of the Bologna Process', *Comparative Education*, 42, 1, 93–111.

Parekh, B. (2003) 'Cosmopolitanism and global citizenship', *Review of International Studies*, 29, 3–17.

Park, H. (2010) 'The stranger that is welcomed: Female foreign students from Asia, the English language industry, and the ambivalence of "Asia rising" in British Columbia, Canada', *Gender, Place and Culture*, 17, 3, 337–355.

Park, J. and Bae, S. (2009) 'Language ideologies in educational migration: Korean *jogi yuhak* families in Singapore', *Linguistics and Education*, 20, 366–377.

Paunescu, M. (2008) 'Students' perspectives upon their mobility: The experiences of Romanian, Polish and Bulgarian outgoing students', in Byram, M. and Dervin, F. (eds) *Students, Staff and Academic Mobility in Higher Education.* Newcastle: Cambridge Scholars Publishing, pp.184–203.

Peck, J. and Tickell, A. (2006) 'Conceptualising neoliberalism, thinking Thatcherism', in Leitner, H., Peck, J. and Sheppard, E. (eds) *Contesting Neoliberalism: Urban Frontiers.* New York: Guilford Press, pp.26–50.

Pe-Pua, R., Mitchell, C., Iredale, R. and Castles, S. (1996) *Astronaut Families and Parachute Children: The Cycle of Migration between Hong Kong and Australia.* Wollongong, Centre for Multicultural Studies: University of Wollongong.

Philips, D. (2006) 'Mapping the European Union agenda in education and training policy', *Comparative Education*, 42, 1, 1–4.

Popkewitz, T. and Rizvi, F. (2009) 'Globalization and the study of education: An introduction', in Popkewitz, T. and Rizvi, F. (eds) *Globalization and the Study of Education (108ᵗʰ Yearbook of the National Society for the Study of Education).* Malden, Massachusetts: Wiley-Blackwell, pp.7–28.

Prague Communiqué (2002) *Prague Summit of the European Ministers of Higher Education*, May 18–19, 2002.

The Quality Assurance Agency for Higher Education (QAA) (2007) *Institutional Review Reports – By Overseas Country.* Available online at: http://www.qaa.ac.uk/reviews/ reports/btoseascountry.asp (Accessed 31 January 2008).

Raikou, N. and Karalis, T. (2007) 'Student mobility from a Greek perspective: Benefits and difficulties as expressed by the participating students', *Higher Education in Europe*, 32, 4, 347–357.

Reay, D., David, M. and Ball, S. (2005) *Degrees of Choice: Social Class, Race and Gender in Higher Education.* London: Trentham Books.

Recchi, E. (2006) 'From migrants to movers: Citizenship and mobility in the European Union', in Smith, M. and Favell, A. (eds) *The Human Face of Global Mobility.* New Brunswick: Transaction Publishers, pp.53–77.

Rivza, B. and Teichler, U. (2007) 'The changing role of student mobility', *Higher Education Policy*, 20, 457–475.

Rizvi, F. (2000) 'International education and the production of global imagination', in Burbules, N. and Torres, C. (eds) *Globalisation and Education. Critical Perspectives.* New York: Routledge, pp.205–225.

Rizvi, F. (2009) 'Global mobility and the challenges of educational research and policy', in Popkewitz, T. and Rizvi, F. (eds) *Globalization and the Study of Education (108th Yearbook of the National Society for the Study of Education).* Malden, Massachusetts: Wiley-Blackwell, pp.268–289.

Rizvi, F. and Lingard, B. (2006) 'Globalisation and the changing role of the OECD's educational work', in Lauder, H., Brown, P., Dillabough, J. and Halsey, A. (eds) *Education, Globalization and Social Change.* Oxford: Oxford University Press, pp.247–260.

Rizvi, F. and Lingard, B. (2010) *Globalizing Education Policy.* London: Routledge.

Roberts, A., Chou, P. and Ching, G. (2010) 'Contemporary trends in East Asian higher education: Dispositions of international students in a Taiwan university', *Higher Education*, 59, 149–166.

Robertson, Shanthi (2009) 'Student switchers and the regulation of residency: The interface of the individual and Australia's immigration regime', *Population, Space and Place* (Advance online publication).

Robertson, Susan (2005) 'Re-imagining and rescripting the future of education: Global knowledge economy discourses and the challenge to education systems', *Comparative Education*, 41, 151–170.

Robertson, Susan (2009) 'Europe, competitiveness and higher education: An evolving project', in Dale, R. and Robertson, S. (eds) *Globalisation and Europeanisation in Education.* Oxford: Symposium Books, pp.65–83.

Robinson-Pant, A. (2009) 'Changing academies: Exploring international PhD students' perspectives on "host" and "home" universities', *Higher Education Research and Development*, 28, 4, 417–429.

Robison, R. and Goodman, D.S.G. (1996) (eds) *The New Rich in Asia; Mobile Phones, McDonalds and Middle-Class Revolution.* London and New York: Routledge.

Rouse, R. (1995) 'Questions of identity: Personhood and collectivity in transnational migration to the United States', *Critique of Anthropology*, 15, 4, 351–380.

Rubenson, K. (2008) 'OECD educational policies and world hegemony', in Mahon, R. and McBride, S. (eds) *The OECD and Transnational Governance.* Vancouver: British Columbia University Press, pp.293–314.

Salt, J. (2005) *Current Trends in International Migration in Europe.* CDMG (2005) 2 Council of Europe.

Savage, M., Bagnall, G. and Longhurst, B. (2005) *Globalization and Belonging.* London: Sage.

Scott, S. and Cartledge, K. (2009) 'Migrant assimilation in Europe: A transnational family affair', *International Migration Review*, 43, 1, 60–89.

Seth, M. (2002) *Education Fever: Society, Politics, and the Pursuit of Schooling in South Korea.* Hawai'i: University of Hawai'i Press.

Sheller, M. and Urry, J. (2006) 'The new mobilities paradigm', *Environment and Planning A*, 38, 207–226.

Shepherd, J. (2006) 'UK students drawn to US for broad-based degrees', *Times Higher Education Supplement*, 4 August 2006, 1.

Sidhu, R. (2006) *Universities and Globalization: To Market, To Market.* New Jersey: Laurence Erlbaum Associates Ltd.

Sidhu, R. (2009) 'Running to stay still in the knowledge economy', *Journal of Education Policy*, 24, 3, 237–253.

Sin, I.L. (2006) 'Malaysian students in Australia: The pursuit of upward mobility', *Asian and Pacific Migration Journal*, 15, 2, 239–266.

Sin, I.L. (2009) 'The aspiration for social distinction: Malaysian students in a British university', *Studies in Higher Education*, 34, 3, 285–299.

Singh, P. and Doherty, C. (2008) 'Mobile students in liquid modernity: Negotiating the politics of transnational identities', in Dolby, N. and Rizvi, F. (eds) *Youth Moves. Identities and Education in Global Perspective*. New York: Routledge, pp.115–130.

Singh, M., Rizvi, F. and Shrestha, M. (2007) 'Student mobility and the spatial production of cosmopolitan identities', in Gulson, K. and Symes, C. (eds) *Spatial Theories of Education. Policy and Geography Matters*. New York: Routledge, pp.195–214.

Skeldon, R. (ed.) (1994) *Reluctant Exiles? Migration from Hong Kong and the New Overseas Chinese*. Armonk NY: M.E. Sharpe.

Sklair, L. (2001) *The Transnational Capitalist Class*. Oxford: Blackwell.

Sklair, L. (2010) *The Emancipatory Potential of Generic Globalisation*, Presentation to the Sociology Department, University of Surrey, January.

Slaughter, S. and Leslie, L. (1997) *Academic Capitalism: Politics, Policies and the Entrepreneurial University*. Baltimore: John Hopkins University Press.

Smith, A. (2006) 'Harvard launches UK state school recruitment drive', *Education Guardian*, 30 October 2006.

Stoer, S. and Cortesao, L. (2000) 'Multiculturalism and educational policy in a global context (European perspectives)', in Burbules, N. and Torres, C. (eds) *Globalisation and Education: Critical Perspectives*. New York: Routledge, pp.253–274.

Sussex Centre for Migration Research (2004) *International Student Mobility*. Brighton: Sussex Centre for Migration Research.

Szelényi, K. (2006) 'Students without borders? Migratory decision-making among international graduate students in the US', in Smith, M. and Favell, A. (eds) *The Human Face of Global Mobility*. New Brunswick, NJ: Transaction Publishers, pp.181–209.

Tang, N. and Nollent, A. (2007) *UK-China-Hong Kong Trans-national Education Project*. Sheffield: Sheffield Hallam University/British Council.

Taylor, C. (2002) *Geography of the 'New' Education Market. Secondary School Choice in England and Wales*. Aldershot: Ashgate.

Teichler, U. (1996) 'Student mobility in the Framework of ERASMUS: Findings of an evaluation study', *European Journal of Education*, 31, 2, 153–179.

Teichler, U. (2001) 'Changes of ERASMUS under the umbrella of SOCRATES', *Journal of Studies in International Education*, 5, 3, 201–227.

Teichler, U. (2004a) 'Temporary study abroad: The life of ERASMUS students', *European Journal of Education*, 39, 4, 395–408.

Teichler, U. (2004b) 'The changing debate on internationalisation of higher education', *Higher Education*, 48, 5–26.

Teo, S.Y. (2007) 'Vancouver's newest Chinese diaspora: Settlers or "immigrant prisoners"?', *GeoJournal*, 68, 2–3, 211–222.

THE (Times Higher Education) (2010) 'News in brief', *Times Higher Education*, 9–15 September 2010, 18.

Tickell, A. and Peck, J. (2003) 'Making global rules: Globalization or neoliberalism?', in Peck, J. and Yeung, H. (eds) *Remaking the Global Economy: Economic-Geographical Perspectives*. London: Sage, pp.163–181.

Tsoukalas, I. (2008) 'The double life of Erasmus students', in Byram, M. and Dervin, F. (eds) *Students, Staff and Academic Mobility in Higher Education*. Newcastle: Cambridge Scholars Publishing, pp.131–152.

Turner, B. (2002) 'Cosmopolitan virtue, globalization and patriotism', *Theory, Culture and Society*, 19, 1–2, 45–63.

UCAS (2009) *Statistics Online*. Available online at: http://www.ucas.ac.uk/about_us/stat_services/stats_online (Accessed 11 April 2010).

University of Hong Kong (2010) *Enhancing the Student Learning Experience*. Available online at: http://www3.hku.hk/strategic-development/eng/strategic-themes-for-09-14/enhancing-the-student-learning-experience.php (Accessed 6 August 2010).

Urry, J. (2007) *Mobilities*. Cambridge: Polity Press.

Usher, R. and Edwards, R. (1994) *Postmodernism and Education: Different Voices, Different Worlds*. London: Routledge.

Venn, C. (2002) 'Altered states: Post-enlightenment cosmopolitanism and trans-modern socialities', *Theory, Culture and Society*, 19, 1–2, 65–80.

Vertovec, S. (1999) 'Conceiving and researching transnationalism', *Journal of Ethnic and Racial Studies*, 22, 2, 447–462.

Vertovec, S. (2004) 'Cheap calls: The social glue of migrant transnationalism', *Global Networks*, 4, 2, 219–224.

Vickers, M. (1994) 'Cross-national exchange, the OECD and Australian education policy', *Knowledge, Technology and Policy*, 71, 25–47.

Vincent, C. and Ball, S. (2006) *Childcare, Choice and Class Practices: Middle-class Parents and Their Children*. London: Routledge.

Vlk, A., Westerheijden, D. and van der Wende, M. (2008) 'GATS and the steering capacity of a nation state in higher education: Case studies of the Czech Republic and the Netherlands', *Globalisation, Societies and Education*, 6, 1, 33–54.

Wächter, B. (2003) 'An introduction: Internationalisation at home in context', *Journal of Studies in International Education*, 7, 1, 5–11.

Wächter, B. and Wuttig, S. (2006) 'Student mobility in European programmes', in Kelo, M., Teichler, U. and Wächter, B. (eds) (2006) *Eurodata – Student Mobility in European Higher Education*. Bonn: Lemmens Verlags, pp.62–181.

Wacquant, L. (1996) 'Prologue (p. iv)', in Bourdieu, P. *The State Nobility: Elite Schools in the Field of Power*. Stanford, California: Stanford University Press.

Warrington, M. (2005) 'Mirage in the desert? Access to educational opportunities in an area of social exclusion', *Antipode*, 37, 766–816.

Waters, J. and Brooks, R. (2010a) 'Accidental achievers? International higher education, class reproduction and privileged in the experiences of UK students overseas', *British Journal of Sociology of Education*, 31, 2, 217–228.

Waters, J. and Brooks, R. (2010b) '"Vive la différence"? The "international" experiences of UK students overseas', *Population, Space and Place* (Advance online publication).

Waters, J.L. (2002) 'Flexible families? "Astronaut" households and the experiences of lone mothers in Vancouver, British Columbia', *Social and Cultural Geography*, 3, 2, 117–134.

Waters, J.L. (2003) '"Satellite kids" in Vancouver: Transnational migration, education and the experiences of lone children', in Charney, M.W., Yeoh, B.S.A. and Tong, C.K. (eds) *Asian Migrants and Education*. Dordrecht: Kluwer Academic Publishers, pp.165–184.

Waters, J.L. (2005) 'Transnational family strategies and education in the contemporary Chinese diaspora', *Global Networks*, 5, 4, 359–378.

Waters, J.L. (2006) 'Geographies of cultural capital: Education, international migration and family strategies between Hong Kong and Canada', *Transactions of the Institute of British Geographers*, 31, 2, 179–192.

Waters, J.L. (2007) '"Roundabout routes and sanctuary schools": The role of situated educational practices and habitus in the creation of transnational professionals', *Global Networks*, 7, 4, 477–497.

Waters, J.L. (2008) *Education, Migration and Cultural Capital in the Chinese Diaspora: Transnational Students between Hong Kong and Canada*. New York: Cambria Press.

Waters, J.L. (2009) 'Transnational geographies of academic distinction: The role of social capital in the recognition and evaluation of "overseas" credentials', *Globalisation, Societies and Education*, 7, 2, 113–129.

Waters, J.L. (2010) 'Becoming a father, missing a wife: Chinese transnational families and the male experience of lone parenting in Canada', *Population, Space and Place*, 16, 1, 63–74.

Waters, J. and Leung, M. (2010) 'Transnational students and (im)mobilities in Hong Kong'. Presentation at the *Association of American Geographers Annual Meeting*, Washington DC, USA.

Wielemans, W. (1991) 'Erasmus assessing ERASMUS', *Comparative Education*, 27, 2, 165–180.

Wiers-Jenssen, J. (2008) 'Does higher education attained abroad lead to international jobs?', *Journal of Studies in Higher Education*, 12, 2, 101–130.

Williams, A. (2006) 'Lost in translation? International migration, learning and knowledge', *Progress in Human Geography*, 30, 5, 588–607.

Williams, A. (2009) *International Migration and Knowledge*. London: Routledge.

Williams, A. and Baláž, V. (2008) 'International return mobility, learning and knowledge transfer: A case study of Slovak doctors', *Social Science and Medicine*, 67, 1924–1933.

Xiang, B. and Shen, W. (2009) 'International student migration and social stratification in China', *International Journal of Educational Development*, 29, 513–522.

Yeates, N. (2002) 'Globalization and social policy: From global neoliberal hegemony to global political pluralism', *Global Social Policy*, 2, 1, 69–91.

Yeoh, B. and Willis, K. (2005) 'Singaporean and British transmigrants in China and the cultural politics of "contact zones"', *Journal of Ethnic and Migration Studies*, 31, 269–285.

Yonezawa, A. (2007) 'Stratigies of the emerging global higher education market in East Asia: A comparative study of Singapore, Malaysia and Japan', *Globalisation, Societies and Education*, 5, 1, 125–136.

Yonezawa, A., Akiba, H. and Hirouchi, D. (2009) 'Japanese university leaders' perceptions of internationalization', *Journal of Studies in International Education*, 13, 2, 125–142.

Zhou, M. (1998) '"Parachute kids" in Southern California: The educational experience of Chinese children in transnational families', *Educational Policy*, 12, 6, 682–704.

Ziguras, C. and Law, S.F. (2006) 'Recruiting international students as skilled migrants: the global "skills race" as viewed from Australia and Malaysia', *Globalisation, Societies and Education*, 4, 1, 59–76.

# Index

Printed and bound by CPI Group (UK) Ltd, Croydon, CR0 4YY